Language and Materialism

Language and Materialism

Developments in Semiology and the Theory of the Subject

Rosalind Coward and John Ellis

Routledge & Kegan Paul

London, Henley and Boston

First published in 1977
by Routledge & Kegan Paul Ltd
39 Store Street,
London WC1E 7DD,
Broadway House,
Newtown Road,
Henley-on-Thames,
Oxon RG9 1EN and
9 Park Street,
Boston, Mass. 02108, USA
Set in 10 on 11 pt IBM Journal
by Express Litho Service (Oxford)
and printed in Great Britain by
Unwin Brothers Ltd
The Gresham Press, Old Woking, Surrey
A member of the Staples Printing Group

British Library Cataloguing in Publication Data

Coward, Rosalind

Language and materialism.
1. Semiotics
I. Title II. Ellis, John
001.56   P99

ISBN 0—7100—8620—2
ISBN 0—7100—8627—X   Pbk

Contents

tive grammar. Their failure to deal with the extra-linguistic: the concerns of psychoanalysis.

Psychoanalysis has changed the object 'language' for linguistics.

Negation and the function of judgment.

The relation of the drives, conscious subject and contradictory outside in Kristeva's work: the Semiotic and the Thetic.

The implications for a theory of practice: position, destruction, renewal.

Poetic language: modes of signification which transgress the positions necessitated by sociality.

Acknowledgments

We would like to acknowledge here the help given us by very many people, particularly the following: Stephen Heath, Parveen Adams, Steve Butters, Paul Lester, the members of the Lacan Study Group in London, and the Language and Ideology group in Birmingham.

We would also like to acknowledge the practical help and encouragement received from: Richard Johnson, Pam Taylor, Stephen Hayward, D. J. and K. S. Coward, Dr Maurice and Hilary Webb.

1 The philosophical context

Perhaps the most significant feature of twentieth-century intellectual development has been the way in which the study of language has opened the route to an understanding of mankind, social history and the laws of how a society functions. In this chapter, we attempt to summarise the philosophical movements involved in the development of this perspective. As an overview, this chapter asserts what the remaining chapters substantiate.

The study of language has taken two forms. First, there has been a massive development of synchronic linguistics whose particular object of knowledge is language's own laws of operation. It makes possible the reflection on speech as a 'language', a specific system with its own laws of functioning. Scientific knowledge of language has also been extended to all social practices which can then be studied as languages, as for example with structural anthropology. This second development is based on the assumption that all social practices can be understood as meanings, as signification and as circuits of exchange between subjects, and therefore can lean on linguistics as a model for the elaboration of their systematic reality.

Both these aspects can render the concept 'mankind' a concept accessible to scientific analysis. Because all the practices that make up a social totality take place in language, it becomes possible to consider language as the place in which the social individual is constructed. In other words, man can be seen *as language*, as the intersection of the social, historical and individual. It is for this reason that work on language has created consideration of man as 'subject', that is, the individual in sociality as a language-using, social and historical entity. Such a consideration can only lead to a demystification of the complex and imprecise realm of the 'human': it makes possible, for the first time, a scientific analysis of the concept of the 'human' which we suggest is fundamental presupposition of bourgeois ideology. This is then an advance for materialist philosophy with its fundamental tenet of 'infinite matter everywhere in movement'. The 'human' can be analysed as a socially-constituted process which plays a material role in society. The category of 'human essence' (a conception which belongs to the opposing philosophic tendency of idealism) is no longer necessary as a founding part of the materialist theory of ideology. Materialist philosophy is thus able to provide a scientific analysis of history and the subject. Ideology is conceived as the way in which a subject is produced in language able to represent his/herself and therefore able to act in the social totality, the fixity of those representations being the function of ideology. (Reference to the notion of 'subject' creates the very problems of language which this book is dealing with. Since the term refers both to an individual in sociality, and more generally to the space necessitated by ideological meanings, we have chosen to designate the subject with the pronoun 'it'. But where this confuses the meaning of a sentence, we use the term 'he'. In accepting this convention, we are aware that it is an ideologically determined use. It is the work of a specific discourse — patriarchal discourse — which inscribes a 'he' as the generalised representative of the species.) Structural linguistics and semiology were not able to carry through this criticism of idealist thought, even though they provided the basis for doing so. This was because structuralism failed to produce a genuinely materialist theory of language, and ultimately rested on idealist presuppositions. It is important to understand the reasons for this failure since they illuminate many problems of Marxist thought, and indeed the attempt to find their solution has led to a reconceptualisation of Marxism.

Idealism depends on notions of 'human essence' which somehow transcend and operate (indeed, cause) the social system, and are not constructed in this system. The idealist 'deformation of thought' mobilises notions of 'mankind' and the 'human' as the specific language-using entity. They underlie the idea of identities which pre-exist the individual's entry into social relations. Idealism has, in other words, an idea of identity which is in complete opposition to the materialist tenet of the subject resulting from its construction in sociality. The idealist assertions underlie the fundamental assumption of bourgeois ideology with its necessity/will to present society as consisting of 'free' individuals, whose social determination results from their pre-given essences like 'talented', 'efficient', 'lazy', 'profligate', etc. The conception of language as a transparent, neutral milieu — a conception which enables bourgeois ideology to construct such representations of essences — was shaken by the extension of a materialist analysis to language itself. Reflection on language in relation to history and to representations of social relations opened the route towards considering the individual as a part of a materialist process. It therefore moved towards a materialist theory of how this individual then appears, that is, as a subject. But as we see in the development of structuralism (from structural linguistics) and semiology in France, it became evident that this theory was constantly inhibited from developing any real materialist understanding of language and ideology in the social process. The emergence of mechanistic tendencies from structuralist analyses revealed its complicity with the idealism of bourgeois ideology. The recognition of this led Barthes, Kristeva and others associated with the *Tel Quel* group to rethink the foundations of structuralism and semiology. In doing so, they have moved in a direction that is of vital importance for any future elaboration of materialism.

Structural linguistics and the possibility of analysing all social practices as languages both emerged from the examination of the 'sign': the relation between the means of expression, e.g. sound (the signifier) and the concept (the signified), neither of which pre-exists the other nor has any meaning outside their relation. It was a matter not simply of realising their interrelatedness as categories, but also of suggesting their separation. This separation, glimpsed by Saussure, made possible a study of the relations entered into amongst the signifiers themselves in the production of meaning. The analysis of the proper relations of the signifier led to the conclusion that 'no meaning is sustained by anything other than reference to other meaning' (Lacan, *Ecrits*, p. 498). The signifier cuts out or articulates the signified only by relations entered into with other signifiers: meaning is only produced by a systematic arrangement of differences.

The possibility of thinking of the signifier and the signified as separate in the concept of the sign had two results. On the one hand, it was responsible for the production of structuralism as the synchronic analysis of a system, that is, the analysis of structural relations. On the other, it had a more radical potentiality since the signifier could be seen to have an active function in creating and determining the signified. It was the concentration on the first aspect to the exclusion of the second which resulted in the failure to develop the radical potentiality of Saussure's theories, and became the central problem for semiology in its exploration of the *avant-garde* text. Structuralism, the first aspect of the examination of the sign, was the analysis of meaning from the perspective of its production by the interaction of various elements in a network of differences. It ascertained the precise rules of functioning of a given structure, and the precise rules of structural transformations. This was the basis for understanding the production of meaning from a system of differences, and the regulation of the relations of difference to fix a specific meaning. In the cases where this type of analysis was carried out, these meanings were generally cultural meanings, for example, the kinship system of Lévi-Strauss. The lesson of this development of structuralism was that man is to be understood as constructed by the symbol and not as the point of origin of symbolism. The individual, even prior to his or her birth, is always already subject-ed to the structure into which he or she is born. The structure is what sets in place an experience for the subject which it includes. This demands a radical re-estimation of the position of the individual; it should no longer be possible to adhere to the notion of the individual as embodying some ideal pre-given essence. Being always subject-ed, the subject can never be the transcendental, punctual source of a symbolic system. It is de-centred within this structure, constructed in a specific system of differences and their arrangements.

However, structuralism tended to gravitate towards a mechanistic theory of the action of the structure. Concentration on the interactions of various elements of the structural network resulted in a separation of the product from its production. The relations between the various elements were then conceived as relations of exteriority. The universe of structuralism was made up of fully constructed objects and subjects; their 'presence' was affirmed by the naive, empirical reference to 'concrete' evidence, to 'social life', to culture, to anthropology, etc. This direction of structuralism blocked the realisation of the radical potentiality of Saussure's work, since it removed any emphasis from productivity, stressing instead a pre-given meaning. Two tendencies resulted from this. Either the system was considered to be imposed on the subject who is then only its support: such is the foundation of mechanical materialism. Or else meaning was seen as produced in the structure by the transcendental consciousness which always already intends that meaning. This is the foundation of idealism.

Any mechanistic account of structural relations is reductive since it reduces the process of structuration, the action or process of the structure, and the process of the subject in this action. It rests, finally, on the implicit assumption of a centre or a fixed origin which organises or limits the action of the structure to produce fully-finished subjects and objects. This centre originates, balances and organises the interaction of the elements of the structure. Derrida (in *The Structuralist Controversy*, ed. Macksey and Donato, pp. 247–65) points out how the history of the concept 'structure' can be seen as a series of substitutions of centre for centre. The centre is given different names, such as 'essence', 'existence', 'transcendentality', 'consciousness', 'God', 'man', etc. But although this appears as a centre, it is in fact a transcendent notion of being which supports the structure. It is therefore finally outside the structure and operating it. Such a contradiction – that of a centred structure achieved only by resorting to the idea of transcendence – expresses the will to find a reassuring certitude, an affirmation of the limitation of what otherwise appears as the endless process of structural causality. This certitude is in direct antagonism to the philosophy of Marxism, whose lesson of dialectic materialism stresses precisely process; everything that exists consists in contradiction and in the process of transformation. The 'will' of the idealist 'deformation' of structuralism can be seen to be the will of bourgeois ideology, a will which seeks to reinstate idealism against materialism.

These politically regressive elements of structuralism quickly became apparent in semiology's attempt to pursue a 'dream of scientificity' basing itself on Saussure's work. Transcendency was implicit in Saussurean linguistics, and those disciplines which drew their influence from it, as the result of understanding the individual simply as a 'user' of the social code. The structure of language (*langue*) is mobilised in the individual speech act (*parole*). In this way, the productivity of meaning from a system of differences is abandoned, and meaning can only be understood as what the individual 'intends'. It is therefore the individual's intention which produces the specific relations of difference. This theory returns us to the idealist premise of the individual belonging to the realm of the transcendent, beyond scientific analysis. The attempt made in the early work of semiology to understand the specific relations of difference from the point of view of the social relations which produced it, led Barthes and Kristeva to recognise this idealist premise. Any consideration of the ideological connotations of specific articulations raises the question of the status of language. Is it superstructural (all ideology) or not? It was soon realised that to propose the former would collapse language and ideology together in a totally mechanistic way. It would deny the very notion of productivity which, at another level, was the specific object of knowledge for semiological analysis.

The problems of language as a specific practice, together with its articulation with ideology, appeared in the analysis of literature. Structural analysis proved to be inadequate to account for the differences between texts. Attention to what distinguishes one text from another necessitated attention to the full complexity of the speech act, to the transformations witnessed in the speaking subject. Such attention clearly demonstrates that language and ideology cannot be collapsed together. The complexities of 'poetic language' equally show the inadequacy of the (simplistic) idea of language as a transparent, neutral milieu (this would be the arbitrary sign) which is taken over by the ideological or scientific metalanguage. However, the early work in semiology had been able to unveil the ideological form of realism by using this idea of the metalanguage. The 'appearance-as-natural' of a certain ideological representation appeared to be realised in a process through which the 'arbitrary' relation between the signifier and the signified (the sign) is taken over to form a new signifier in an ideological discourse. This presupposed an original neutrality and innocence of language, which was used to inform the ideological signified with its 'naturalness'. Barthes gave the name '*écrivance*' to this complicity of realist writing with bourgeois ideology and it seemed relatively simple to demonstrate. It was, however, the attempt by Barthes, Kristeva and others to deal with writing which did not re-present reality in quite this way, that made problematic the fundamental assumptions such as identity that form the basis of the 'arbitrary' sign in structural linguistics.

It was in analysing texts by Mallarmé, Lautréamont, Joyce, Robbe-Grillet, Bataille, etc., that semiology's assumptions about the speaking subject (*parole*) and its relation to the system of language (*langue*) became increasingly untenable. Often, these texts turned their attention to their own material, to language. The effect of this attention was to expose the production of meaning from the activity of the signifiers. The fixed relations of the sign and meaning in the realist text are displaced and redistributed. Every enunciation is seen to be a practice, transforming and renewing positions of meaning. These texts expose the inadequacy for literature of the model of 'communication' (addressor/ addressee). Communication can only conceive of an author as source of meaning. But texts like these refuse the possibility of a conventional 'I' behind or outside the text: they refuse any sense of the plenitude of being and meaning behind the text. These texts destroy all unity both of reader and of author. The identity of the subject of the text (i.e. the space necessitated by the meanings of the text) is dissolved. This dissolution is a function of the dissolution of the fixed system of meanings found in classic representations. In this way, textual practice makes it felt that meaning and the subject are only produced in the discursive work of the text, and the subject is only experienced in process. In other words, language emerges in all its materialist implications as the specific milieu of productivity, practice and transformations.

Barthes's *S/Z* was a crucial turning point between early semiological analyses and full acceptance of the complexities of the speaking subject in signifying practices: an acceptance that has itself necessitated a radical re-examination of traditional Marxism, structuralism and notions of ideology. It was realised that the complexities of the text result from the fact that poetic language gives itself to the expression of certain aspects which are entirely ignored by formal linguistics. The sense of the *montage* of the subject in language, the musicalisation and the multiplication of meanings, all imply a far greater determinacy of the signifier than can be accounted for by formal linguistics. The text deals with the rhythmic or musical functioning of language: it is therefore no longer analysable in terms of structural transformations and instead necessitates attention to discursive reality as the movements of consciousness and the unconscious processes. Experimental texts demonstrate the productivity of new meanings in the discursive work and, for this reason, they could be seen to be significantly similar to the forms of signification which Freud described. He had shown a form of signification, such as the dream work, that could not be recognised by formal linguistics. The processes of condensation and displacement clearly demonstrate the active function of the signifier in the production of meaning. Meaning, then, is no longer a matter of a pre-given, arbitrary relation between signifier and signified, but rather the fixing of the chain of signifiers to produce a certain meaning. Nor is it a question of an innocent sign being 'taken over' by an ideological discourse. Attention is reoriented towards discursive work, to the productivity of meanings, to meanings being cut out, articulated, from the signifying system. In this way, the idea of the metalanguage became untenable.

It was seen that a metalanguage could only present itself in language; there is no neutral milieu on which it unfolds itself. Every identity between signifier and signified is the result of productivity and a work of limiting that productivity. The identity of signifier and signified had to be analysed from elsewhere than a purely natural or a purely ideological relation, if idealist thought was to be dispensed with.

What emerged was a need for a theory of the production of the positions by which the chain of signifiers becomes attached to a specific signified, and what is demanded is a theory of the process and positions occupied by the subject in relation to language and ideology. The realisation that specific meanings are produced with specific identities points to the need for a radical re-estimation of the place of the subject in the structure. This would be what Barthes conceived as a 'political theory of language' which would 'bring to light the processes of appropriation of the system of language (*langue*) and study the "ownership" of the means of enunciation, something like the *Capital* of linguistic science' (Barthes, *Promesse*, no. 29, 1971, p. 25). In other words, no materialist theory of language can be produced without consideration of the process of the subject in the relation between identity and sign. The political implications of this are clear: the domination of bourgeois ideology can no longer be seen as control of ideas by a class, it is a function of those positions established in relation to meaning. A genuinely materialist understanding of language and ideology needs an analysis of the process by which fixed relations of predication are produced for/in the subject. It is this necessity which can be met only by psychoanalysis, since positions/identifications are produced in the socio-familial construction of the subject.

Lacan's re-reading of Freudian theory involves a similar attention to the productivity of language as that demanded by the *avant-garde* text. As well as reaching similar conclusions about meaning, psychoanalysis has begun to account for these conclusions from a genuinely materialist position. In turning to psychoanalysis, Barthes and Kristeva were in no way demonstrating their allegiance to psychoanalysis as a bourgeois practice. This contemporary mode of analysis dramatises the limits imposed by sociality in order to return the individual to these limits. Contemporary psychoanalysis thus has a specific ideological character. It is this political pessimism which has provoked the extreme and justifiable hostility from Marxists and, especially, feminists. But Lacan's theoretical work is very different from this form of psychoanalysis. Its ultimate effect is a complete undermining of the notion of a unified and consistent subject, the assumption on which all bourgeois ideology is founded. This critique is based on an analysis which emphasises the more radical tendency in Saussurean linguistics: Lacan claims that Freud had already anticipated this in his work on dreams. Freud's discovery that unconscious signification is accessible and objectifiable for an analysis in language has made it possible to demonstrate the active function of the signifier in the determination of meaning. In dreams, for example, either several thoughts appear condensed in one symbol, or the representation of unconscious desire is displaced into another symbol to accommodate dream censorship. Meaning disseminates itself in the dream according to the position of the subject (its socio-familial construction) and the arrangement of the signifying chain in relation to this position. Because of this, it is never possible to separate the domains of consciousness and unconscious. The fixed relation of signifier and signified which is the object of linguistics is shown as only one moment of a process. It becomes fixed when the conscious subject is constructed in a certain position in relation to the signifying chain. The unconscious is constructed in the same process as that by which the human animal enters the symbolic universe. This unconscious is what makes accessible the knowledge of the 'price paid' for the splitting by which the individual becomes a language-using subject. It is the constitution of a subjectivity which necessitates the splitting which produces the unconscious. And it is this splitting which produces the subject as able to be in a fixed relation to the sign. This constitution, therefore, has to be taken into account if we are to found a materialist theory of ideology. It specifies the determination of a construction into symbolic relations, into a position of predication, which involves the mirror-phase and the castration complex. There is no possibility of a mechanical materialist collapse of language with ideology, or of any obscurantist notion of the unconscious as the 'unknown'. The determining force of the unconscious at certain moments in history is now acknowledged, e.g. in relation to the reactionary character of certain groups of women, or in relation to fascism. These political forces demand attention to unconscious desires and familial and sexual attitudes as much as to economic determinants.

Lacanian theory is grounded in materialism because the constitution of the language-using subject is a continuation of the same process as that by which the ego is constructed: according to the defensive, economic functioning of the pleasure principle. The conscious position of the subject is constructed from the process of the interaction of the somatic drives with the movement of the contradictory outside (in the Marxist sense). It is here, as Kristeva has realised, that Lacan's work rejoins the logic of dialectical materialism, since it is able to account for the process of the subject in its relation to the motor of all historical movement: contradiction. This demonstrates the way in which the unconscious makes itself felt in consciousness, indicating what society has to repress in order to reproduce itself. It is now possible to construct a theory of practice. This theory would no longer be crippled by the ambiguity of traditional Marxism: the ambiguity of showing the place of the subjective moment in the transformation of society when subjective actions are initially posited as simply mirroring the objective processes of history. The production of the subject, and therefore its ideological positions, can now be shown in the place of objective contradictions. Practice is seen as the interaction of new objective contradictions with a subject formed in the place of old contradictions and old representations of contradictions. Kristeva's work is moving towards a theory of revolution as well as being a revolutionary theory. It is a re-examination of ideology and practice from a materialist perspective; and it is the inadequate thinking of these two areas which has constantly returned Marxism to an idealist problematic where subject and object are unresolvably separated.

These concerns relate directly to contemporary thought in the fields of linguistics, literary criticism, social sciences, political philosophy and psychoanalysis. The ambiguities outlined above have not only inhibited the work in these fields but have also had political consequences, in that materialism can only lose ground if the corrosive influences of bourgeois idealist thought are not eliminated. The problems encountered in the development of semiology, and the kinds of solutions which are beginning to emerge, are exemplary for the whole perspective of the 'human sciences'. The articulation of language and ideology is the single most important area for materialism to develop. Its failure to do so has become increasingly a political lack as well as a theoretical absence in the years following 1968: such an absence has been exposed in the political and intellectual developments in Europe over the last decade. In the forefront of these developments is what could be called a renaissance of Marxist theory in the face of increasing political reaction. In the last few years, setting out from the work of Louis Althusser, a consistent attempt has been made to deal with the question of ideology: an attempt to fight against the crude economism of early Marxism, which is still inhibiting political development, and its concomitant mechanistic versions such as dogmatism, idealist humanism, etc. Such an attempt has resulted partly from a political disillusion with the official history of Marxism, as established by orthodox communist parties. These resort, in the final analysis, to the formulation of, 'it is the masses which make history': a 'belief' that 'truth' is to be found in the progress of the working class. At its most crude, history is distorted into a series of resistances by the working class on their ineluctable march towards socialism. This tendency is particularly true of British Marxism and its contributions to sociology, cultural and communications studies. Here this tendency predominates. History is the material advance of the working class; ideology simply mirrors the economic base; and bourgeois ideology will cease to exist with the overthrow of that class. The latter is asserted on the premise that the current dominance of bourgeois ideology is only a consequence of its production by the ruling class and its maintenance in their interests. Such mechanistic views of history are exposed in the inability, displayed by this form of Marxism, to provide anything more than the most economistic account of such phenomena as fascism, or of the problems connected with sexual politics. It is only very recently – and certainly as a direct result of the work on language discussed in this book – that these questions are being raised by Marxism. (See, for example, *Eléments pour une analyse du fascisme I and II*, transcriptions of the seminars held by M. A. Macciocchi.) Until this work, the problem of fascism has been, on the whole, abandoned since Reich's *Mass Psychology of Fascism*. What Marxism has consistently refused to face is precisely the popular appeal of fascism; a popular appeal which could, and still can, motivate a class to act against its own material interests. It cannot be accounted for by solely economic analyses nor by any mechanistic theory which does not credit the material force of ideology and the unconscious.

This inadequacy has recently become glaringly obvious in the development of a theoretical debate concerning the oppression of women. Until very recently, Marxist theory had only made rather insignificant excursions into this question, and there are no founding texts even to indicate its mechanisms in the way that *Capital* could be said to lay the foundations for an understanding of the oppression of the working class through wage-relations. One important tendency has been that of simply transposing the mechanisms outlined in *Capital* and applying them to the work performed by women in the home. Women are considered to be in a situation analogous with the working class, and models of productive and unproductive labour, the production of surplus value, etc., are applied. The determinant in the subordinant role of women is seen, from this perspective, to be the relations of production, and the familial relations act as a sort of secondary mirroring of this determinant. Several factors make this thesis untenable. The most obvious is that it is no longer possible to equate women's subordination with capitalist exploitation. Indeed, the equal pay and rights of women can be seen as a rationalist exigency of capitalism. In addition, in a society such as China, where the capitalist relations of production have been transformed, it is nevertheless acknowledged that women still have a subservient role and that a criticism of ideology is necessary for any change to be accomplished. In recognising these problems, the women's movement could be said to have become the political *avant-garde* since 1968, because the specificity of its problems – the sexual and familial construction of women – has raised in a political arena precisely the problems which the developments of semiology have encountered.

Thus the political significance of the theoretical developments we are examining are very great. In pointing to the need for a theory of ideology *and* language that accounts for the construction of the subject in representations by which he or she can act, these developments have pointed to a central failing in Marxist thought and practice. This has hindered the development of a mass movement for radical change, because Marxist theory in its present form does not provide a means of criticising the '*petit-bourgeois* mode of transformation'. It thus cannot clearly recognise the working of bourgeois ideology either in its own practice or in the social totality.

2 Structuralism

Language, as Lévi-Strauss claims, in some sense lays the foundations for culture as it is made of the same material: structural relations, systems of difference, signs, relations of exchange. Structuralist thought bases its analysis of the social process upon this analogy between society and language as it is conceived in structural linguistics. For Lévi-Strauss, linguistics presents itself as a systematic science, whose methods are exemplary for the 'human sciences'. The discipline of anthropology, along with the other human sciences, can exploit the fundamental discoveries of modern linguistics. These reveal that signification, which appears to be a natural relation, is in reality an arbitrary system of differences in which elements gain their meanings only from their relation with all other elements. This conception of language, with its concomitant modes of study, was originated by Ferdinand de Saussure in his lectures from 1907 to 1911, published after his death as the *Course in General Linguistics*.

Saussure's initial gesture was to introduce an order into the inchoate mass of speech acts that compose a language. He produced the distinction between *langue*, the system of language, and *parole*, the individual acts of realisation of that system. The speech act is only comprehensible on the basis of the whole system from which it gains its validity; and the system itself only exists in the multitude of individual speech acts. The structure of language is the systematicity which informs every individual act of speech: it is a system which can be constructed by an analyst but has no concrete existence as such. The system only exists in the fact that the potential infinity of individual utterances is comprehensible. In Saussure's initial distinction, language is revealed to be a system whose only reality is its realisations. This is the preliminary definition of a structure.

The elements of the structure of language are signs, and it is the notion of the sign which provided the founding moment for structuralism. The sign has long been recognised to be the fundamental kernel of language, from ancient Greece until modern times. C. S. Pierce, the American philosopher, first attempted a categorisation of the functions of the sign, but it was Saussure who developed the first thorough and scientific analysis of the linguistic sign in modern thought.

Saussure demonstrated that signs are composed of two faces, two sides, neither of which pre-exists the other nor has any meaning outside their relation. These are the sound-image or *signifier*, and the concept, or *signified*. Thus the sign /cat/ consists of a signifier the sounds 'k-a-t' and a signified, the conception of a cat. These two, the signifier and signified together, comprise the sign, and neither has any meaning outside their relation in the sign. In French, there are different signifiers, 'chat' or 'chatte', and a difference introduced into the signified, as French is capable of making a sexual differentiation where English has no gender system. From this example, two aspects of the sign can be deduced. First, the link between the signifier and the signified is an arbitrary convention. Nothing 'in nature' decrees that a certain signifier should articulate a certain signified. There is no so-called natural link between a particular sound and its concept, for even onomatopoeic sounds, which are meant to resemble their signifieds physically, still differ from language to language. The sign is constituted in the social fixing of the appearance of a relation of equivalence between signifier and signified: in language the signifier and the signified appear as symmetrical. Second, the concept and sound-image are produced in the same movement: the signifier cuts out, articulates, a certain space which becomes through this articulation, a signified, that is, meaning. The linguistic signifier in isolation has no intrinsic link with the signified: it only refers to meaning inasmuch as it forms part of a system of signification characterised by differential oppositions.

It is therefore artificial to speak of 'a' sign, as signs are only comprehensible within systems of signification and not in any ideal way 'on their own'. The structure is that which endows signifiers and signifieds with the possibility of signification: they are constituted in a process of differentiation from each other.

> In language there are only differences *without positive terms*.
> Whether we take the signified or the signifier, language has neither ideas nor sounds that existed before the linguistic system, but only conceptual and phonic differences that have issued from the system (Saussure, op. cit., p. 120).

Thus the structure not only sets in place but also creates both signifiers and signifieds, and the structure is a system of difference. Each signifier differs from others that sound similar but are not identical; and it differs from those that precede and follow it in the signifying chain. Language is a structure whose elements constitute each other in difference. Hjelmslev defines this structure as 'an autonomous entity composed of internal dependencies', and adds that

> the analysis of this entity allows one constantly to disengage the elements which condition each other reciprocally, each of which depends on certain others and could neither be conceived nor defined without these other elements. This analysis returns its object to a network of dependencies by considering linguistic facts

as proportional to each other ('Linguistique structurale' in *Acta Linguistica*, IV, 1944).

Structural linguistics abandoned the question of bourgeois linguistics, the question of the origin and history of language, to make its object the relational composition in the interior of language itself. In this, it implied two dominant modes of analysis. One mode analyses the structural form at any one moment, the substitutions that are possible within it, the analysis of a particular state of *langue*. This is analysis of the paradigm, synchronic analysis of that which exists at a certain moment or during a definite epoch. The second form of analysis is that of the actual combinations that are generated, the signifying chains that are produced, the analysis of *parole*. This is analysis of the syntagm, the diachronic analysis of that which unfolds through the passing of time. It can be seen that whereas syntagmatic analysis deals with the combination of elements that are actualised in the sentence, paradigmatic analysis reveals the sets and codes to which these elements belong, any member of which could be legitimately substituted for them. If this is conceived spatially, syntagmatic analysis deals with a horizontal axis of present elements; paradigmatic analysis deals with the vertical axis of the system which renders each element intelligible. This separation of modes was initially necessary for linguistics in order to combat the atomistic historicism which dominated the late nineteenth century, and it has proved valuable in other disciplines to overcome similar tendencies, as Lévi-Strauss's work demonstrates. However, the distinction is in some ways too rigid as it fails to deal with the productivity of structures: it tends to separate the product from its production, the subject from the structure. For example, in structural linguistics this separation has produced an almost exclusive concentration on the paradigmatic mode of analysis.

Modern linguistic tendencies share a common idealist basis, that of seeing language as a logical synthesis, as an act of understanding which ensures communication and social exchange. In their general principles they have a common tendency to look at language as a strictly formal object; they concentrate on either syntax or mathematical structures. Here, linguistics has followed Saussure's lead very closely. Language is seen as a systematic arrangement of parts; 'it is made up of formal elements put together in variable combinations, according to certain principles of structure' (Benveniste, *Problems in General Linguistics*, p. 19). This conception sets out from the premise that language always has a limited number of basic elements but that these elements, although few in number themselves, yield a large number of combinations. Methodological analysis showed that language in fact only uses a small amount of the potentially enormous numbers of possible combinations that would result from these basic elements being freely assembled. The restriction of these possible combinations gives shape to specific forms which vary according to the linguistic system under consideration. This is what is implied by the term 'structure': particular types of relation-ships articulating the units at a certain level. Each of the units in a sys-tem is defined by the relations which it maintains with other units and by the oppositions into which it enters. This 'relational' view of language is oriented towards language as structure, paradigm and synchrony, rather than as the speech act, syntagm and diachrony.

Kristeva points to the formulation of Z. S. Harris, the American structural linguist (in *Mathematical Structures of Language*, Inter-science, London, 1969), as typifying a conception of language, generally agreed on by those for whom language is a strictly formal object. He defined language as: (1) the arbitrary relation between signifier and sig-nified, (2) the acceptance of the sign as substitute for the extra-linguistic, (3) its hidden character, (4) capable of being enumerated and analysed. Julia Kristeva has undertaken a detailed analysis of these tendencies in linguistics; looking at the developments of Saussurean linguistics of the Prague circle (Jakobson, etc.), the Copenhagen circle (Hjelmslev, etc.), American structuralism (Bloomfield, etc.), and generative grammar. In all these, at the most general level, she finds the same distrust of the signified. Together with this is the tendency not to explain language but to put forward a uniform description which is blind to its own founda-tions and the techniques of its own procedures. Language is made out to be static, without history and at first sight without a subject. This is because language is conceived of as a structural transformation, and for this reason the subject is foreclosed. It is either ignored or seen to take up its position unproblematically as simple language-user. The impetus of linguistic practice in this perspective can only be the ex-change between the structure of language (*langue*) and the individual speech act (*parole*). The subject is therefore left to the realm of the individual and the non-scientific; it is left, according to Lévi-Strauss, as 'personal identity, poor treasure' (*Mythologiques IV*, 'L'Homme nu', p. 614).

The strengths and weaknesses of the structuralism which developed from Saussure's linguistics are well demonstrated by the work of one of the originators of modern structuralism, Lévi-Strauss. He transposed the structuralist conceptions to the study of anthropological data, rely-ing on the sign as a central term. It was not simply an analysis of the transmission of signs which functions within sociality, but also a matter of envisaging structures as symbolic systems, that is, the structural arrangement as productive of meaning: 'any culture may be looked upon as an ensemble of symbolic systems, in the front rank of which are to be found language, marriage laws, economic relations, art, science and religion' (Lévi-Strauss, *Introduction à l'oeuvre de Marcel Mauss*, 1950).

Lévi-Strauss's work is paradoxical: it uses rigid structural models which emphasise a synchronic moment in a process rather than the diachronic process of production and change, yet his writing seethes with evocation of the specificity of each moment, which, he claims, analysis cannot reconstruct. This tension has to be remembered throughout this schematic account of his structuralism: it is a tension that cannot be resolved except by a radical transformation of the structuralist mode of thought.

As an anthropologist, Lévi-Strauss examines the multitude of different forms of social organisation that, despite the remorseless spread of Western bourgeois modes, still exist in the world. He sees his task as taking these societies on their own terms; then to translate their terms into ours, to explain the logic by which the people of these societies conceive of and organise their relations to each other and to the world. This necessarily entails going behind the subjective accounts given of these relations, to find the basic relations which generate them. So, with his analysis of kinship structures, he takes the mass of disparate evidence from various cultures and deduces the basic 'unit of kinship' that gives rise to this multitude of different forms. Similarly, when analysing myths he finds oppositions which, whilst they reduplicate themselves to infinity in a body of myths, nevertheless express a basic contradiction or relation which underpins the attitudes and behaviour of a particular society. Summarising this method of analysing basic structures in a society, he wrote that

the method we adopt . . . consists of the following operations:

(i) define the phenomenon under study as a relation between two or more terms, real or supposed;

(ii) construct a table of possible permutations between these terms;

(iii) take this table as the general object of analysis which, at this level only, can yield the necessary connections, the empirical phenomenon considered at the beginning as being only one possible combination among others, the complete system of which must be constructed beforehand (Lévi-Strauss, *Totemism*, p. 16).

His analysis of kinship systems demonstrates this method and its contrast with previous approaches.

'The error of traditional anthropology, like that of traditional linguistics, was to consider the terms, and not the relations between the terms' (Lévi-Strauss, *Structural Anthropology*, p. 46). Traditional anthropology ran up against a problem with kinship structures: it had to explain the recurrence of instances such as special relationships which exist between sons and their mother's brothers, the maternal uncle. Anthropologists like Radcliffe-Brown encountered this problem because they thought kinship from the point of view of a Western bourgeois family: a unit consisting of a man, wife and children; this results in three special relationships, those between parents, between children, and between parents and children. The special relationship of children to the maternal uncle in certain societies is thus inexplicable. Lévi-Strauss begins not from the established 'family unit', but by positing the 'universal' incest taboo and resulting exchange of women. The incest taboo is the prerequisite of any form of social organisation whatsoever: Lévi-Strauss claims that women are exchanged between one family and another, creating bonds of mutual obligation and relation, instead of being kept by the brother for himself. He can find no society where this does not take place: there is always exchange of women by men, and for this reason it has been asserted (e.g. Kristeva in *Des Chinoises*) that despite varied forms of descent (matrilinear, patrilinear, matrifocal, etc.), all known social organisations have been patriarchal. It is an exchange (one woman for another) which takes place over generations, amongst a whole social group, and for small tribes it is the principal form in which the society is held together. The mechanisms take place in a variety of forms in differing societies, and they are expressed in the often complex taboos on marriage with cousins: it is possible to marry a cousin on the father's side, but not on the mother's and vice versa. It is clear from this way of viewing kinship structures that the place of the maternal uncle is no anomaly: he is the brother who gives his sister in the exchange, expecting, as his 'natural right', a wife in a similar exchange with another member of the society. In this analysis of the social formation, the maternal uncle is a structural function from the start.

The result is that Lévi-Strauss distinguishes a basic unit consisting of four relations: brother/sister, husband/wife, father/son, mother's brother/sister's son. Furthermore, this structural functioning makes it possible to predict and analyse the forms of those relations, for they always occur in two contrasting pairs. There are modifications to this model, concerning the different forms of relationships that are possible (mutuality, reciprocity, rights, obligations), but it reveals the basic pattern of kinship systems, based not on the 'biological family' of traditional anthropology but on the incest taboo and the resultant exchange of women. The traditional view only describes what appears to be the 'biological reproduction' of the species and does not account for the reproduction of social structures and their role in determining the form of reproduction of the species. Lévi-Strauss's methods accomplishes both by revealing the way in which the demands of sociality form the kinship structure. This description of what structures interhuman reality, introduced by Lévi-Strauss, is referred to as the symbolic order. The assertion is that the human subject is inserted into a preexistent linguistic order, which forms its relation to 'meaning' (in this case, the forms of familial relations). Lacan takes up and elaborates this term, as we will see later, to describe the construction of the subject in relation to meaning; but, in opposition to Lévi-Strauss, Lacan stresses that a signifier can never be permanently bound to any signified.

Kinship structures are one element in the organisation of a society. Men need at once to form relations with nature (of which they are a part), and to mark themselves off from nature. This complex relationship between Nature and Culture, together with the taboos and preferred forms of behaviour that it entails, are expressed in the form of myths and totemism. Similarly, the form of kinship and its taboos are explained in these practices. Myths themselves are oblique, repetitive tales of men intermingling with animals, fabulous events in the cosmos, strange distinctions made between apparently homogeneous materials, etc. Lévi-Strauss shows how myths cannot be understood singly, but only – like language – as a corpus of differences and oppositions. Each myth is incomplete, full of irrelevant details and events; when understood as a part of a corpus, it is seen to carry basic oppositions, messages about the organisation of nature, culture, and their interpenetration and difference. These relationships are expressed in the form of relations between: men, animals and supernatural beings; forms of food; useful animals and plants; categories of landscape, climate, heavenly bodies, etc.; sounds and silences; smells and tastes. The material of myth is not necessarily words; the signs also include such totemic substances as food, as the example of honey and tobacco demonstrates.

Food is particularly important since it is a direct manifestation of the interpenetration of man and nature: it is a natural process for man to consume food (as animals do), but the ways in which it is consumed are entirely cultural. So Lévi-Strauss elaborates a system of difference between kinds of cooking that expresses an opposition between Nature and Culture. The system has two poles, constituted by the two ways in which raw food can be transformed: the cultural use of fire to cook, and the natural method of rotting. He then shows that, in the mythology of the South American Indians of whom he writes, there exist two crucial kinds of food which transgress this system of differentiation. One is honey, which is naturally pre-cooked, and requires no cultural intervention to make it edible; the other is tobacco, which has to be entirely consumed by the cultural means of fire before it can be enjoyed as smoke. Honey is over-natural; tobacco is over-cultural. Each of these then becomes a totemic substance for this reason: as transgressors of the differentiation between Culture and Nature, their transgressing power has to be neutralised in rituals which confirm this basic division of the world into two categories, with man as irreducibly different from animals.

The structural analysis of myth emphatically does not 'pin down' the meaning of a myth system, even if that meaning were only ascertainable from a whole corpus of individual cases. Myths are endlessly transformable into each other: any structure is a structure of transformations, not of eternally fixed oppositions between terms. As Lévi-Strauss puts it: 'all our analyses show – and this is the very justification for their monotony and proliferation – that the divergent differences worked by myths do not inhere so much in things as in a body of common properties which can be expressed in geometric terms and transformed one into another through operations which are already an algebra' (*Mythologiques II*, 'Du Miel aux cendres', p. 407). Thus myths are not a static system of prohibitions, but a dynamic logic for explaining the world and the society of the subject tribe. The complexity of this transformational logic is shown in the four volumes of *Mythologiques* (published 1964—8). Its subject is the myth-system of South American Indians. The first volume begins with the birth of culture, which according to the myths comes about with the cooking of meat. This demands an alliance between man and the master of fire, the jaguar. The relation is established and elaborated above all in the codes of cooking and kinship, because they deal with the interpenetration of Culture and Nature. In the second volume, it is the excessive modes of cooking which confront each other: honey and tobacco draw the balance between man and nature in their very excessiveness. These excesses are found again in the myths of the Honey-Mad-Woman, who consumes honey, disregarding all the rules for its correct usage. In these myths, the 'mad' consumption of honey corresponds to a breaking of the rules of marriage, for she is 'consumed' sexually in defiance of the kinship system. Thus the third volume deals with the rules that men impose upon women: table manners, on the level of the transformation of myth, are seen as one of the possible ways of introducing order into a menacing disorder that has woman as its centre. Woman transgresses the division between Nature and Culture by her very reproductive capacity: she is at once natural, because of reproductive capacities, and equally entirely cultural, speaking, thinking and acting as a human. Thus there is a disorder within the classification of Culture and Nature; and myth, with its endless transformations, exists to express such contradictions and to provide (ritual or religious) ways of settling them. The endless transformations of myth work towards producing this ordering of the world in which men and women can act.

Thus we see how it is that the central categories of Nature and Culture themselves are transitory, or as Lévi-Strauss puts it, the very distinction itself is a *'product of culture'*: the activity of signification. The structural system appears to have no fixed points, but rather a play of differences in which the establishment of fixed points is one moment in the endless transformations of the system.

> There exists no real end for the analysis of myth, no secret unity that can be seized at the end of a work of deconstruction. The themes divide to infinity. When it seems that they have been untangled and are held separately, this is the very moment when it is realised that they knit together again in response to unforeseen affinities. As a result, the unity of myth is only tendential and projective, it never reflects a state or moment of the myth. As an imaginary phenomenon implicated in the effort to interpret, its role is to give a synthesising form to myth, and to prevent it from dissolving into a confusion of contraries (Lévi-Strauss, *Mythologiques I*, 'Le Cru et le cuit', p. 139).

This process of difference and of transformation means that human beings cannot be regarded as the transcendent subjects of this system, operating it from outside. They are defined by the systems of kinship, myth and ritual: they do not rest undefined by these systems, full and complete subjects born to operate them. A structure is what 'sets in place an experience for a subject which it includes' (J. A. Miller, 'Action de la structure', *Cahiers de l'analyse,* vol. 9, 1968, p. 95). The structure defines the human subject within its play of transformations. The subject is, then, not a full and self-sufficient 'I' in the sense of classic bourgeois philosophy:

> What Rousseau asserts — a truth which is surprising even though psychology and ethnology have made it more familiar to us — is that there exists an 'it' which thinks in me, and makes me doubt whether it is I that think. To the 'what do I know' of Montaigne (from which everything sprang), Descartes thought himself able to reply that I know what I know because I think; to which Rousseau's response is a 'what am I?', to which there is no certain solution, inasmuch as inner experience provides us only with that 'it' which Rousseau discovered (Lévi-Strauss, 'J.-J. Rousseau, fondateur des sciences des hommes' in *Jean-Jacques Rousseau,* Editions de la Baconnière, Neuchâtel, 1962, p. 241).

Thus Lévi-Strauss's structuralism shows us that the human subject is not homogeneous and in control of himself, he is constructed by a structure whose very existence escapes his gaze. The self-presence of the human subject is no longer tenable; instead the subject is seen as subject to the structure and its transformations.

To see the subject as subjected, constructed by the symbol, is the most radical moment of this structuralism. However, this very structuralist method prevents Lévi-Strauss from going any further: the implication of seeing the structure as a process of production should be that the subject is also constructed by and in an imaginary relation to the real relations which produce that subject which they include. This implies a diversity of structuring practices, including imaginary relations, real relations, and relations between these two. These relations are necessary if the subject is to produce itself at all in the structure, when the action of the structure presupposes that the subject (as what seems to 'produce' the structure) is absent from the activity of the structure. Only the articulation of psychoanalysis and Marxism can hope to give an account of such practices. Such a philosophy has no ultimate full stop, or centre, to its process of structuring: it has no 'God', no 'human essence', no 'presence' as the transcendent term which makes the system possible. There is only the play of difference, and the multiplicity of mutually conditioning contradictions. Instead of moving to this conception of structuration, Lévi-Strauss finally posits a transcendent centre to his structures: he locates them in the 'human mind', a term which by definition remains beyond analysis.

And if we are asked to what final signified do these significations return, significations which signify each other, but which must finally relate together to something else, the only answer suggested by this book is that myths signify the mind which elaborates them by means of the world of which it is itself a part. Thus simultaneously the myths themselves are generated by the mind that causes them, and through the myths is generated an image of the world that is already inscribed in the architecture of the mind ('Le Cru et le cuit', p. 346).

The generalised human mind becomes the repository of these structures, and this human mind constitutes the unconscious of each individual. In this way, Lévi-Strauss's structuralism does not have to conceive of the structure as a continuous process of production. In spite of the radical potentiality of structuralist thought, therefore, there remains the danger of thinking of an immanent structure made up of fully finished subjects and objects. Lévi-Strauss can therefore conceive of structure in terms of a spatial diagram. On the surface, there is empirical richness, whose multiple specificity always escapes analysis; this is assigned to the uniquely individual. This is the realm of diachronic analysis, the place where time passes and events occur. The notion of process is left at this level. Beneath (or behind) this is the structure which generates this surface empirical richness: this structure is itself only comprehensible as a totality of relations, it is constituted by oppositions between terms, and undergoes transformations and substitutions. This structure is englobed by the human mind, which constitutes the play of the structure yet remains outside it. Hence the form of his analysis of kinship structures: there are many societies with a huge number of different kinship relations between individuals, but these are generated by a basic arrangement of relations. Although it is explicit that this kinship structure functions to reproduce society and individuals within it, the model constructed exists on the level of one generation of parents and children. In other words, the diachronic development of the structure and the actual engendering of children, is left out of the model which thus deals with the synchronic only. There are mere gestures to the diachronic. As J. A. Miller put it, in a seminal essay, this form of structure,

> demands an 'empirical' content from a 'natural' object to which it adds 'intelligibility'. If one is content to display an object using the dimensions of a framework so as to describe the interaction of elements, then the product is isolated from its production, a relation of exteriority is established between them (op. cit., p. 94).

Lévi-Strauss's structuralism can be expressed in terms of a spatial model, just as it uses geometric forms to explain its structures. But the notion of process cannot be expressed in this way, as will become clear.

We have seen that, in the most radical moment, the categories of Nature and Culture are no more than products of a system of difference which provides their interrelation and intelligibility. For instance, the kinship system, the foundation of society, straddles the division between Nature and Culture, being at once natural (universal) and cultural (a system of taboos and customs). The difference, Nature/Culture, has to be produced across this discrepancy; it is in no way inherent. However, such moments are finally treated as transgressions of the system, a notion around which the explication of the role of honey and tobacco finally rests. These moments are treated as transgressions of an already-constituted system, rather than as evidence of its very process of constitution, which then would have to be analysed as a continuous process of contradiction. Rather than objects and subjects which are constituted of contradictions (as in both Marxist and psychoanalytic thought), this structuralism thinks in terms of systematic oppositions between objects that are already fully constituted, held in a system of oppositions that gains its internal balance and limits from a transcendent subject. The structuralist system relies on the sign having a real referent: the arbitrary relation between signifier and signified is established in this schema by a natural bond between the human mind and a real referent. What is arbitrary in this schema, is the signifier produced for that reference. This is a tendency implicit in Saussure, who, despite realising that the designated object was not important — replacing it with the notion of a 'referent' — nevertheless, still seemed committed to the idea of a real referent. This was clear from his assertion that several signifiers have the same signified. By establishing the separability of signifier and signified, Saussure left the way open for linguistics and structuralism to found themselves on the basis that meaning, the signified, pre-existed the realisation of it in the individual speech act. By this, structuralism bypasses the question posed by materialism which asks, what relation exists between the linguistic symbol, in its totality, and the real outside that it symbolises? This question can only be posed if the radical potentiality of Saussure's separation of the signifier and signified is realised. The separation would make it possible to ask what is arbitrary in the relation of the sign (signifier/signified) to the reality which it names.

The limitation, imposed by a 'real referent' appears in much of Saussure's work; and his less radical followers exploit this side of his work exclusively. His rigid division of language into synchronic structure and diachronic change, obscures his fundamental discovery that the establishment of signification by a process of difference is not static, but is a constant process of articulation of new signifieds by the signifying chain. This idea of difference has two implications. In emphasising the indissolubility of the signifier and the signified in the sign, it is also necessary to stress their separation. In other words, it is the signifying chain which produces the chain of signifieds. Language, then, becomes a ceaseless productivity. As we shall see in the following chapter, this radical rethinking of Saussure's dichotomies (synchrony/diachrony, signifier/signified) came about when his schema was applied to the analysis of those uses of language which exceed communication: poetry, the *avant-garde* text and the discourse of the unconscious. These practices also reveal the second aspect of language as a continuous productivity: the social use of language necessitates the fixing of certain positions for the speaking subject in order that predication can take place, in order that an 'I' is constituted who can utter a remark. It is psychoanalysis which shows how this subject is constituted in the positions that enable predication, precisely through the limitation of the productivity of the signifying chain. In Saussure's own work, however, the question of the constitution of the subject who speaks, is never asked. Throughout, he assumes a pre-given user for the linguistic system which is the object of his analysis. He assumes, in fact, a transcendent human subject who uses language in order to 'sort himself out': 'psychologically our thought — apart from its expression in words — is only a shapeless and indistinct mass. . . . The characteristic role of language with respect to thought is not to create a material phonic means for expressing ideas but to serve as a link between thought and sound, under conditions that of necessity bring about the reciprocal delimitations of units' (Saussure, op. cit., p. 112). These are consequences of Saussure's initial positing of a transcendent subject, the user of language. Thought is then deemed to pre-exist language in some way.

It can be seen that structuralism can only operate its divisions of synchrony and diachrony, *langue* and *parole*, structure and product, etc. by presupposing a transcendent subject of some kind: the human mind, the language-user, etc. If, on the other hand, the radical nature of Saussure's concept of difference is realised, the continuous productivity of the system of signification becomes clear, showing the ineffectuality of such rigid divisions. The concept of productivity implies that it is the play of difference of the signifying chain that produces signifieds; the fixing of this relation is provided by the positionality of the speaking subject, a subject who is produced in this movement of productivity. Man is constructed in the symbol, and is not pre-given or transcendent.

It is the task of the following chapters to extend this critique of structuralism. First, the development of semiology in France in the late 1950s and early 1960s shows the strengths and limitations of what Saussure had foreseen as 'a science that studies the life of signs within society' (op. cit., p. 16). The problems of this mode of analysis become clear with the examination of literature: it reveals the process of language, both in the fixity of social positions in realism, and in their crisis in texts which exploit language as more than a medium of communication. Then the persistent metaphor of exchange (exchange of meanings between pre-existent subjects) that underlies both Saussure's linguistics and Lévi-Strauss's anthropology is shown to be inadequate through an examination of both Marxism and psychoanalysis. With Marxism, the notion that economic relations are relations of exchange appears as a representation that is produced in a particular social practice, a representation which functions to provide a positionality for subjects within a system of contradictions. With psychoanalysis, the constitution of the human subject is a constant process of splitting as the unformed infant encounters the contradictory outside analysed by Marxism. Finally, this conception of the human subject is shown to undercut any notion of language as a system of exchange between complete individuals. Its notion of the subjective moment and of the productive dissolution of structures is a theory of revolutionary practice.

3 Semiology as a science of signs

Saussure foresaw a 'semiology' of which linguistics would be at once one part and the privileged methodological guide. It was this 'science of the life of signs within society' that saw a rapid growth in France in the 1950s and 1960s, and it was the developments from this basis that led to the critique of the notion of the sign and of the structuralist method outlined in the last chapter.

> Semiology aims to take in any system of signs, whatever their sub-
> stance and limits; images, gestures, musical sounds, objects, and the
> complex associations of all of these, which form the content of
> ritual, convention or public entertainment: these constitute, if not
> *languages*, at least systems of signification (Barthes, *Elements of
> Semiology*, p. 9).

Food and clothes, for instance, carry meanings which organise their usage: there are conventions of eating and clothing, as well as meanings attached to both individual items and combinations of food and apparel. 'Confronted with the "limitless text" of fashion, food, furniture, urban design, all the day-to-day phenomena of life, the semiologist tries to understand the diverse processes of signification by the elaboration of models fitted to realise the system of intelligibility of each object' (S. Heath, *Vertige du déplacement*, p. 62). Semiology was thus an extension of the methods of Saussurean linguistics into new territories.

At first, the tools furnished by linguistics — the conception of signifiers and signifieds caught in a system of difference which provides the very possibility of their being understood — were applied to the systems of, for example, playing cards, traffic lights and menus, as though these were independent of language. It became increasingly evident, however, that they depend crucially upon language for their intelligibility, not only as a relay of their meaning, but, vitally, to found their very system of difference. This necessitated a revision of the basis of the work, a concentration on the study of language itself. Equally, semiology was originally based on what Barthes was able to call, in 1971, 'a euphoric dream of scientificity' (*Tel Quel*, nr 47, p. 97). This describes the structuralist project of drawing up models of the systematicity of each system, such that any possible enunciation (but no impossible enunciations) could be predicted by the operation of the model. This is the basic requirement of science, that it is able to predict. However, this scientificity can only operate with monological systems, whereas social systems are composed of diverse practices whose relation to each other, and mutual effectivity, are in a constant state of mutation. The semiology that does not eventually take account of this process (explored in Marxist thinking) inevitably declines into a sterile formalism, elaborating models whose only relevance is to a world that stands still.

The examination of the systematic nature of social signification was one major aspect of semiology. Barthes's route to it was through another, related, study: that of the forms of representation that bourgeois society gives to itself. In *Mythologies* he found that the systems of signs that are the rituals of eating, dressing, wrestling, going on holiday, etc. are themselves taken over by another system of signification which he calls 'myth'. These are forms of representation that naturalise certain meanings, eternalise the present state of the world, in the interests of the bourgeois class. Thus myth signifies through the system of food or of fashion that is described in semiology, just as the realist myth of the instrumentality of language works over the basic narrative structures discovered in the analysis of literature. In this chapter, we will examine the structural systems of food, fashion, narrative, etc., as well as these myths, and it is with the founding text of *Mythologies* that we begin.

Barthes's *Mythologies* were originally magazine articles in *Lettres nouvelles*, written between 1952 and 1956. They are published with a postface, 'Myth today', which systematises their intuitive method in terms of Saussurean linguistics. The analysis of myth was for him 'the beginning of semiology': it explains how the ruling ideas of a social formation come to seem universal and natural. It therefore joins the analysis of ideology which is proposed by Marx and Engels in their early text *The German Ideology*:

> Each class which puts itself in the place of the one ruling before it,
> is compelled, merely in order to carry through its aim, to represent
> its interests as the common interests of all members of society, that
> is, expressed in an ideal form: it has to give its ideas the form of uni-
> versality, and represent them as the only rational, universally valid
> ones (Marx and Engels, *The German Ideology*, pp. 64—5).

It is this conception of ideology that has undergone a radical change, as we shall demonstrate in our examination of Marxist thought in Chapter 5. *Mythologies* pre-dates these developments in Marxism, conceiving of ideology as a system of ideas, the product of the ruling class, which form the reality of a society. In an initial moment, these ideas inspire even the proletariat to revolution: it was in a large part the actions of the 'mob', inspired by the bourgeois slogan 'Liberty, Equality, Fraternity', that carried through the French Revolution. As the contradictions between bourgeois and proletarian classes developed, a large middle group emerged, the petit-bourgeoisie. They do not live the material reality of the bourgeoisie (who own the means of production), but they live bourgeois ideological reality as the natural, unacknowledged limits of their universe. As Barthes analyses it:

> Petit-bourgeois norms are the residues of bourgeois culture, they are bourgeois truths which have become degraded, impoverished, commercialised, slightly archaic, or shall we say, out of date? The political alliance of the bourgeoisie and the petit-bourgeoisie has for more than a century determined the history of France; it has rarely been broken, and each time only temporarily (1848, 1871, 1936). . . .
>
> The bourgeoisie ceaselessly absorbs into its ideology a whole humanity which has none of its fundamental status, and can only live it in their imagination, that is, through a fixation and impoverishment of consciousness. By spreading its representations across the whole catalogue of petit-bourgeois images, the middle class sanctions the illusory lack of differentiation between social classes (*Mythologies*, p. 140).

The petit-bourgeoisie is 'recruited' to bourgeois reality which appears under such forms as Nation ('national interest'), Essential Man ('it's only human nature'), Morality (immutable good and evil), etc. Myth makes the world immediately self-evident, without contradictions. Bourgeois ideas become the eternal essences of things, they impregnate everyday reality through the mechanism of myth.

Myth takes over the ideas embodied in high culture and makes them homely, comforting: high culture is extended and vulgarised into a kind of public philosophy. The innovatory and exploratory aspects in bourgeois thought are eliminated: the petit-bourgeoisie cannot comprehend the other, that which exists outside its realm and defines the limits of that realm. The petit-bourgeois world is the world of sameness, of endless repetition of identical forms, the world of so-called 'mass culture'. Thus democratic political change takes place within this sameness, according to the rules of 'little by little'. Sollers identifies social democracy as change in a petit-bourgeois mode, altering the structures but maintaining bourgeois relations and therefore, ideology.

Barthes concentrates more on the mechanisms by which these ideas present themselves than on the structures of power and forms of change that they support. It is an attempt to 'go further than the pious show of unmasking' (ibid., p. 9), to provide an analytic method. Barthes identifies many forms of thought as they essentialise various social practices. Things as diverse as cooking and children's toys are submitted to an 'irrepressible tendency towards extreme realism' (ibid., pp. 53 and 78). Election photographs or an exhibition entitled 'The Family of Man' readily display an 'essential humanity' rather than differences (ibid., pp. 91 and 100). And the travel guide, *Guide bleu* writes a picturesque history of Spain which effortlessly integrates support for the Fascist regime (ibid., p. 74). The social productivity of the world, the fact that it is constituted of complex relations which are in constant flux, disappears beneath a system of essences. The real is the immediately visible, and this visible does not appear to be a form of representation. Such is the work of myth.

The mechanism of myth is the way that habitual representations tangle themselves up in everyday objects and practices so that these ideological meanings come to seem natural, the common-sense reality of that object or practice. There are therefore two systems of meaning: the denotative and the connotative, the 'object-language' (the film, the toy, the meal, the car, inasmuch as they signify), and the myth which attaches itself to it, which takes advantage of the form of this denotative language to insinuate itself. In Barthes's famous example, there is a magazine cover, showing a black soldier saluting the French flag. This photo has one fully adequate denotative meaning ('Here's a black soldier saluting the French flag'), but this meaning is invaded by a second sense, which is precisely its intended sense: the connotative meaning which springs from a mixture of colonialist nationalism and militarism. It says — at the time of the Algerian war of independence — 'Colonialism must be right: there are negroes perfectly willing to defend it to the death.' The connotation leans on the denotation; there is a perpetual to-and-fro movement between them so that they appear as a natural unity. The connoted myth is successful exactly when it 'goes without saying', when it confirms an established position from doubt or attack, when it universalises history by saying 'That's the way it must be'.

In semiological terms, the whole of the denotative sign is used as the signifier by the connotative system. Whatever may be the form of an object or practice, as soon as it signifies, as soon as it is endowed with meaning, it submits to the differentiating system of language. It becomes a unity of concept and signifier: a sign. It then opens to the connotative process. The sign as a whole is taken up to be the articulator of a second concept, the ideological concept. Barthes represents it using the diagram shown as Figure 1, 'it being understood, of course, that the spatialisation of the pattern is here only a metaphor' (ibid., p. 115).

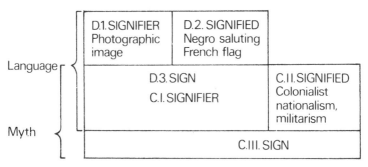

Figure 1

For the innocent consumer of the myth, the relationship between denotation and connotation is a constant swivelling movement which presents first one and then the other as a two-faced unity. It appears as though there is a causal link between them, a process by which the myth is inferred from the denotative language. In contrast, semiology reveals a process by which socially-defined equivalence is established between two meanings. For myths themselves are a product of a process of signification:

What the world supplies to myth is a historical reality, defined, even if this goes back quite a while, by the way in which men have produced or used it; and what myth gives in return is a natural image of this reality. . . . The world enters language as a dialectical relation between activities, between human actions; it comes out of myth as a harmonised display of essences (ibid., p. 142).

Myth serves as a particular process of conceptualising and sign-ifying the world, a process that is motivated by the necessity for a dominant order (its law and its thought) to present itself as a natural order. Myth is a particular use of the faculty of language which takes over denotative language to use it to naturalise and dehistoricise a humanly-created reality.

Semiology treats myth as one element in the social sign systems it examines. As well as connotation, it studies what *Mythologies* calls the 'object-language', or denotative language. The initial formulation in that book is somewhat naive, implying that a kind of pure, pre-mythic signi-fication is possible. This presupposes a natural link between the signifier and signified which constitute the denotative sign. The development of semiology increasingly exposed the contradiction of a science based on systematicity and differentiation whilst still attempting to operate the distinction between denotation and connotation. It demonstrated in-creasingly that the connotative system is an integral part of the signify-ing system that gives intelligibility to each sign. Barthes's *Système de la mode* eventually showed how both denotation and connotation are inseparable in the functioning of the system of fashion.

Semiology, then, aims to give an account of the structure of meaning of social practices and objects, like furniture, table manners, chess, etc. The initial systematisation of the method of this semiology was provided by Barthes's *Elements of Semiology*, originally published in the review *Communications* in 1964, and later as a short book. In it, he demonstrates the form of such signifying systems, using a method which is close to that of Lévi-Strauss:

The food system . . . is made up of (i) rules of exclusion (alimentary taboos); (ii) signifying oppositions of units, the type of which re-mains to be determined (for instance, the type of *savoury/sweet*); (iii) rules of association, either simultaneous (at the level of a dish) or successive (at the level of a menu); (iv) rituals of use which function as a kind of alimentary rhetoric (Barthes, *Elements of Semiology*, pp. 27–8).

This then is the system which allows many individual speech acts to take place: you order (in a restaurant of a certain class) steak and chips followed by ice-cream, but not steak and rhubarb followed by spinach and cream, although there is nothing in the material nature of these foods to prevent such a combination. With this system comes a whole set of meanings which immediately accrue to it: the connotative system of *Mythologies*. Hence the food statement 'steak-and-chips' comes to connote full-blooded nature and French patriotism (cf. *Mythologies*, pp. 62–4).

This is a simple system compared to cinema or the novel, yet it still demonstrates the relation proposed between this semiology and both language and sociology. Like language, these systems have two terms, the signifier and the signified, but the substance of the signifier can have a simply utilitarian function: 'the function of a dish can be to signify a situation and also to serve as food' (*Elements of Semiology*, p. 41). There is a kind of double movement involved: there is an immediate semantisation of all social functions 'as soon as there is society', Barthes writes, 'every usage is converted into a sign of itself; the use of a raincoat is to give protection from the rain, but this use cannot be dissociated from the very signs of an atmospheric situation' (ibid., p. 47). Here we have the more cautious attitude to language: it is seen as a model for the examination of these systems, and these systems seem to have a linguistic admixture, 'they pass through the relay of language, which extracts their signifiers (in the form of nomenclature) and names their signifieds (in the form of usages or reasons)' (ibid., p. 10). Equally, this demonstrates the status of semiology in relation to sociology. Semiology intervenes 'before' sociology (never instead of it): it examines the system of sense which is exploited by socio-economic forces. The example of Fashion shows this clearly.

Barthes's *Système de la mode* is a detailed examination of Fashion magazine writing. He examines the written system of Fashion because this is the only way in which the distinction between Fashion and non-Fashion is founded. Photographs are always accompanied by writing which points out important factors in clothes, and crucially gives them the connoted (and sometimes the denoted) concept of Fashion. The clothes themselves cannot do this: they remain, like plates of food, on the level of utility and are only able to signify simple concepts. For more complex differentiation, and the concept of Fashion itself, they have to pass through language:

> If you go beyond a few rudimentary signs (eccentricity, classicism, dandyism, sport, ceremony) can clothes, in order to signify, go without a speech that describes them, comments on them, gives them signifieds that are abundant enough to constitute a real system of sense? (*Système de la mode*, p. 9).

This luxury of words, this system of signification which is given to clothes through the medium of writing, has a social and economic function:

> Itself calculating, industrial society is condemned to developing consumers who do not calculate; if the producers and purchasers of clothes had an identical consciousness, then an item of clothing would only be bought (and produced) at the — very slow — rhythm of its wearing out; Fashion, like all fashions, rests on a disparity between two consciousnesses: one must be foreign to the other. To cloud the calculating consciousness of the purchaser, a veil of images, reasons, meanings must be stretched in front of the object; this elaborates a mediating substance around it that acts like an appetizer, in sum creates a simulacrum of the real object by substituting for the weighty period of wearing-out a sovereign time which is free to destroy itself in an annual suicide (ibid., p. 9).

It is the task of semiology to examine this system of sense which enables the whole sociology of fashion to take the form it does: then it is possible to examine the actual ways in which clothes are worn, sold, manufactured, used.

At the time of writing of these texts, semiology was conceived as a 'metalanguage', a system of language which takes over established system as a network of formal rules and constraints. Metalanguage functions in much the same way as connotation (in that it takes in charge an already-constituted sign system), but with one important difference. Connotation uses denotation as its signifier, to convey and naturalise its own meaning; metalanguage uses the denotative signs as its signified, articulating the systematicity of the denotative system in the face of the naturalisation and essentialisation to which language is open.

> On the one hand, it seems that every society engages in an endless activity to penetrate the real with signification and constitute strongly and subtly organised semiological systems by converting things into signs, the sensible into the signifying; on the other hand, once these systems are constituted (or more exactly, in the course of their constitution), men engage an equal activity to mask their systematic nature, to reconvert the semantic relationship into a natural or rational one (ibid., p. 285).

At this stage, the political purpose of semiology was conceived as that of demasking this process wherever it takes place. This is evident both in the writing of *Mythologies* and in the critique of realist writing examined later in this chapter: both examine the moment of naturalisation of a socially-constituted language. Despite the changes that have now taken place in its methodology, semiology was never conceived as an innocent science designed simply to provide a systematic analysis which is as inert as it is exhaustive. It requires a certain stance within history: in order to expose this process of naturalisation, it is necessary to see society as a process of structuring that is created by the interdependence of human activities. This structuring is not objective or benevolent, but is a complex process of reproduction of relations of unequal power between capital and labour. This is why systems of meaning are masked, why they become natural and rational rather than arbitrary. They articulate this 'structure in dominance' that is society, and must therefore in the same movement justify it, provide it with reasons, make it seem innocent. Because of the separation denotation/ connotation, bourgeois semiologists can produce a semiology that is itself innocent, describing systems that seem to be hermetically sealed. Two attempts at this in different fields are Pierre Guiraud's *Semiology* (Routledge & Kegan Paul, 1975) and Jonathan Culler's *Structuralist Poetics* (Routledge & Kegan Paul, 1975). Analysts who rather see the social position of the sign systems they examine simultaneously take a historically specific stance towards them. They produce a knowledge of sign systems and their naturalisation which can be the basis for a constant demystification of established systems of meaning: showing that what appears to be unchangeable is humanly created and can be recreated in certain directions.

The form taken by early semiology somewhat constricted the full realisation of the extent to which this naturalisation goes. As Stephen Heath has put it:

> The simple separation of signifier and signified . . . corresponds to a certain regime of sense (the system of the sign, the closure of Western thought) and to the mode of its analysis (*Mythologies* and *Système de la mode* are proof of this). The danger is that of not understanding this closure, of remaining in the representation of the signified, on which is then erected a whole mythology of 'demythication' (*Vertige du déplacement*, p. 51).

The method of 'demythication' is that of creating a metalanguage which can unveil the systematicity of another language. The language analysed is put in the position of a signified, re-presented by the metalanguage. However, this method becomes untenable with the realisation of the primacy of the signifier within signification; signification then appears to be a productivity (which presupposes the production of certain positions for the speaking subject), rather than a system that can be operated, or 'summed up' in a metalanguage by a transcendent subject. *Système de la mode* in its very detailed attention to one system of signification shows the strains suffered by this distinction between connotation and denotation, and between object-language and metalanguage.

The discussion of language and Fashion moves from the various functions of the written texts in relation to fashion photographs (functions of pointing out, naming and evaluating) to a more radical stance whereby these captions are no longer a mediating tautology of the photograph but submit it to their own play of difference:

> The clothing-image can certainly be fashionable (it is so by definition),

but it cannot be directly Fashion . . . in fact the specific aim of the description is to direct the immediate, diffuse knowledge of the clothing-image by a mediated and specific knowledge of Fashion (*Système de la mode*, p. 27).

This difference Fashion/non-Fashion is produced in more than one way. It appears as the connoted concept in statements that link clothes to fashionable situations (e.g. 'Prints win at the races'); and it appears as the denoted concept in statements that are confined to detailed descriptions: whole statements like 'A red and white cotton dress' are signifiers whose signified concept is 'Fashion'. Denotation and connotation are thus shown to be inseparable in practice: they both constitute the original system of signification which cannot function without both 'forms' of signification. The separation between them is shown to be superfluous: ideology enters into the very constitution of the sign.

In this way, the sign systems whose structuring semiology had originally tried to define by borrowing linguistic tools came to be seen as 'secondary modelling systems, that is, semiotic practices organised on linguistic foundations (denotative language being the primary system), but constituted in complementary, secondary and specific structures' (Kristeva, *Semiotiké*, p. 44). This perspective was developed utilising some of the methods of Russian Formalism, and concentrated on the most complex of these secondary modelling systems, writing and the institution of literature. It was through this kind of study that the whole system of the sign (and not just connotation) was exposed in its complicity with forms of thought specific to Western society. To explain these developments, we must examine the 'literary face' of early semiology.

In 1962 Barthes wrote an article (reprinted in his *Essais critiques*) which described three attentions to the process of signification, three 'imaginations of the sign'. Semiological research into literature proceeded unevenly along these three axes; and it was not until the crucial work of Kristeva and Derrida in the later 1960s that it was possible to present the synthesis and reconceptualisation of their insights. Barthes describes these three attentions:

Every sign includes or implies three relationships. First, an interior relation, which joins signifier to signified; then two exterior relations: the first is virtual, it unites the sign to a specific reserve of other signs, from which it is extracted to be inserted into discourse; the second is actual, it joins the sign to the other signs of the enunciation which precede or follow (*Essais critiques*, p. 206).

The first is the symbolical relationship, which in literature sees the work as the sign of a certain historical reality, etc.; the second is paradigmatic, examining the structure of the narrative, forms of writing, etc.; the third is the syntagmatic, examining the specific structure of the literary work, the individual relations that give sense to the elements.

It can be seen that there is a certain discrepancy between these (especially between the generality of the second and the hermetic specificity of the third), but it required a major change in perspective from the idea of structure, of elements already produced and in place, to overcome this problem. This change in perspective is demonstrated in Barthes's *S/Z*, the subject of the following chapter. We will now summarise the work that has been produced within these 'three attentions to the sign'.

The symbolical thinking of the sign suspends the sterile dichotomy between form and content. No longer is it a matter of the text having two faces which can legitimately be examined separately: its form (some kind of unique shape) and its content (summed up as either a 'picture of the world' or an essentialising platitude like 'men are men' depending on the political position of the analysis). This distinction is based on a convenient confusion of modes of signification which the symbolical attention to the sign rethinks. This attention is based on the idea that literary texts are signs complex enough for the sense not to be satisfied with designating one meaning, but equally signify larger realities across their ostensible content.

One version of this attention sees literary texts as wholes which act as tokens, standing for wider social situations and forces. This is the area of classic Marxist aesthetics whose epochal visions show how a text is intimately connected with its times. They show how the text expresses, stands as a symbol of, deep historical contradictions. Thus Lucien Goldmann succinctly situates his innovatory work:

> If I now examine the works of literary criticism inspired by the Lukacsian school to which I subscribe, I would say that . . . the disciples of this school have felt compelled to demonstrate scientifically and positively, in a certain number of specific instances, the unity of a work of art, the world vision to which it corresponds, and the relations between this world vision and the social groups (notably social classes) of which it is an expression. If I take as an example my own case, I can say first of all I confined myself to showing the existence of unitary and coherent world visions around which the works of Racine, Pascal, Malraux and Genet revolve (in *The Dialectics of Liberation* (ed. D. Cooper), Penguin, Harmondsworth, 1969).

And Lukács, too, writes in *The Historical Novel*:

> This work is intended to show how the historical novel in its origin, development, rise and decline follows inevitably upon the great transformations of modern times; to demonstrate that its different problems of form are but artistic reflections of these social-historical transformations (*The Historical Novel*, p. 13).

Illuminating as these works are, their kind of symbolical attention returns too smoothly and easily to history; it depends on a view of

language as transparent, as an easy covering of the real whose conceptualisation was somehow pre-linguistic. *How* a text means is no problem;
they find *what* (in a certain situation) it means, and why. It is indicative
of this that Goldmann's work on the French 'experimental' *nouveau
roman* should manage to discover 'the degree to which these writings
carried a realistic, critical and perfectly coherent vision of contemporary
society' (Goldmann, in *The Dialectics of Liberation*, p. 147), whereas
Stephen Heath sees 'the drama of writing, against the natural representation of linear writing, against the fixity of stereotype and repetition'
(*The Nouveau Roman*, p. 39).

At the basis of this are different conceptions of the historical process
and the role of language and ideology within it. Lukács and Goldmann
both see history as a process of becoming through which the world view
of a class attains its full expression. Art is a reflection of this process, a
realisation of this vision. It is an 'emancipation from daily practice similar to . . . the emergence of the scientific form of reflection' (Lukács,
1963, quoted in George Lichtheim, *Lukács*, Fontana, 1970), a contem-
plation which reveals the complexity of the ideology, the world view,
of a social group.

The structuralist view conceives of history as a complex process of
contradictions within and between economic, political and ideological
practices, a process whose development is uneven. Within this, the
particular practice of ideology at any one time is determined by the
overall relations between practices within the social formation. Art is
a practice of language within ideology: as such its task is to contribute
to the building of a particular reality. It uses language in particular
ways to carry this out. Here lies the difference between the two interpretations of the *nouveau roman*: Heath sees representation itself (the
idea of art as a reflection) as being ideological. Because realist writing
is a particular way of using language, the dominant mode in bourgeois
society, it is seen as inevitably tangled up with the particular social
forms of that society. Thus the novel stands as a symbol not for 'a
historical reality' as classic Marxist aesthetics have it, but rather for the
particular real which a society constructs for itself. As Stephen Heath
puts it:

'Reality', that is, needs to be understood not as an absolute and
immutable given but as a production within which representation
will depend on (and, dialectically, contribute to) what the French
Marxist philosopher Louis Althusser has described as 'practical
ideology', a complex formation of *montages* of notions, representations, images and modes of action, gestures, attitudes, the whole
ensemble functioning as practical norms which govern the concrete
stance of men in relation to the objects and problems of their social
and individual existence; in short, the lived relation of men to their
world. In this sense, the 'realistic' is not substantial but formal (a
process of significant 'fictions'), and, in connection with the novel, it

may be described in the notion of the *vraisemblable* of a particular society, the generally received picture of what may be regarded as 'realistic'. . . . Evidently, this *vraisemblable* is not recognised as such, but rather as, precisely, 'Reality'; its function is the naturalisation of that reality articulated by a society as *the* 'Reality' and its success is the degree to which it remains unknown as a form (op. cit., p. 20).

The triumph of the bourgeois novel is precisely to act as a mirror of the world; to use language as a tool that conveys the world without problems (i.e. in total complicity with the established *vraisemblable*). The success of this *vraisemblable* is shown by the way in which it remains unknown as a form to critics like Lukács and Goldmann who take an unequivocal stance against the nature of bourgeois society. They favour classic bourgeois realism as the form for socialist novels, precisely because they present an overall view of the whole reality of the world. They think in terms of a real world 'out there' which is accessible to reason, rather than a world which is produced by the whole ensemble of social activities, including that of conceptualisation in language. Although they show clearly the historical conditions in which literary texts were produced and which they come to reflect, they see no problem in this process of 'coming-to-reflect'. This leads Lukács into direct dispute with Brecht, whose theatre is a constant un-covering of this process of coming-to-reflect (see *New Left Review*, 84, March 1974).

Brecht's theatre consists of putting into crisis the normal forms of thinking and representation in bourgeois society. He was concerned that the spectator should not be put in the normal relationship with the text and the spectacle that is exploited in realism. This is essentially a relationship of consumption: the reader moves along a smooth pro-gression from one predominantly emotional event to another. It appears that events engender each other, that the progression from one to another is a causal link. This causality is far stronger than the wide historical causes which may be shown as acting on that situation, and the fiction is thus self-justifying. Against this, Brecht's theatre brings the spectator constantly into a relationship of criticism with the events depicted. The events themselves are incomplete; they point to the socially constructed reasons for their existence, and the spectator's critical attention is needed to realise these. There are many techniques used to achieve this situation in Brecht's theatre, but it is not a theatre of isolated techniques which can be appropriated as gimmicks. Its fundamental movement is to put into crisis the very forms of realist theatre. *The Mother*, as Barthes shows (*Essais critiques*, p. 143), is a complete reversal of the realist theatrical model of the young person who comes to full consciousness through the transmission of his cul-tural heritage from his parents. The central action of *The Mother* is of the Mother moving away from her fatalistic attitude towards a revolu-tionary stance because of the example of her son Pavel. Pavel is silent for the most part; the separate episodes show his mother dealing with various problems and, through the action, growing more aware of her position. The power and originality of Brecht's vision is starkly demonstrated by comparing the role of Pavel and the interaction of the disjoint scenes in his play with Pudovkin's 1926 film of the same Gorky story. Powerful as it is, the film flattens out the conflict and coming-to-consciousness that Brecht shows, and instead makes Pavel the central character. His heroism inspires his mother to one heroic gesture of her own at the end of the film. The effect is emotional and strong, but transitory; Brecht's is exemplary and moving.

Barthes was involved in the review *Théâtre populaire*'s crucial defence of Brecht's theatre after his Berliner Ensemble had visited Paris in 1954. He saw that this theatre was a comprehensive criticism of realism as a natural use of language in bourgeois society, as a constituent part of the (mostly fatalistic) 'natural attitude' of people within this society.

> Brechtian dramaturgy, the theory of the epic theatre, distantiation, and the whole Berliner Ensemble practice with regard to decor and costume pose an explicitly semiological problem. What the whole of Brechtian dramaturgy postulates is that, today at least, dramatic art has less to express the real than to signify it (*Essais critiques*, p. 87).

Brecht's attitudes have remained very important during the development of semiology, as is demonstrated by the special issue of *Screen* devoted to Brecht and a revolutionary cinema (Summer 1974), as well as Barthes's continuing interest. These attitudes demand a putting into crisis of realism, showing it to be a signification of reality and not an innocent conveying of it. And in early semiology, it was the task of the symbolical attention to the sign to uncover this process by which a particular way of writing becomes naturalised, an invisible form whose overall meaning is the perpetual statement 'this is reality'.

The paradigmatic attention to the sign demonstrates that realism is not simply a system whose overall aim is to construct a *vraisemblable*, as though each text presented itself as just a mirror of the world. Realism is complex and contradictory within itself; it is an overall form of writing that is normal in bourgeois society. Realism has its own forms, even forms to encompass the unreal (fantasy, the grotesque, science fiction, certain forms of comedy): the point is that all these forms use writing in a certain way, as the instrument to convey something else: the real.

The paradigmatic attention to the sign uncovers two kinds of forms used by realism: its forms of writing and the structure of the narrative which, when analysed as a structure composed of elements, was considered to be a 'universal' form similar to that of kinship in Lévi-Strauss's work. The basic model for the paradigmatic attention is Saussure's couple of *langue* and *parole*: the system and its activation in individual speech acts. Narrative structure exists as a *langue* itself, a system whose use is sharply delimited. However, the forms of realism occur between *langue* and *parole*: they are *écrivance*, forms of writing complicit with ideology, natural forms which do not have the same systematising status as *langue*. With both the narrative and the forms of realism, each text is a repetition of basic forms which exist only in the diversity of the texts themselves.

In the early *Writing Degree Zero*, Barthes described the development of the institution of Literature. In line with the general ideological project of the bourgeoisie (the universalisation of their ideas), a transparent writing was developed during the eighteenth century, part of the ideological preparation for the French Revolution, part of what Gramsci calls the establishment of hegemony. As capitalism developed, the contradictions between capital and labour became more apparent, and the Europe-wide revolutions of 1848 split bourgeois societies into three mutually hostile groups. 'These circumstances put the bourgeoisie into a new historical situation. . . . Henceforth, [its] ideology appears merely as one among many possible others . . . the writer falls prey to ambiguity, since his consciousness no longer accounts for the whole of his condition' (Barthes, *Writing Degree Zero*, p. 66). Transparent language cannot be maintained in the complex field of fiction writing; instead it is replaced by a conspicuous display of the craft of writing, the beginnings of the institution of Literature, a multiplication of modes of writing. Any account of modern literature has to take into account the different modes of writing (modes far wider than so-called good forms of writing given the label of literature; though radical texts, like Joyce's *Ulysses* can pass through many of them). These modes of writing are a particular system of which each piece of writing is an individual realisation. This seems uncontroversial enough, but its consequences have been difficult for orthodox literary criticism even to understand.

A mode of writing is pre-eminently social, it is a use of language which pre-dates the writer and forms the writer like language itself: it is a sociolect. The innovatory freedom for the user of the system is greater than in language, but still it is a freedom which is profoundly constrained by the historical situation of which these sociolects are a part. Dickens is an early example of a writer who utilises all the forms of writing available in his society, and is able — through a certain freedom in language — to question them. His *Hard Times* (1854) is within one such sociolect: the nineteenth-century social reform novel, known from writers like Mrs Gaskell, Disraeli, Mrs Trollope and many others who have not been admitted to the literary pantheon. The basis of the genre is to treat reality as a spectacle, society as a passive framework within which individuals move. This is achieved by repeating an established form of intelligibility, using stock ways of articulating the world. So the trite opposition of individual to society forms this sociolect: the result is a novel which portrays the ills of industrial society (misery, exploitation, ugliness) but shows any mass movement of workers organising against this as inevitably destructive. The only remedy is for the individual worker, Stephen Blackpool, to present his grievances to his employer on a personal basis.

However, his previous novel, *Bleak House* (1853) acts as an interrogation of the very ways of articulating reality that found the sociolect of *Hard Times*. The story is a search for connections between various people thrown together by the Court of Chancery, itself a logic running beyond individual understanding, without reason. The only link that is found is negative, that of disease and death. Thus in trying to make society intelligible (instead of reflecting it), *Bleak House* shows the apparent anarchy of capitalism; a society composed of isolated individuals whose only connection is the endless circularity of capital. To construct this interrogation of the limits of intelligibility of his society, Dickens breaks with the normal method of unilinear, impersonal narration, and inserts a second narrative: Esther's narrative. This is an innocent recounting of the spectacle of society which eventually moves towards the knowledge of the central narrative. It is the situating and unveiling of a particular sociolect: that of the governess novel (a well-known example is *Jane Eyre*). In this way, a particular form is shown for what it is, a way of knowing the world. Such forms of writing have their own logic and carry with them a way of thinking the world which can only be avoided by clear-sighted and constant work of criticism. Thus Brecht's work was always in tension with, a critique of, the form of tragedy whose particular logic is to lead to a resolution of grimly accepting history as eternal, the cultural as natural.

The way in which these forms of realist writing achieve their pre-eminence is by repetition. They are the accepted, normal ways of writing, endlessly diffused across all communication media. Their weight of social accretion, of normality and naturalness, far outweighs what one writer can achieve within them: thus radical writers resort to a 'raiding', an interruption and unveiling of forms whose life as a critical work lasts only so long as this interruption is not contained and transmuted into something fashionable (e.g. the dilution of Surrealism from the outrage of Bunuel/Dali's *Un Chien andalou* to the fashionable prints of Dali and the critical acclaim heaped on the latest Bunuel film).

Underlying these forms of realist writing, as well as 'articulate language, spoken or written; pictures, still or moving; gestures and the ordered arrangement of all of these ingredients' is the narrative. The structural analysis of the narrative claims to discover basic and trans-historical narrative relations applicable to all narrative texts. It was originated by Propp (in his classic *Morphology of the Folk Tale*, University of Texas Press, Austin, 1969) and the Russian Formalists; we shall merely sketch its basic features, following Barthes's 'Introduction to the structural analysis of the narrative' in *Communications*, 8:

either the narrative is a simple hotch-potch of events, in which case
it can only be discussed by referring it to the art, the talent or the
genius of the narrator (the author) — all mythical forms of chance —
or it shares with other narratives a structure which can be analysed,
however much patience it may require; there is a deep gulf between
the most complex product of chance and the simplest construction
of the mind, and no-one can build (produce) a narrative without
reference to an implicit system of units and rules (p. 2).

He then summarises extensive research as 'three levels of description':
functions, actions, and narrations. The activities these describe perpetually feed each other to produce the structure of a narrative.

Functions are small units of information which are either denoted or
connoted, and assume different importance according to the way in
which they are emphasised, and how the unfolding of the narrative
takes them up. Thus, in *Goldfinger*, we are told that Bond saw a man of
about fifty, and immediately this conveys two kinds of information:
first, a character trait (age) which feeds into the description of an actor;
second, that Bond does not know the man he is about to speak to (implying, in this novel-form, the beginning of a threat and the need to
identify; it opens certain narrations). Similarly, 'Bond picked up one of
the four phones' connotes Secret Service and technological efficiency,
as well as opening on to one of the possible sequences of actions to do
with telephone calls. Every item in a narrative performs some kind of
function.

The analysis of actions deals with the '*dramatis personae* or *actants*
[who] form a necessary level of description, outside which the smallest
related actions cease to be intelligible' (Barthes, op. cit.). A. J. Greimas
schematises these as six modes (which may be combined into single
characters or distributed amongst several). The *subject* is he who seeks,
desires, undertakes, and the *object* is that which is sought; the *giver*
sends the object and the *receiver* is the place to which it is sent; the
helper aids the action, and the *opposer* blocks it. These six modes,
expressed through very complex mediations, make up one of the bases
for all narratives according to this analysis.

The final level is that of narrations: the organisation both of the
attributes and the various expressions of the *actants* into sequences.
The narration takes place through an opening and closing of activities:
thus 'Bond picked up one of the four phones' inevitably opens onto the
sequence 'Conversation' from which will spring information, orders,
etc., which will lead to further sequences. Different analyses treat this
in various ways: Propp sees it as a simple unrolling; Lévi-Strauss and
Greimas see it as based on a set of oppositions; Bremond considers it
as governed by a logic of alternatives, each action implying various
choices of outcome which themselves lead to further choices. These
narrations are given a hierarchy (marked as either important or un-
important) by the 'attitude' of the other two levels as well as from the

accumulation of probabilities from the preceding narration. Thus 'He lit a cigarette' is incidental unless it is given extra importance in that the character involved fulfils an important action; has the attribute of only smoking under stress; or if the lighting of the cigarette itself initiates or furthers a sequence of narration.

The aim of the structural analysis of the narrative is to construct a kind of grammar for the narrative which could contribute to a (structural) linguistics of the discourse. Linguistics itself only deals with the sentence as its largest unit. This analysis therefore aims to demonstrate that vast numbers of narratives are constructed from basic rules. It is a transhistorical analysis, taking no account of the specificity of the language of the texts it analyses. The analysis of sociolects, on the other hand, aims to show that various modes of writing exist which give intelligibility to groups of texts, and that these sociolects are complicit with the established *vraisemblable* of society.

The paradigmatic attention to the sign returns texts to structures whose existence is of necessity constructed by the analysis: the syntagmatic attention tries to deal with the fullness of a text or small corpus in its individuality. It therefore uses certain aspects of the analysis of the narrative (in particular the narration in its perpetual opening and closing of events) in order to examine the work of a particular text within it. But this analysis of the singularity of a text tends towards a hermeticism, a tendency to think of the text as closed in the construction of its own rules. This is what traditional literary criticism means by 'the structure of the text': a formalisation of the pattern of action or meanings which stands as a sophisticated paraphrase of the text itself. Treated carefully, the syntagmatic attention outlines the way in which the text organises itself. It shows the text as a complex of differentiation, of oppositions which set in motion the creation of meanings. The syntagmatic attention aims to describe the conditions of meaning in a text, not any particular meaning(s): it is concerned with how a text means, not what it means.

Such is the project of the essays published by Barthes in his *Sur Racine*. Using a method similar to that of Lévi-Strauss's examination of myth, he outlines the sets of oppositions which govern Racine's plays: the action takes place in the antechamber, suspended between the chamber of power and the exterior of destruction and events. These oppositions immediately set in movement the pattern of the plays. But the aim of the book is not just to outline them, but to show how they generate meanings:

> Let us try on Racine, by virtue of his very silence, all the languages that our century gives us: . . . we shall not hide behind a 'truth' of Racine which our time is the only one (by what presumption?) to discover; it is enough that our response to Racine engages, rather than ourselves, all the languages through which our world speaks to

itself and which are an essential part of the history it gives itself
(Barthes, *Sur Racine*, p. 12).

This early formulation sees the text as a formal structure which is
activated by the languages which the reader reads in it. Already, this implies that traditional criticism based on the idea of the author is radically misconceived. Instead of showing the richness of the text in its
openness, its readability in the meanings that can be produced from it,
it aims at a particular sort of closure. It aims to establish *the* meaning of
the text, to reduce the text to a monologue whose function is to repeat
something else. That something else is the individuality of the Author
rather than the social institution of language. The Author becomes the
punctual source of the text (thus writing out history and society); the
meaning of the text is what the author intended, albeit unconsciously
(so the productivity of language and the autonomy of the text are cen-
sored). Criticism based on this notion of the Author-as-source has a
disturbing circularity even at its most sophisticated: it elides the complexity of the text in favour of simplistic psychology and fake historical
analogy. The question should not be 'Did Marlowe write Shakespeare?'
but 'Through and against what languages are those texts written?'

Yet, though this approach can carry through a radical critique of
literary criticism, it is, like the symbolical and paradigmatic attentions,
finally limited in what it can achieve.

In an initial moment . . . two complementary tendencies could be
noted in the thinking of textual semiotics: the attempt to construct
general descriptive models to account structurally for a mass of individual narratives, to define . . . a narrative *langue*, and, the second
tendency, the assumption of a structural closure of a given text and
the consequent attempt to render account of its coherence (and it is
here that old notions of organicism crept in again) in the description
of the structure *it proposes*. Pursued rigorously, there is a friction
between the two tendencies: if a *langue* may be defined to describe
the realisation of a mass of individual texts, how can a particular
text be seen as closed in the proposition of its own structure? (Heath,
The Nouveau Roman, p. 211).

There was a tendency for the general descriptive model of narrative
langue to become completely a-historical, a form valid for all time
despite any historical change. As a result, the historicity of an individual text had to be proposed as something closed, a matter of individual quirks which could only have resulted from some internal structuring. The transhistoricism of the first was answered by the hermeticism
of the second.

This discrepancy became most evident in dealing with texts which in
some way disturb the realist schema, or even the fixed relations of language itself. It is possible to consider texts like those of Robbe-Grillet,
or *Bleak House*, as unveiling the logic of realism, pushing it to its absurd
conclusion. But there exist more radical texts that can be seen in no

sense as 'closed in the proposition of their own structure', and cannot by any contortion be referred to a narrative structure or any other such system. These are texts like *Finnegans Wake*, or those of Mallarmé or Artaud which are witness to something more than a crisis in the relations of bourgeois representation. They work within the productivity of signifiers, to the extent that the word and grammatical relations are dissolved in the play of signifiers which is seen to produce multiple meaning in the process of reading. This is more than a crisis of bourgeois representation because it reveals the productivity of signification, and dissolves the identity of signifier and signified upon which the whole of Western discourse is ultimately based. This crisis reveals what is repressed in order that the sign should function as the representative of something. As Philippe Sollers announces it:

> Real — i.e. materialist — history cannot do without a *semantic materialism* . . . which, if it were founded, would open a very wide field of research. What is contested, here, is linear history which has always enslaved the text to a representation, a subject, a truth; it represses the enormous work undergone by limit-texts by using the theological categories of sense, subject and truth. The limits worked by these texts seem to me to be characterised by those names which linear history — within which we speak — has given them: mysticism, eroticism, madness, literature, unconscious. . . . In all these texts the theory of writing (*écriture*) is there, immanent, proved: but it is generally perceived as delirium, fantasy, poetry, obscurity, individual deviation etc. (*L'Ecriture et l'expérience des limites*, pp. 6—7).

What is revealed in these texts is that part of language which is beyond communication of content: it returns as musicality, rhythm, and productivity. Ultimately, it is psychoanalysis which can analyse this activity of language. The constant sliding of signifiers that constitutes *Finnegans Wake* gives a vague indication of this textual practice to which we refer: '(Stoop) if you are abcedminded, to this claybook, what curios of signs (please stoop), in this allaphbed!' (p. 18). This enunciation is itself transformed later in the book to 'Please stop if you're a B.C. minding missy, please do. But should you prefer A.D. stepplease' (p. 272). This play within and between enunciations produces many meanings, none of which could ever be called 'the' meaning, yet it still preserves grammatical relations. In other such texts (e.g. Artaud) even the relations between subject and predicate, action and object, are dislocated.

At first, semiology conceived of this textual practice as a practice of writing (*écriture*) which was contrasted with *écrivance*, writing which is devoid of productivity, complicit with dominant sociolects, and repeats itself within dominant ideological forms. However, as the work of the group involved in *Tel Quel* magazine progressed, it became evident that this view of the nature of *écrivance* was untenable. Instead of being conceived as an ensemble of structures composed of interrelated terms, realism itself was seen in terms of the productivity of relations within the signifying chain. Realism, *écrivance*, are then a limitation of the productivity of language through the establishment of certain positions for signification. It is the establishment of these positions which necessitates a repression which establishes for the human subject the discourse of the unconscious, analysed by Lacan. It is these repressed signifiers which return in the *avant-garde* text in the forms that Sollers outlines; in rhythm and musicality; in the sliding of signifiers exhibited in Joyce's writing.

The examination of realist texts now takes the form of an interrogation of their structuration rather than their structure. This is the method of Barthes's *S/Z*, examined in the following chapter. In seeing each text as an activity of production (including, therefore, the production of its own limits, its positionality and fixity), the two antithetical forms of structuralism are no longer possible. The transhistorical tendency of the structural analysis of the narrative is rendered obsolete. Barthes now describes it as an attempt

> to see all the world's narratives (and there are a multitude of them) within a single structure: we shall, they thought, extract from each tale its model, then out of these models we shall make a great narrative structure, which we shall reapply (for verification) to any one narrative: a task as exhaustive . . . as it is ultimately undesirable, because the text thereby loses its difference (*S/Z*, p. 3).

It is the *difference* which constitutes the text: each signifier opens onto a perspective of reference from which it differs, upon which it depends. These codes give the text its meanings and establish its positionality. Barthes speaks of the difference of the text rather than its individuality: individuality is a hermetic concept, whereas difference indicates the way in which a text at once *differs from* (is not the same as) other texts, and *defers to* (relies upon) them. This conception of difference (developed by Derrida) encapsulates the form of textual analysis advanced in *S/Z*: 'it is necessary at once to bring out the totality and the exteriority of the text' (ibid., p. 12). It is no longer a question of structure and instance (semiology), but of structuration (difference).

4 S/Z

S/Z aims to demonstrate how language produces the realist text as natural. It examines not the structure of the text but its structuration. The text is seen as a productivity of meaning which is carried on within a certain regime of sense: realism. The productivity of language which is dramatically revealed in the unconscious and in *avant-garde* texts is given a fixity, a positionality, so that it functions to 'denote' a 'reality'. Thus realism is more than a 'natural attitude', it is a practice of signification which relies upon the limits that society gives itself: certain realist texts, like the novella analysed in S/Z are consequently capable of dramatising these limits at certain moments.

Initially, Barthes expresses this new perception of the text by reformulating the distinction *écriture/écrivance*. He bases it on the 'practice of writing' (Barthes, S/Z, p. 3) in which realism is the normal mode, submitted to the need to represent. He speaks of 'writable' texts (the translation, unhelpfully, has 'writerly'): those texts that 'make the reader no longer a consumer, but a producer of the text': the texts of the *avant-garde* which deconstruct language. Face to face with this floating, open practice is the dominant mode of writing, a fixity, a process where the reader's role is that of consumer, able only to 'accept or reject the text'. This is the area of classic realist texts, the normal mode of writing. It is none the less possible to see that they are based on a certain, limited plurality of language; and it is precisely the task of S/Z to reveal this plurality, 'to appreciate what plural constitutes it' (S/Z, p. 5), as well as the closures of plurality which make possible its discourse. Some texts rely on the moment of closure more than others. Some veer towards the mere repetition of sociolects, but even these rely to some degree upon the productivity of language merely in order to function as a realist text. Barthes sees the liberating function of a criticism that shows the production of meaning at work in the realist text itself. Conventional criticism aims at a closure of the troubling plurality: it aims at an interpretation, fixing a meaning, finding a source (the author) and an ending, a closure (*the* meaning). This form of criticism plays the game that the text proposes: that the text is nothing except what it can denote or describe and the rhetorical grace with which it can do so. Barthes's liberatory criticism intends to discover what the rules of this game are (for writers and readers), in order to enter into a more serious and vital play: to find ideology out in the moment that it is produced.

To found this liberatory criticism, Barthes produces a 'slow-motion' reading of a text which is set within the realist form. It is formed by Balzac's aesthetic in which 'the art of literature is composed of two distinct parts: observation—expression' (*Comédie humaine* XI); the act of writing is the mere transcription of what has been observed. Yet at the same time, this particular text dramatises the limits of the realist form by introducing elements that question its whole basis: the text in question is *Sarrasine*, a novella written in 1830, concerning a castrato. The narrator is at a party given by the *nouveau riche* Lanty family. The woman who accompanied him has a brush with a mysterious debilitated old man, who is treated with exaggerated care by the family. The narrator undertakes to tell her the story of this character, in exchange for a night with her. It is the story of a sculptor, Sarrasine, who falls in love with Zambinella, a famous singer in Rome. Eventually, he can no longer avoid the fact that 'she' is a castrato: and he is murdered by the henchmen of the Cardinal who protects him/her. This castrato is the old man, whose singing was the source of the family's wealth. In horror at this unnatural tale, the woman refuses the narrator. Even in this brief summary, the troubling is reproduced: there is no 'neuter' personal pronoun; the castrato is a physical fact that unsettles sexual categorisation.

Sarrasine is a 'limit-text' of realism, a text which uses all the mechanisms of realism to produce a narrative which dramatises its very founding presuppositions. So, basing his aesthetic on the practice of writing (*écriture*), Barthes reveals realism as a social practice of representation which exploits the plurality of language in a limited way. It is a practice that has its own sociolects, a form which can generate texts which dramatise their own limits, a form that can be rebuffed by texts of unveiling, hesitation and productivity.

To understand *S/Z* as anything other than a superior formal method (and every indication is that this is how it has been received in Britain), it is necessary to understand what linguistic and ideological practices produce these various kinds of text. We must first understand the relation between realism and the plurality of language.

First, realism stresses the product and not the production. It represses production in the same way that the mechanism of the market, of general exchangeability, represses production in capitalist society. It does not matter where a product comes from, how it was made, by whom or for what purpose it was intended. All that matters is its value measured against the general medium of exchange, money. In the same way, it does not matter that realism is produced by a certain use of language, by a complex production; all that matters is the illusion, the story, the content. What we value is its truth to life, the accuracy of its vision. We do not read Agatha Christie or John Braine for the productivity of their language, we read for the story, the impression we produce of a real world. When we pay attention to the 'style' of writers like Raymond Chandler or Len Deighton, it is because this style produces the illusion of a character: the hard-boiled individualist using his limited powers against a social system he does not fully understand. We do not look at the production, but the product; hence the shock of reading an unusual book like *S/Z*, which goes against the 'natural' way of reading realist texts, and looks precisely at the way in which the illusion is produced. It treats realism as an effect of language, and not language as a (rhetorical) effect of realism.

This repression of production takes place because realism has as its basic philosophy of language not a production (signification being the production of a signified through the action of the signifying chain), but an identity: the signifier is treated as identical to a (pre-existent) signified. The signifier and signified are not seen as caught up together in a process of production, they are treated as equivalents: the signifier is merely the equivalent of its pre-established concept. It seems as though it is not the business of language to establish this concept, but merely to express or communicate it. 'Not only do signifier and signified seem to unite, but in this confusion, the signifier seems to be erased or to become transparent so as to let the concept present itself, just as if it were referring to nothing but its own presence' (Derrida, *Positions*, pp. 32−3). Language is treated as though it stands in for, is identical with, the real world. The business of realist writing is, according to its philosophy, to be the equivalent of a reality, to imitate it. This 'imitation' is the basis of realist literature, and its technical name is *mimesis*, mimicry. The whole basis of mimesis is that writing is a mere transcription of the real, carrying it over into a medium that exists only as a parasitic practice because the word is identical to, the equivalent of, the real world. Realism naturalises the arbitrary nature of the sign; its philosophy is that of an identity between signifier and signified on the level of an entire text as much as that of a single word.

There are many texts which question this instrumentalist view of language, some written even when it was first being established. A crucial part of the attempt by the emergent bourgeoisie to establish its hegemony in the late seventeenth and early eighteenth centuries was the creation of several institutions of language. In England, there was the Royal Society with its official, 'scientific', philosophy of language, as well as the institutions of journalism and the novel, etc. Swift satirised instrumentalism with his vision of people carrying round literal objects with which to converse (*Gulliver's Travels*), and Sterne, in *Tristram Shandy* (1759−66), unmasked its presuppositions in play. His comedy consists of taking the realist form too seriously, at its face value. He forces its claims of 'fidelity to reality', 'mirroring reality' to their absurd conclusion. For instance, he attempts to equate the time taken to read a passage with the time it took in reality to carry the action forward to the next episode (vol. IX, chs 17–20). In direct contrast these chapters are followed by the briefest possible mention of a set of actions, a mere signalling: 'My uncle Toby's map is carried down into the kitchen', which comprises a whole chapter (vol. IX, ch. 27).

But the challenge to mimesis is carried on almost at a deeper level, the level at which the troubling of *Sarrasine* occurs. *Tristram Shandy* is concerned with what it cannot speak both because of censorship and the nature of realist language: sexuality and castration. The book begins, logically according to the realist schema, with the first appearance of the central character: that is, with his conception. This account of *coitus interruptus* is obscure only because the text cannot in all propriety name what act is taking place. But the real problem that the book has is not so much sexuality as castration, the same problem as *Sarrasine*. Uncle Toby received a wound 'in the groin' whose exact nature intrigues many; and he himself devotes much of his time to dramatising the moment of this castration in his war-game. Tristram had his nose flattened, a statement whose overt meaning is constantly subverted by the presence of sexual puns on the word 'nose', like Slawkenbergius's Tale, a discourse from outside that opens vol. IV. The book plays on castration as a lack it cannot name if it is to comply with the canons of decency. It employs the constant metaphors to which it must resort to express castration as a perpetual undermining of realist language's claim to imitate. In *Tristram Shandy* this realist language becomes treacherous, the signifier is no longer linked to the signified in a relationship of identity. There is a constant sliding of signifiers; substitution, relationships of metaphor; a dissolution of the realist signifier–signified equivalence. The attempts at exact, detailed description try to restore this equivalence, but finally they confirm its impossibility. *Tristram Shandy* thus plays with mimesis, attempting to give a full and accurate picture of reality, but instead showing up the repressed area of production of meaning.

Its way of doing this is distinct from *Sarrasine. Tristram Shandy* is obsessed with convention, with the correct way of behaving and of writing. With *Sarrasine*, seventy years later, the realist convention is no longer visible as a convention; it has become natural, identical with reality. So anything that disturbs its naturalness, its ability to imitate the real, inevitably disturbs that real as much as its instrumental language. For *Tristram Shandy*, realist language is still visible as a convention (the desirable way of writing rather than natural). The comedy of the book is thus to show the inadequacy of conventions (social and literary) in the face of a multiple reality that cannot be fully comprehended. Without this element of play, Sterne lapses into the dominant mode for expressing the incomprehensibility of reality: sentimentalism (*A Sentimental Journey*, etc.). Balzac's habitual mode is the fully-fledged language of realism, the language of mastery, of the 'science of reality' as he described it.

The identity between signifier and signified which is established in realist writing is the precondition of its ability to represent a *vraisemblable*, an accepted natural view of the world. It does not mean that all writing is absolutely transparent, but rather that the narration, the dominant discourse, is able to establish itself as 'Truth. The narration does not appear to be the voice of an author; its source appears to be a true reality which speaks. The value of other discourses in the text (the speech of various characters, descriptions of subjective processes, etc.) is measured against this voice of truth. Thus a general evaluation of the discourses of the writing is established. The absolute value is that of reality itself, and the discourse of the narration attains this through the creation of an identity between signifier and signified. The other discourses of the text then contain varying degrees of truth or even none at all. Through this position of dominance, based on its equivalence with reality, the narration can then attribute points of origin for subsidiary discourses, appearing itself to have a point of origin in reality. So fragments of writing are confidently attributable to one character or another. And as we shall see with the analysis of *S/Z*, the narration also establishes the basic positionality for these characters, by setting up antithetical oppositions between them, creating a system of mutually-defining, separated spaces.

The realist narrative functions to uncover a world of truth, a world without contradictions, a homogeneous world of appearance supported by essences. But as Stephen Heath has pointed out in his seminal analysis of the film *Touch of Evil* (*Screen*, vol. 16, nos 1, 2), the process of narration is itself necessarily a statement of contradiction and heterogeneity: although the narrative-as-product displays a harmonious world of reality, the process of unfolding is the continuous statement of contradiction which will be more or less closed at the end.

The beginning of the narrative action depends on a violence as interruption, as the violation of a state of homogeneity . . . the point of the action, the goal of its advance, is the recovery of homogeneity according to a movement of reconvergence—reinvestment which, precisely, realigns, contains the violence anew (Heath, op. cit., no. 2, p. 91).

The paradox of such a narrative is then this: aimed at containment, it restates heterogeneity as the constant term of its action — if there is symmetry, there is dissymmetry, if there is resolution, there is violence; it contains as one contains an enemy, holding in place but defensively (ibid., no. 1, p. 49).

It is this movement of process and of opening that *S/Z* attempts to capture in its analysis of the structuration of the text.

This process of narration, a process that opens and closes with homogeneity, depends on 'the inscription of the subject as the place of its intelligibility' (ibid., no. 2, p. 98). The whole process is directed towards the place of a reader: in order that it should be intelligible, the reader has to adopt a certain position with regard to the text. This position is that of homogeneity, of truth. The narration calls upon the subject to regard the process of the narrative as a provisional openness, dependent upon the closure which the subject expects as the very precondition of its pleasure. In order that the narrative is intelligible at all, it is necessary that the subject regards the discourse of narration as the discourse of the unfolding of truth. The subject must operate the identity between signifier and signified: and as we shall see, the construction of the subject as homogeneous in ideology places it in an imaginary position of transcendence to this system. So the subject is constructed in such a way that it is not questioned by the flux of the text (something that is regarded as an 'aberrant reaction'); neither is it thrown into process by the sliding of signifiers which disestablish social positionality, as with the *avant-garde* text. Narration rather sets the subject in place as the point of intelligibility of its activity: the subject is then in a position of observation, understanding, synthesising. The subject of narration is a homogeneous subject, fixed in a relation of watching. It is precisely this relationship of specularity that becomes clear in the analysis of films, hence the importance of magazines like *Screen* which analyse narration in the cinema and the positions for the subject that it includes.

Texts which do not depend on placing the subject in this kind of position are as rare in the cinema as in literature itself. For reasons of convenience, we shall confine our account to literature, where a text like Joyce's *Ulysses* appears at certain points to be creating 'that breach of the "I" [exhibited in] the explosion of modern literature: a plurality of languages, a confrontation of types of discourse and ideologies, with no conclusions and no synthesis — without "monological" or axial points' (Kristeva in *Twentieth Century Studies*, no. 7—8, p. 111). In the 'Nighttown' sequence of *Ulysses* (Penguin ed., pp. 425—532), this lack of positionality takes the form of a dramatisation: the theatrical form is appropriate because the positions of realist language become a performance, they are shown as arbitrary, shifting and confusable roles. The names which 'utter' discourses are not origins, they are no more than points that are criss-crossed by discourses that are no longer stratified. Hence the descriptions of characters are constantly changing; fantasies of total power, abasement, sexuality, Samaritanism, etc. move with expressions of repressed elements: guilt; obscenities; everyday exchanges; oratory; songs; political, medical and academic discourse; revision of previous 'points of view'; catalogues of disparate items and names. It is no longer possible for the reading subject to establish a comparative valuation of these discourses according to the points which utter them, and the positions they express. Bloom changes shape, sex and appearance so often that even the illusion of a physical presence as the ultimate grounding point of a character completely disappears. What the 'Nighttown' sequence does is to dramatise the production of positions in language, showing them to be woven of multiple contradictions.

Thus realism has two basic features: mimesis, the imitation of reality based on fixing the signifier/signified identity, and the stratification of discourses around this which set the subject in the place of mastery. But these mechanisms take place over a multitude of different texts, and are supported by a practice of reading and writing. So how does realism find its social hold, how does it appear multiple and always changing, as the immediate 'spontaneous' mode of writing and reading? The practice of reading and writing are determined by the widest forms of behaviour, the basic attitude of capitalist society: reading is a consumption, writing is a purely instrumental use of language. Reading as consumption presupposes that the text is read once, for its imitation of reality: 're-reading is an operation contrary to the commercial and ideological habits of our society which would have us "throw away" the story once it has been consumed ("devoured"), so that one can move on to another story, buy another book' (*S/Z*, p. 15). This reading pays a certain attention to the text, because some discourses, some pieces of information, indicate themselves as incidental, as the confirmation of the illusion: messages 'whose very gratuitousness serves to authenticate the fiction by what is called the reality effect' (*S/Z*, p. 182). *Tristram Shandy* draws attention to this, but only once, as persistence would endanger the text's whole game with mimesis: 'How could you, Madam, be so inattentive in reading the last chapter? I told you in it, *That my mother was not a papist*' (vol. 1, ch. 20). An argument ensues between Shandy and this inattentive reader; she is sent back to re-read the chapter, because, we are told whilst she does so, ' 'Tis to rebuke a vicious taste, which has crept into thousands besides herself, — of reading straight forwards, more in quest of the adventures, than of the deep erudition and knowledge which a book of this cast, if read over as it should be, would infallibly impart with them.' The information could only have been gleaned by drawing out all the implications of each remark and not following the narrative onwards, for it is contained in 'the last line but one of the chapter, where I take upon me to say, "It was *necessary* I should be born before I was christened". Had my mother, Madam, been a Papist, that consequence did not follow.' A footnote is needed to elucidate the theological nicety involved.

The way of writing complementary to this mode of consumerist reading is that of *écrivance*, instrumental use of language. It is a use of language that calls up a vast reserve of echoes from similar texts, similar phrasings, remarks, situations, characters. This process is not one of pure repetition therefore, but, rather, a limited exploitation of the plurality of language, through a controlled process of echoing, re-calling.

Kristeva introduced the term *intertextuality* for this process — which applies as much to reading as to writing — a term first used by Mikhael Bakhtin.

In order to analyse the structuration of the novel rather than the structure, we shall situate it within the totality of previous or synchronic texts. . . . So as to study the structuration of the text as transformation, we shall picture it as a textual dialogue, or better, as an intertextuality. We shall therefore state that consideration of the novel as a transformation implies that it is approached as 'a system that is not adequate in itself and which must refer to its surrounding environment' (Lévi-Strauss) Kristeva, *Le Texte du roman*, pp. 67–9).

This environment is understood as the whole limitless corpus of writing, for 'what lies behind the paper is not reality, the referent, but Reference, "the subtle immensity of writing" ' (*S/Z*, p. 122). The naturalness of realism derives from its echoes of other writing that represent reality through a transparent language, whether novels, journalism or treatises, etc., as well as from modes of speaking, proverb, etc. Intertextuality designates, for the realist text, the process by which it uses language in order to appear real and natural: natural because it leans on the density of writing which becomes ordinary and invisible as writing; real because it calls on the whole *vraisemblable*. This realness is constructed precisely by the constant re-presentation of the same relations in a different guise, the constant cross-echoing of texts, of writing, 'a circular recollection. And this is precisely the inter-text: the impossibility of living outside the infinite text — whether this be Proust, the daily newspaper or the television screen: the book makes sense, sense makes life' (Barthes, *Le Plaisir du texte*, p. 59). Each text is suspended in the network of all others, from which it derives its intelligibility. Realism is 'a copy of a copy', supported by connotation, a 'perspective of citations'. It is silent quotation, without inverted commas, with no precise source.

Intertextuality cannot indicate a monolithic process without change. Writing involves the constant reformulation and repositioning of the signifying process that is being called up:

the term *intertextuality* designates this transposition of one (or several) system(s) of signs into another. . . . The passage from one signifying system to another demands a new articulation of the *thetic* — of enunciative and denotative positionality . . . [this] transposition is the possibility for the signifying process to pass from one system to another, to exchange them and to permutate them (Kristeva, *La Révolution du langage poétique*, pp. 59–60).

The continual process of writing is not a mere addition, a piling-up of citations onto other citations to form an ever more compact tissue of realist language; it is a constant process of displacement and revision. Each new citation alters those that have gone before; imperceptibly, the form of the realist illusion is changed, new sociolects emerge and others have their particular energies scattered and redirected. It is this aspect of intertextuality that is exploited in *avant-garde* texts: they throw together scraps of phrases, etc., but without a unifying, totalising position. They play with and in ideology.

This intertextual process of citation operates by connotation: connotation describes the way in which the intertextual space is articulated in one text. It is not a matter of an 'association of ideas', something that is personal, a-social, arbitrary; it is rather the way in which the whole corpus of realist knowledge (a social knowledge) is called upon to support the fiction, to give it its necessary solidity. Barthes likens this process to that of a limited 'noise' (in the technical sense of interference, disturbance in the material of communication):

> In contrast to idyllic communication, to pure communication
> (which would be for example that of the formalised sciences), read-
> able writing enacts a certain 'noise', it is the writing of noise, of
> impure communication; but this noise is not confused, massive and
> unnameable; it is a clear noise, made up of connections and not
> superimpositions: it is a matter of a distinct 'cacography' (*S/Z*,
> p. 132),

that is, a comprehensible cacophony of writing. Connotations are sown throughout the text, each one the opening for a code, a form of intelligibility. This spread of connotation is enough to ensure the reality of the text without calling attention to its productive, intertextual nature.

Thus the idea of intertextuality conceives of the realist text as calling on a tissue of 'voices' from the whole vast corpus of writing of all kinds. These voices are transposed into the text in question, each usage modifying the corpus slightly. The mechanism by which the voices are called up is that of connotation: each word and group of words reverberates with other and similar uses, opening onto a limitless 'perspective of fragments, of voices from other texts, other codes' (*S/Z*, p. 12). These perspectives, these voices, occur as various forms of intelligibility: the five codes that Barthes identifies as organising the connotations of *Sarrasine*.

Denotation is shown to be a product, an effect, of connotation. It is here defined, in contrast to the naive formulation in *Mythologies*, as 'the last of connotations'. Denotation is the effect of a closure, a limiting of the connotative process, of the productivity of meaning.

> Ideologically, this play [of connotation] has the advantage of
> affording the classic text a certain innocence . . . denotation is not
> the first sense, but it pretends to be; under this illusion, it is ulti-
> mately only the *last* of connotations (that which seems at once to
> found and close the reading), the superior myth by which the text
> pretends to return to the nature of language, to language as nature
> (*S/Z*, p. 9).

The final effect of connotation in the realist text is to produce the illusion of denotation, the illusion that language is incidental in the process of transcription of the real. The 'superior myth' is precisely that of the

identity between signifier and signified, the way in which they are
treated as equivalents. Connotation calls upon the intertextual space
only so as to make that whole process of productivity seem invisible, a
direct imitation of reality. This closure is effected, as we shall see,
through two codes, those of narration and of the enigma, the question
that the text poses. These two codes have an onward thrust which ensures that the text is read progressively 'from beginning to end', cream-
ing off denotative meaning sufficient to accomplish the reading of a
story.

The point at which the process of denotation is expressed most
clearly is in the repetition without variation of stereotypes, something
that takes place throughout our culture:

> Encratic language, (that which is produced and spread under the pro-
> tection of power) is by definition a language of repetition; all the
> official institutions of language are recapturing mechanisms: school,
> sport, advertising, pulp novels, pop songs, news, always repeat the
> same structure, the same sense, often the same words: stereotypes
> are a political fact, the principal aspect of ideology (Barthes, *Le
> Plaisir du texte,* p. 66).

Stereotypes are immediately identifiable, concrete common-sense definitions; they are solidified language, the point where connotation is
closed:

> A stereotype is a word that is repeated without any magic, any en-
> thusiasm, as if it were quite natural, as if by some miracle this
> recurring word was adequate every time for different reasons, as if
> imitation was no longer felt to be imitation: an over-familiar word,
> which claims consistency and does not know its own insistency.
> Nietzsche remarks that 'truth' is nothing other than the solidifica-
> tion of old metaphors. In this way, stereotypes are the contem-
> porary path of 'truth', the way in which the original rhetorical effect
> is transformed into the canonical, constraining form of the signified
> (ibid., p. 69).

The contemporary example of this solidification of rhetorical effect
into endlessly repeated truth is the opposition 'moderate/extremist'.
This 'turn of phrase' now provides the basic positionality of present-day
political life. Its connotations become richer with every use, and the
metaphor solidifies until it becomes reality itself.

Barthes sees five forms of connotation, five codes that organise the
intelligibility of *Sarrasine*. They correspond to the five major critical
languages of our time: narrative, thematic, psychological, sociological
and psychoanalytic criticisms. But they are not conceived as five independent ways of looking at a text, but as five organisations all of which
are essential for any act of reading a text. The five critical methods
mentioned above merely privilege one over the others in their operation. Barthes's analysis splits up the story into 'lexies', sometimes
phrases, sometimes groups of sentences, which imply at most three of

these codes in their reading, in the way that their connotations are organised. He then identifies the codes and analyses their precise function at that moment; sometimes he adds further commenting and synthesising passages. The result is a 'slow-motion reading', watching the production of meaning.

Two of the codes are responsible for giving the text its forward impulsion, moving it from point to point, towards its inevitable end. These are the *proiaretic* code and the *hermeneutic* code. The proiaretic code composes the actions, the narrative. This moves from one action to another, constantly opening on to already-known narrative actions (seduction, orgy, conversation, etc.). This opening presupposes a continuation and a closure, an ending, and it is this pressure to finish that pushes on the narrative. Even the opening of a door presupposes its closing and offers possibilities of someone coming through, description of an interior, etc. Gradually these minute, named actions build up into a sequence which can continue for a long period, or indeed compose the narrative of the book (seduction is the subject of many books; in *Sarrasine* it is a brief episode). It is a constant process of naming, of defining sequences (whether they are from 'real life' or from novelistic convention) which makes the proiaretic code: it is this naming and the consequent impulsion to finish the sequence which guarantees the readability of the realist text as a story. It is not, therefore, a matter of narrative structure that is generated from a closed system, but of an activity of intertextual connotation, of production of sequences, and the ability to recognise and name them.

The hermeneutic code constantly reformulates the problem that the text represents. In *Sarrasine*, this problem is an engima, 'What is Zambinella?'; in other texts it can be an incompatibility between social forces or, 'Who done it?', etc. They are all questions which are answered when the text ends (whose answer constitutes the end of the text):

> To narrate (in the classic fashion) is to pose a question as if it were a subject which one delays predicating; when the predicate (the truth) arrives, the sentence, the narrative, are finished, the world is adjectivised (after we had a great fear that it wouldn't be) (*S/Z*, p. 76).

So as not to answer its question too soon, the hermeneutic code delays the answer in various ways: by constant reformulation; by the promise that there will be an answer (the narrator undertakes to tell the story); by various traps; by equivocation, by half-truth and half-trap; by asserting the insolubility of the enigma; by providing a suspended response, a reply that is broken off; by a partial answer, giving only one of the characteristics necessary to construct the truth. The hermeneutic poses an enigma and then teases through the progression of the narrative actions until the enigma is resolved, the truth is revealed.

These codes give the text its forward thrust, but they are nothing in themselves. Three other codes provide the vital information, produce the connotations necessary to complete the intelligibility of the text. These are the cultural, semic and symbolic codes. Of these, the symbolic code is the most difficult for us to understand, both because it is the source of the troubling in *Sarrasine* and because it depends on Lacanian psychoanalysis.

The *cultural code* is the way in which the text refers outwards to general knowledge (of art, medicine, politics, literature, etc., as well as to proverb and cliché). It is the realm of 'mythology', of ideology when it is considered as a system of ideas:

The very numerous codes of knowledge or of conventional wisdom to which the text ceaselessly refers (*S/Z*, p. 18).

They form a kind of scientific vulgate which it would eventually be valuable to describe: what do we 'naturally' know about . . . youth? —'it is turbulent', etc. If you collect up all these knowledges, all such vulgarisms, they form a monster, and this monster is ideology. As a fragment of ideology, the cultural code *inverts* its (social and school) class origin into a natural reference, into a proverbial assertion (*S/Z*, pp. 97–8).

The interweaving of the references in this code forms the sense of reality of the book; for these ideas themselves form the natural, the *vraisemblable* of their culture. They are what everybody knows, naturally.

The *semic code* deals in characteristics, whether they are psychological, of character or of atmosphere. Their naming is an important moment in the closure of the play of meaning. At no point does *Sarrasine* say directly that the Lanty family is very rich, but every indication says that they are (they live in a fashionable area of Paris, they give sumptuous parties, their money is discussed). From these indications, the seme of 'richness' is constructed. But the moment that this seme is named, the remarks have fulfilled their (realist) function and are not investigated any further. The narrative continues.

The seme is a connotator of persons, places objects, of which the signified is a characteristic. . . . Even though the connotation may be clear, the nomination of its signified is uncertain, approximative, unstable: how the naming of the signified is stopped depends largely on the critical pertinence to which we adhere: the seme is only a *departure*, an avenue of sense (*S/Z*, pp. 190–1).

These characteristics are sown throughout the text; they are fixed to a character by grouping themselves around a name. Hence Sarrasine attracts the semes of Genius, Impiety, Wildness, Excess. These can migrate between characters or apply to whole groups.

The *symbolic code* is the field in which the basic positionality of the text and the reader is charted. In the realist text, positions are inevitably constituted according to psychoanalytic principles. At the beginning of *S/Z*, Barthes shows how certain semes (inside/outside; hot/cold) are organised into an antithesis that gives the basic positionality of the text: either masculine or feminine. No position is possible between or outside them: they are the normal (ideologically constructed) positions of society. Thus the shock of Zambinella's castration: the introduction of a castrato, straddling the division between these irreconcilable elements of the antithesis masculine/feminine, disturbs both language and the positions it constructs.

But it is not only the rhetorical device that provides the positionality. Usually, this is the textual expression 'of the biological axis of the sexes (which would force us, quite pointlessly, to put all women in this story in the same class)' (*S/Z*, p. 35). This relationship of positions is defined around the 'to have' or 'to have not' of the phallus, which according to Lacan is the sign around which the dialectic of identifications of the subject is made. For the phallus functions as a signifier whose reference is the cultural order. It is by taking up positions around it that accession to the symbolic is achieved. Sexual relations are grouped around the phallic symbol, and positions of exchange are established by identifications made by the ego in relation to it. For the particular text of *Sarrasine*, this relationship would provide 'a complete structure of the sexes (two opposed terms, a mixed term and a neutral term) . . . (1) being the phallus (the men) . . . (2) having it (the women) . . . (3) having it and being it (the androgynes) . . . (4) neither having it nor being it (Zambinella)' (*S/Z*, p. 35). However, a normal arrangement does not hold for this text: at some moments, women are opposed to each other in relations of power/subservience (e.g. mother to daughter); and none of the men represent a full virility, being in accessory positions, subjected, or behaving maternally. Thus it appears that the positionality is arranged around castration rather than the phallus, around the division active/passive, castrator/castrated. The active woman, together with the motherly sculptor who shields Sarrasine from sexuality, etc. are on the side of the castrated; 'as far as the castrato himself, we would be wrong to place him of necessity among the castrated: he is the blind and mobile flaw of this system; he moves back and forth between the active and the passive: castrated, he castrates' (*S/Z*, p. 36). So, here, positionality is established not around the normal opposition fullness/lack (phallus), but around active/passive (castration).

Though the introduction of castration at this level is consistent with the theme of the book, it nevertheless disturbs normal positionality, making problematic the basic sexual antithesis of positions which underlies most realist texts. The relations between positions are now established not according to fullness, presence, but according to a lack, a deficiency. It is this orientation of the text that shakes the entire system of exchange, equivalence, identity and fullness upon which the realist text is founded. Instead of fullness, there is lack; instead of identity, difference; instead of exchange, refusal. The realist text is normally a system of equivalence; the signifier stands as the equivalent of the signified (this equivalence gives rise to mimesis, the identity of signifier and signified). The book, the story itself is a saleable commodity that is exchangeable with something agreed to be of the same value. But all of this is disturbed here: the story that the narrator tells is too shocking, and the woman refuses to pay him for it. This is just one expression of the break in the circuit of equivalences which enables exchanges to take place. Marx shows that recognised socially-fixed positions are necessary for the exchange of commodities;

> In order that these objects may enter into relation with each other as commodities, their guardians must place themselves in relation to one another. . . . They must, therefore, mutually recognise in each other the rights of private proprietors. This juridical relation, which thus expresses itself in a contract, whether such a contract be part of a developed legal system or not, is a relation between two wills (*Capital*, vol. 1, p. 88).

Equally, the positionality established in the realist text is necessary for its system of equivalence to function. So what is the result of this troubling orientation of the positionality of *Sarrasine* around a lack rather than a fullness?

On the level of the writing itself, the identity between the signifier and the signified is disturbed. Then, the sexual opposition which is necessary for reproduction is displaced by the entry of a third, troubling term. Finally, gold is shown as being a troubling form of wealth, a new form that is no longer simply the index of physical wealth. These three forms of disturbance are three 'routes of entry' into the symbolic code, 'none of which is privileged' (*S/Z*, p. 215). They are equally the three major forms of exchange by which society reproduces itself (language, sexuality and economics), each of which requires a fixed positionality (addressor–addressee; masculine–feminine; buyer–seller). The disturbance in this text originates in the area of sexual positionality, but its effects are felt equally and necessarily in each of these areas: positionality is disturbed, so each of these modes of reproduction becomes impossible.

Language is questioned because the signifier and signified are no longer freely interchangeable: their identity is challenged. 'The economy of language (is) usually protected by the separation of opposites' (*S/Z*, p. 215), but here a third term intervenes in the antithesis masculine/feminine, which abolishes the bar between them. It is a situation that can be named, but cannot be described. The descriptions of the castrato vary wildly from the most feminine semes to the most masculine. This confounding of semes constantly transgresses the antithesis: it is impossible to say what Zambinella is. We are aware of a signified which can be pointed to (the barest and least satisfying form of signification), but realist language cannot reproduce it. It would have to resort to a different strategy of writing to do so, a strategy which would be aware of how it constructs positionality. This was not historically possible until much later: here, it is a disturbance, a dramatisation of the impossibility of a truly mimetic writing, which spreads into the account of other arts. The statue and the painting of Zambinella are both mistaken: they reproduce a full femininity, not realising that they should attempt the impossible, to represent and imitate a castrato.

Sexuality is disturbed because the division of the sexes which is necessary for reproduction is confounded: in 'the economy of the body, parts cannot interchange, the sexes cannot be equivalents' (*S/Z*, p. 215). The intervention of a neuter term into this opposition is the introduction of a different kind of body which can be desired (Sarrasine desires Zambinella), but is sterile, useless for reproduction. Thus 'the contract of desire [is] falsified' because 'the neuter claims to be human' (*S/Z*, p. 215). The 'seller' Zambinella (who performs on stage) has tricked the 'buyer' Sarrasine by taking a position that is not rightfully hers/his. But the trick cannot be revealed satisfactorily by returning Zambinella to a correct position because such a position does not exist. Thus the sexual antithesis is rendered uneasy.

Economic exchange itself is shown to be disturbed by the intervention of the wealth of the Lanty family and their like: 'Parisian gold produced by the new social class, speculative and no longer land-based — such gold is without origin, it has repudiated every code of circulation, every rule of exchange, every line of propriety' (*S/Z*, p. 215). This troubling is the irruption of the financial bourgeoisie, whose wealth is not the traditional form of feudal and early bourgeois society, the index of property and of social position: it comes from exchange, is wealth itself. The troubling of traditional social positions is the creation of a new social positionality where social place is not determined by land, title and heredity, but by the possession of money and the skill in its use. The political attitude of *Sarrasine* can thus be called 'reactionary' because it takes the side of old positions by showing new social forces as destructive. What takes place in the 1830s of this novella is a development in the economic role of gold, from being a particular equivalent alongside others (land, title, etc.), to being the universal equivalent:

> Like all other commodities, [gold] was also capable of serving as an equivalent in isolated exchanges, or as a particular equivalent by the side of others. Gradually it began to serve, within varying limits, as universal equivalent. So as soon as it monopolises this position in the expression of value for the world of commodities, it becomes the money commodity, and then, and not until then, does . . . the general form of value become changed into the money form (Marx, *Capital*, vol. 1, p. 75).

Gold gains a new economic meaning (the money commodity) which brings with it new social positions (finance capitalists). This is an alteration in the chain of difference of social meaning, and as such it supports and produces new positions.

Shifting from monarchy based on land to an industrial monarchy,
society changed the Book, it passed from the Letter (of nobility)
to the Figure (of fortune), from title deeds to ledgers, but it was always subject to a writing. The difference between feudal society and
bourgeois society is this: the index has an origin, the sign does
not. . . . Replacing the feudal index, the bourgeois sign is a metonymic confusion (S/Z, pp. 39—40).

Sarrasine's political stance can be called reactionary for this reason; it
looks backwards to old social positions, seeing new positions as a disturbance of the chain of exchange, of substitution.

However, *Sarrasine* is in no way a simply reactionary text, because
several forms of positionality are involved in its disturbances. The
presence of the castrato

abolishes the power of *legal substitution*, on which meaning is based:
it is no longer possible to oppose in a regular way one contrary to
another, one sex to another, one commodity to another; it is no
longer possible to safeguard an order of just equivalence; in a word it
is no longer possible to *represent*, to make things *representative*,
individuated, separated, assigned: *Sarrasine* represent the very
troubling of representation, the unbridled (pandemic) circulation of
signs, of sexes, of fortunes (S/Z, p. 216).

Sarrasine dramatises the limits of the social positions necessary for
realist language, for sexuality directed towards reproduction, for the
form of exchange of feudal and early bourgeois society. It is in the
symbolic code that these positions are established.

S/Z demonstrates how a 'limit-text' disturbs the positionalities upon
which the representations of bourgeois society depend, positionalities towards which these representations contribute. However, such a limit-text
can only dramatise the existence of positionality and representation. It
is the discourse of Marxism and psychoanalysis which can unveil them as
arrangements of an activity of production. Psychoanalysis demonstrates
how the positions of the subject that are necessary for predication are
constructed in the interaction of somatic drives and the contradictory
outside of sociality. It shows how the accession to language is the crucial
moment in the formation of this subject who is able to participate in the
social processes of exchange, communication and reproduction. Marxism
demonstrates how the positionality of exchange is a necessary fixity (a
'contractual relation') within a social process formed by the articulation
of economic, political and ideological practices. Furthermore, ideological
practice shows that this positionality is produced for a subject within a
mode of representation. This fixing of positions for the subject can be
seen to be a part of the process analysed in psychoanalysis. It has been
the research into language (the key to both ideology and to the simultaneous construction of conscious and unconscious) which has made it
possible to develop this crucial area in theory. It is these developments
(many of which underlie the work of *S/Z*) to which we now turn.

5 Marxism, language, and ideology

The previous chapters have shown how semiology and structuralism conceived of society in terms of structure and of language. We have seen various attempts to deal with social systems of signification that result from this thinking, and have indicated some of their short-comings. However, the realms of thought upon which structuralism draws are not full and finished, they are themselves in crisis. It is not possible to think of social structure without taking account of social conflicts, of change and of revolution: in short, without accounting for the constant mutation of structures which are, at any one moment, uneasy and are constituted by forces that are in conflict. The structures are in fact constituted by the very conflict of these forces. It is Marxist thought that has explored this 'double reality' of solid social structures which are at the same time constituted by conflicting forces. Marxism has problems of its own, problems which are not mere academic puzzles, but imply very different forms of politics in their solution. The chief problem encountered here is that of the subject: Marxist theory, implicitly or explicitly, has several conflicting conceptions of the human being which find their theoretical expression in the conception of the subject. Marxism conceives at once of a subject who is produced by society, and of a subject who acts to support or to change that society. We shall see several attempts to show how this human subject is constituted in ideology and by history, and at the same time acts to make history and change society, without having a full and self-sufficient knowledge of or control over the actions it undertakes. Marxism cannot conceive of a subject who remains outside the structure, manipulating it or acting as a mere support; if it did so, it would cease to be a revolutionary philosophy. So already we have two 'crises of thought': a social crisis, in that society is constituted by the (uneven) conflict of forces; a crisis in Marxist thought of this process, in that Marxism is forced to examine its notion of the revolutionary subject in order to know its political orientation to individuals who try to act within the social crisis.

The same problem of the subject has asserted itself within linguistics. Recent linguistics has been able to formalise its object to the extent that the social nature of that object has been almost completely eliminated from the theorising. But certain linguists, Jakobson and Benveniste among them, have shown how this fails to account fully for the reality of language: for instance, Jakobson shows that there exists a category of signifiers which depend entirely on their context for their meaning, words like 'I', 'here', 'now', etc. Language then, is not reducible to a formal system. Attention has to be paid to the moment of enunciation, to the specific production of an utterance and not just its abstract, formal character. If the moment of enunciation is seen only in terms of an opposition text/context, then there are still no problems for formal linguistics. However, if the text and context are seen as mutually determining, caught in the same process of production, then the interrelation between the speaker and the spoken has to be examined. It is no longer enough to posit the speaking subject as outside the system, operating it and unaffected by it. The subject is caught in the moment of enunciation, and is in some way constructed by it, put in place by it. This can be seen as another crisis, this time in linguistics. Its character is similar to that of the crisis in Marxism, in that it demands a new attention to the subject, hitherto assumed or elided in both spheres of thought. The problem is again that of the constitution of the productive subject who is at the same time determined by forces which he or she does not manipulate or control totally.

We shall now examine both Marxism and language in the light of the problem of the subject. For Marxism, this entails examining both its conception of the social structure-in-process, and its philosophy of dialectical materialism to see what notions of the subject are contained within them. As for language, we have first to indicate how it represents a problem for Marxist theory, which can give no adequate account of its place in the social process; then we have to show the way in which psychoanalysis provides an account of the construction of the subject of the enunciation from the perspective that the process of the subject is the process of signification. This then makes possible an account of the subject of revolutionary change.

The Marxist analysis of the construction of the capitalist social structure is indicated in this short quotation:

> We have seen that the capitalist process of production is a historically determined form of the social process of production in general. The latter is as much a production process of material conditions of human life as a process taking place under specific historical and economic production relations, producing and reproducing these production relations themselves, and thereby also the bearers of this process, their material conditions of existence and their mutual relations, i.e. their particular socio-economic form (*Capital,* vol. 3, p. 818).

Several fundamental conceptions can be drawn from this quotation.

First, what finally determines the social process is the production of 'the material conditions of human life': it is the need, to survive which brings this about. This statement (which may appear to be a banal truism) sharply differentiates Marxism from any idealist philosophy that holds that the origin of all things is a single point, God, the Idea, etc. Marxist materialism begins from the basis that 'men themselves begin to distinguish themselves from animals as soon as they begin to produce their means of subsistence' (Marx and Engels, *The German Ideology*, p. 42). Production can be defined as the transformation of specific raw materials into specific products by labour using specific tools. It is productive activity that marks human society, and the form of the production of the material means of subsistence that *finally* determines the form of a particular society.

However, the production of the means of subsistence is not the only determinant; neither is it, under many conditions, the principal determinant. For production, according to the above definition, assumes the simultaneous renewal of tools and producers so that production can continue. Equally, the form of production is determined by what has gone before, by history: raw materials are themselves the products of previous productive activity in the same way as both tools and producers themselves. In other words, a specific social formation is in fact a complex and uneven relation of elements within one historic mode of production. Marx indicates several modes of production that have developed through a process of revolutionary change: the primitive, feudal and capitalist modes; equally, he indicates that the capitalist mode of production can itself be overthrown. This is because each social formation is constituted by unequal elements that are in contradiction with each other: movement and change are provided by the struggle between elements. 'The fundamental cause of development of a thing is not external but internal; it lies in the contradictoriness within the thing' (Mao Tse-Tung, 'On Contradiction', p. 26). This internal struggle produced by a particular historical development is overdetermined by other contradictions outside in a complex process, so development does not proceed smoothly but comes about through breaks and ruptures, through revolution. So what Marxism (historical materialism) speaks of is social formations constituted by material production and determinate practices. The existence and transformation of each mode of production implies definite economic, political and ideological practices.

The quotation also shows that Marxist thought takes account of three practices within a mode of production. The term 'practice' here designates a particular form of productive activity by which the social formation is produced and transformed. The idea is latent in this quotation: it has since been developed by Engels, Mao and Althusser. Each practice is constituted by elements which provide each other's conditions of existence. First, in the quotation, is economic practice, the production and reproduction of the material means of subsistence, and of 'the specific historical and economic production relations'. This practice is constituted by the form of the productive forces, and the form of the relations of production. Second, political practice produces the 'mutual relations' of social groups, the forms of social organisation, and the relations of dominance and subordination between these forms. This practice is constituted by the contradiction between classes, in capitalism that between the bourgeoisie and the working class. Third, ideological practice produces positions which enable subjects to act within the social totality. Before explaining the character of these practices in more detail, it is necessary to emphasise that these three practices alone do not account for the whole of human existence: they go a long way towards delineating a social process which does not have man at its centre, but rather constructs man as he attempts to construct the system. Historical materialism details the first half of this process, including the forms in which people 'live' the social formation. What it fails to show is how the human subject is constructed, a construction which is specified by ideological practice. This problem of the subject will become clearer when we outline the role of ideological practice. First, it is necessary to give a fuller account of economic and political practices.

The capitalist economy consists of forces of production and the relations of production; that is, resources in terms of raw materials, machinery and men combined in a certain way to produce on the one hand; and the functions fulfilled by individuals and groups in the manipulation and control of these means on the other hand. Each presupposes the other (no machinery is possible without a division of labour, etc.), yet they develop unevenly, each blocking the other and forcing their form of mutual development. Marx demonstrates that the specific contradiction within capitalism is between the increasing socialisation of the means of production and their enduringly private nature, owned by a certain class with specific interests. What began as the concentration of the means of production into the hands of one entrepreneur − a progressive movement that enabled expanded production to take place − gradually becomes, as this very production ceaselessly expands, innovates and spreads its influence, a force which holds back the productive forces from their full potential:

> The contradiction, to put it in a very general way, consists in that the capitalist mode of production involves a tendency towards absolute development of the productive forces, regardless of the value and surplus-value it contains, and regardless of the social conditions under which capitalist production takes place; while, on the other hand, its aim is to preserve the value of the existing capital and promote its self-expansion to the highest limit (i.e. to promote an ever more rapid growth of this value) (*Capital*, vol. 3, p. 249).

The contradiction, then, is between the potential for unlimited expansion of the productive forces (which could produce for need), and the way the relations are set up within the system: the productive forces are controlled by the owners of capital whilst their character makes them less and less dependent on that form of control, more and more organised to be controlled by society as a whole.

Private ownership and capital are interdependent: the concentration of the means of production into the hands of a controlling group enables an expanding production to take place through a certain kind of exploitation of wage-labourers. This exploitation is the production of surplus-value by the worker within capitalist relations. This system is a historically-created situation in which,

> for the conversion of his money into capital . . . the owner of money must find in the commodity market a free worker, free in the double sense, that as a free man he can dispose of his labour power as his own commodity, and that on the other hand he has no commodity for sale, and lacks everything necessary for the realisation of this labour-power (*Capital*, vol. 1, p. 166).

Already in this description we see implied both political and ideological practices: the fact of two classes (capital and labour) necessitates a political instance which is the necessary space of representation of their conflicting positions within definite organisations (political parties, trade unions, etc.). In addition the worker is presented as 'free', a representation that covers both his 'free will' and his deprivation of any means of production: this representation is the product of ideological practice. But the mechanism that is the real concern of economic practice is different from this particular ideological representation: it is the production of surplus-value. In the representation, the worker is selling his labour at a fixed price. In fact, what he is selling is his labour-power:

> the value of the labour-power, and the value which that labour-power creates in the labour process are two entirely different magnitudes; and this difference of the two values is what the capitalist had in view when he was purchasing the labour-power. . . . What really influenced him was the specific use-value which this commodity possesses of being a source not only of value, but of more value than itself. . . . The seller of labour-power, like the seller of any other commodity, realises its exchange-value, and parts with its use-value (*Capital*, vol. 1, p. 188).

It is labour that creates new value in the process of production:

> the action of labour power not only reproduces its own value, but produces value over and above it. The surplus-value is the difference between the value of the product and the value of elements consumed in the formation of that product, in other words, of the means of production and the labour-power (*Capital*, vol. 1, p. 201).

Surplus-value is what is left after the means of production, machines, raw materials, etc. have been paid for, and the labour-power has been bought at its socially-fixed rate, that is at a rate sufficient to reproduce the worker himself, and to reproduce the labour force in the family. What remains is surplus-value, and this is distributed in three ways. Some is paid to the state in forms of taxes, for various purposes; some is the reward for owning capital, which consumed by the possessors of capital; the rest is reinvested to expand the means of production still further. The private appropriation of surplus-value together with the expansion of the means of production characterise the economic practice of capitalism. Every mode of production produces a surplus: it is the mode of appropriation of the surplus (the relations of production) which determines the character of the social formation.

However, this account is meaningless and unworkable by itself. Economic practice cannot and does not exist on its own. It needs both a political and an ideological practice merely to exist at all. In political practice, the struggle between the bourgeois and working classes takes place, not as two monoliths facing each other, but through various groups, fractions of classes, alliances, etc. Political practice is the representation of the relation of power between classes and class fractions, it is the realm of the State: 'The State should be seen (as should capital, according to Marx) as a relation, or more precisely the condensate of a relation of power between struggling classes' (N. Poulantzas, *New Left Review*, no. 95, p. 74). These power relations are organised and exercised in the control of the apparatus of the State: that is, in the legislative aspects of the State (parliament and civil administration) and the repressive apparatuses, the armed forces, police, judiciary, prisons, etc. The State does not 'express' the interest of a given economic class: rather state apparatuses guarantee the continuance of the mechanism of appropriation of surplus labour by the ruling class. Political practice, producing representations, takes place at a particular conjuncture within determinate conditions. And moreover, those political representations are produced within determinate institutional formations (parties, government departments, etc.) which make up the State. Political practice within capitalism forms and promotes the interests of classes and class fractions: thus the series of nineteenth-century acts limiting the employment of children and shortening the length of the working day. These were conceded under pressure from a working class that had no direct parliamentary representation, through an alliance with the humanitarian wing of the (efficient capitalist) Liberal Party. Such apparent victories are, however, formed within the given political representations of the capitalist social formation. Existing political representations have their own level of determinacy: in order to transform the mode of production, 'the proletariat must seize State power in order to destroy the existing bourgeois State apparatus and, in a first phase, replace it with a quite different, proletarian, State apparatus, then in later phases set in motion a radical process, that of the destruction of the State' (Althusser, *Lenin and Philosophy*, p. 135). Thus runs the classic Marxist theory, summed up by Althusser. Political practice is not just a matter of the State, it is equally that of the constitution and organisation of class forces in various kinds of organisation: trade unions and revolutionary political parties.

As necessary to the social formation as political and economic practices is a third: ideological practice. We have seen this already in the conception of the 'free worker', a way of conceiving the role of the wage worker that produces a relation to the social formation, the necessary way in which the system (production of surplus value and its appropriation by capital) presents itself to the individual. But ideology is not a slogan under which political and economic interest of a class presents itself. It is the way in which the individual actively lives his or her role within the social totality; it therefore participates in the construction of that individual so that he or she can act. Ideology is a practice of representation; a practice to produce a specific articulation, that is, producing certain meanings and necessitating certain subjects as their supports. In considering the developments of the analysis of realism, we saw the increasing untenability of a simple notion of ideology operating through a system of connotations imposed on an original 'natural' language. In the analysis necessitated by such texts as *Sarrasine*, it became obvious that the conventional representation of realism was disrupted by the fracturing of the identity of the sign, that is, the identity of signifier and signified. The production of an ideological *vraisemblable* which is effective precisely for the reason that it appears as 'natural', 'the way things are', is the result of a practice of fixing or limiting of the endless productivity of the signifying chain. This fixing is the result of the limiting of certain signifiers to a certain signified or meaning. Limitation does not rely on the imposition of a system of ideas on a natural pre-given sign, but on the construction of a certain subject in relation to a discourse; a subject who then becomes the place of its intelligibility. Ideology is not perceived as such. It does not appear that ideology is the production of representations (ideas and positions) in social practice. It appears as certain 'natural' ideas, a certain horizon, an ordinary way of thinking, 'common sense'. It is not perceived as a limitation, a closure. Ideologies then are not perceived as systems of ideas (though they can be elaborated as systems, 'natural' systems, in, for example, law books); they govern the way people normally act, their feeling of themselves as individuals.

Practical ideologies are complex formations of montages of notions—representations—images on the one hand, and of montages of behaviours—conducts—attitudes—gestures on the other. The whole functions as the practical norms which govern the attitude and the taking-up of concrete position by men with respect to the real objects and the real problems of their social and individual existence, and of their history (Althusser, 1968, quoted in Heath, *The Nouveau Roman*, p. 190).

The practice of ideology has succeeded when it has produced this 'natural attitude', when for example the existing relations of power are not only accepted but perceived precisely as the way things are, ought to be and will be.

It is with the problem of the construction of the subject *for* these representations that the question of ideology becomes much more complex than previously recognised. What is produced in ideology is the very basis of the subject's activity, the conditions of its positions *as* subject, and the coherency of that subject in the face of contradictions which make up society. Ideology produces the subject as the place where a specific meaning is realised in signification. It is thus an active part of social relations since it creates their intelligibility, an intelligibility which in a capitalist society tends to serve the interest of one class. This process of production of representations and subjects for those representations is reinforced by certain material apparatuses, which ensure and support the physical reproduction of ideology and social contradictions. However, its real effectivity is established in a more complex movement of the production of a subject as place where an ideological signified is realised. Thus the socio-familial positioning in relation to discourse is likely to have primary importance in determining the definition and the reproduction of individuals as agents (subjects) for the mode of production from the place it assigns to them. In this way, bourgeois ideology can sustain a plurality of articulations (even apparently oppositional ones) which do not alter the basic relation to social relations. The conception of 'freedom' is recognised to be produced and reproduced for the worker and the employer alike in education, law, ethics and morality. But it is more than a system of representations operating a distortion which can be corrected by the assertion of the so-called real relations. It results from a process of production of subjects who think and feel themselves to be free; it is because ideology can presuppose a consistent subject, the origin of ideas and actions, that we can represent ourselves as free even when there is evidence to the contrary. It is this coherency, this sense of a unified being which is produced in the work of ideology and fixes identifications and representations, and subjects in relation to these. This is not to imply that the consistency refers to the individual who expresses one single coherent ideology. The individual can occupy a plurality of sometimes conflicting subject positions, given in a plurality of representations. Each practice of representation, however, presupposes a perpetual retotalisation in a process of movement. It is this coherent subjectivity which is specifically emphasised in bourgeois ideology. The social relations of capitalism are only possible with this notion of the subject as 'free' and consistent.

  Ideological practice has not been dealt with extensively by Marxist thought. It is often referred to as being merely a 'system of ideas', 'false consciousness', etc. These crude ideas result from Marx and

Engels's early formulations in *The German Ideology*. The (dialectical materialist) idea that the production of representations necessarily entails the production of subjects for these representations has only been developed occasionally by such writers as Brecht, Mao and Althusser. And these writings have often been misunderstood or described as just too difficult, especially where they deal with questions of ideology. It is always this consideration which receives the least attention when these writers are discussed. It is therefore the aim of this chapter to elaborate the idea of ideological practice, and to show how in Marxist thought it has not been extended to provide an adequate explanation of the social formation of the individual. We attempt to suggest some of the more advanced work in this area, and also to point out some of the drawbacks to this work; and we assert that it is only psychoanalysis which has gone any way to analysing the formation of the subject which receives its specific subjectivity in the work of ideology. The importance of understanding ideological practice in the way suggested by the articulation of Marxism and psychoanalysis is very great. The politics which flow from radical and Marxist thought can then be rid of any economic determinism, that is, the idea that economic practice is more important than political or ideological processes in the social process. As long as Marxists still think of ideological practice as somehow subservient to the economy (as a 'superstructure' built on the economic 'base'), then their politics will always stress the economy as the principal determinant, and see economic crisis as the principal (or only) cause of social crisis. Engels was very clear about the nature of determination within the social process:

> According to the materialist conception of history, the ultimately determining element in history is the production and reproduction of real life. More than this neither Marx nor I have ever asserted.
> Hence if somebody twists this into saying that the economic element is the *only* determining one, he transforms that proposition into a meaningless, abstract, senseless phrase (Letter to J. Bloch, September 1890, published in Engels, *Correspondance vol. II, 1887–90*, Progress Publishers, Moscow).

An analysis of the social totality as composed of three practices which *together* 'produce and reproduce real life' goes a long way to remedying this economic determinism. For it is no longer a matter of politics and ideology being superstructures which are supported/produced by the economic base, presupposing that they will be forced to undergo their revolutionary change when the economic base is in revolution. It is rather a matter of seeing the articulation of the three practices which depends on the historically specific conjuncture. For the contradictions within each practice weigh upon the specific contradictions of the others: the whole historic situation impinges upon each moment. As Althusser says:

> The Capital–Labour contradiction is never simple, but it is always

specified by the historically concrete forms and circumstances in which it is exercised. It is specified by the forms of the superstructure (the State, the dominant ideology, religion, politically organised movements and so on), specified by the internal and external historical situation, which determines it on the one hand as a function of the national past . . . and on the other as functions of the existing world context (Althusser, *For Marx*, p. 106).

According to the precise historical situation, a crisis can occur within and/or between political, economic and ideological practices: their specific contradictions are *overdetermined* (as Althusser puts it) by other contradictions, so that they become the arena of crisis, the principal contradiction, the contradiction whose struggle determines the future direction of the social whole. This idea of structural causality means that the results of history are never decided in advance: there is no inevitable end of capitalism, no final outcome of the class struggle. The various Marxist faiths are thus distortions, expressions of a will rather than a reality: the economy will not develop according to its own contradiction and finally liberate the working class (as turn-of-the-century German socialists believed); capitalism will not necessarily be superseded (it persistently shows adaptability to 'working-class demands').

At certain moments in history, it is therefore ideological practice which is overdetermined in a revolutionary direction. One situation is that of China: the Cultural Revolution of the late 1960s was born of the fact that ideology does not follow meekly after the revolution of the relations of production: if the forms of representation of the old social order persist, they reproduce the social relations of that order in both political and economic practice. Ideology therefore became the practice which was overdetermined in the Chinese social situation: the outcome of ideology would determine the whole form of Chinese society:

> The Cultural Revolution is nothing other than an implacable war against all the values that found the traditional division of labour, its method of management, everything that had been left to China by a capitalist and then post-Stalinist industrialisation. The struggle between Mao and Liu Shao-Chi is a bitter and definitive battle on the level of ideology above all. But, closely linked to the ideological choice, what is at stake in the struggle is the future of China itself (Macciocchi, *De la Chine*, p. 95).

The recognition of the determinacy of ideology — both that it can be the site of an overdetermination, and that it has a concrete role in every social totality — is the core of the difference between China and Russia. In Russia, the revolution in ideology is seen to have taken place more or less as a result of the revolution in production relations. In China its full complexity and determinacy is acknowledged.

Since 1968, the Marxist theory of ideology in the West has been developing to produce an analysis which can begin to deal with the real historical role of ideology. It is still the French communist philosopher Louis Althusser who has produced some of the most advanced formulations, notably in two essays: 'Marxism and Humanism', dating from 1965 (*For Marx*, pp. 231–6), and 'Ideology and Ideological State Apparatuses' (*Lenin and Philosophy*, pp. 121–73). The formulations given there are to be considered advanced in that they point out certain aspects of the work of ideology: the principal feature being that the subject is constituted as a part of the working of ideology. However, this recognition in itself is not adequately elaborated by Althusser. He limits his account by using the category 'subject' to describe the possible ideological positions for the individual constructed in social relations. When he attempts to account for the construction of the relation between the subject and the social relations (i.e. the articulation of ideology), the inadequacy of his theory is implicitly acknowledged, for he draws on psychoanalytic terms: he calls ideology the 'imaginary relation' of individuals to their real relations of existence, but in no way uses the full implications of the psychoanalytic term 'imaginary'. In the above formulation, Althusser attempts to account for the moment at which the subject acts as if it is the coherent source of meanings – meanings necessitated by the ideological representations which already include that subject. But in doing this, Althusser closes off the possibility of the human subject being constructed in contradiction, which should follow implicitly from his work elsewhere. His notion of the imaginary relies finally on a notion of 'image-production' which can be read as similar to that of *The German Ideology* with its theory of ideology as the distorted representation of real relations. These notions are finally based on a conception of coherent subjectivity. They presuppose an 'empty subject' which mechanically inhabits a specific ideological formation according to a distorted image of real relations produced by those relations. They are limited to a description of the subjective moment of images and representations. The notion of the construction of representations and subjects for them in contradiction is a notion found elsewhere: in the philosophy of dialectical materialism and the theoretical elaboration of psychoanalysis by Lacan.

In order to discuss the notion of ideology as articulations which necessitate certain subjects as support for their meanings, it is necessary to recall some of Althusser's formulations concerning ideology, and to suggest a way of escaping from their limitations. These limitations result from the mechanistic tendency of regarding meaning as produced by a distorted image of reality which functions to reproduce existing relations. Then it is possible to suggest where the important areas of this analysis can be illuminated by psychoanalytic discoveries.

Ideology consists of: a practice of representation, and a subject constructed for that representation – this being a practice with a specific role and effectivity in the social formation, a practice that acts through and is invested in certain material institutions. According to Althusser ideology operates to reproduce the relations of production, the relations between classes, and the relations of men to their world. Every society has to reproduce its conditions of existence whilst it produces, or else it would cease to exist. The conditions of production, it will be remembered, consist at once of the productive forces (machinery, etc.) and the relations of production (the division of labour). In this schema, ideology reproduces the relations of production in two complementary ways. It sets individuals in place, in position, as diversely skilled operatives, by setting them on their 'rung of the ladder', in their 'rightful place'. It equally sets individuals in positions

> of submission to the rules of the established order, that is, a reproduction of submission to the ruling ideology for the workers, and a reproduction of the ability to manipulate the ruling ideology correctly for the agents of exploitation and repression, so that they, too, will provide for the domination of the ruling class 'in words' (Althusser, *Lenin and Philosophy*, pp. 127–8).

Ideology is the practice in which individuals are produced and produce their orientation to the social structures so that they can act within those structures in various ways. Individuals are set in positions as subjects so that they can act, which is the basis for their activity. This first development of Marxist theory — the space inhabited by Althusser's work — represents a break with dominant (vulgarising) thought. Vulgar Marxism has it that ideology is like a 'cloud of ideas' floating above the 'real' structures of society. In indicating that ideology is the basis for the subject's activity in society, Althusser showed it to be a necessary social practice, 'there is no practice except by and in ideology' (ibid., p. 159). Ideology then governs people's activities within economic and political practices; so the idea of a social revolution that is not accompanied by a revolution in ideology is a recipe for disaster; a recipe for a return to the structures that have been overthrown, brought about by the way people habitually and unconsciously act and relate. An essential part of the bourgeois revolution was to remould ideological practice from top to bottom, instituting a new legal system, a new mode of representation in writing and graphics (realism). Thus in China, another revolution in ideology is taking place, overthrowing ideas of delegation, management, the handing over of power to 'representatives', or 'responsible individuals', ideas which are the keystone of capitalist production relations and bourgeois democracy. They are replaced with ideas of collective decision making, of active thinking by all the people, summed up in the ideas of 'philosophy in the factory', 'philosophy is no mystery', etc.

To put the argument exclusively in these terms is, however, still to retain certain aspects of the thinking that sees ideology as a cloud of ideas and the subject as a 'consciousness' which becomes the bearer of these ideas. Ideology is always more than ideas; it is a material force in that it constructs subjects in specific relations to the social relations. The materiality of this force is affirmed by its investment in concrete institutions. Because certain institutions appear to function to reproduce ideology, and therefore individuals as subjects for ideology, Althusser has been led to suggest that the materiality of ideology is the fact of concrete institutions. He calls them 'ideological State apparatuses', entrusted with the regulation of the existing power relations between classes by means of ideas. He lists them as: educational, religious, political, legal, trade union, communications, and cultural apparatuses, and the family. Obviously, some of these apparatuses have important, if not principal, roles in other practices: political parties and trade unions function in political practice, and it is precisely as a function of their role in this practice that they also act as ideological apparatuses, producing the ideas, representations, positions, which are necessary for their political functioning. Equally, Althusser states that the Law is not only an ideological apparatus, but also belongs to the second category of State apparatus that he proposes: the 'repressive State apparatuses'. These are organisations of physical force which are centralised in the State itself. Ideological apparatuses on the other hand have a great degree of autonomy, and (when there is profit to be made from running them) they can be privately owned. However, their function is in no way private: they ensure the reproduction of the existing relations of power in ideas. They function primarily by ideas; repressive apparatuses function primarily by force: thus repressive apparatuses include the government, civil administration, the armed forces, the police, courts, prisons, etc. Just as ideological apparatuses have some repressive functions (school discipline, censorship, etc.), the repressive apparatuses have some ideological functions (the ethics of government, etc.). Thus, in Althusser's formulation, law is poised between the two, with a function that is equally ideological and repressive: it is the linchpin of the system, ensuring by force that the fundamental 'freedoms' are maintained.

However, Althusser's notion of the materiality of ideology reveals a rather distorted view of materialism: it relies on the so-called 'concrete' and empirical. The materiality of ideology should rather be seen as a force in the dynamic of the mode of production, a force which operates to produce a certain subject with a certain meaning, in other words to institute an articulation. Ideological practice is then doubly material: it works to fix the subject in certain positions in relation to certain fixities of discourse, and it is concretised in certain apparatuses. Behind these lie repressive apparatuses, which can be used to ensure the continuance of existing power relations by force if ideological practice fails to do so. The notion of materiality of ideology consisting in its fixing of the subject alters the status of the ideological apparatuses themselves: the family assumes a greater importance than accredited to it by Althusser and ceases to be an ideological state apparatus. It becomes the arena in which the subject is produced in a certain relation to discourse, and therefore meaning; this relation then orients its position within the material institutions of the state. This understanding of ideology has only become possible with the developments of psychoanalysis examined in the following chapter.

Ideology can be seen as the form of representation that society gives to itself, on condition that this representation is seen as an active process of production within material instances, as a material force comprising 'the perceived, accepted, suffered cultural objects: objects of [men's] world' (Althusser, *For Marx*, p. 233). This representation has the character of tending towards a structural closure: it defines the limits for, and works to fix the individual with, a certain mental horizon.

Ideology achieves this closure by fixing the relationship by which the individual represents himself in his world of objects: it provides the positions from which individuals can act and represent themselves and others within the social totality. Ideological practice is necessary to societies of whatever kind because the individual is not the centre of the social whole: the social process has no centre, no motivating force in the sense that Renaissance humanism saw man as the centre of the world, actively willing the events of his social organisation. Instead, society is composed of multiple contradictions in relationships of over-determination. It is necessary, then, that the relationship of people to the structure is produced in a process of representation so that they can act within the structure. Ideology is the practice which articulates this relationship, what Althusser calls the necessarily imaginary relationship between individuals and the social structure in which they act and by which they are constructed. What ideology produces is 'the way [people] live the relation between them and their conditions of existence' (ibid., p. 233). In practical terms, this means that ideology is in no way *false* consciousness: the ideology of the free worker, freely selling his labour at its market value, is a representation which it is necessary to live in order to function within the capitalist system. It is necessary also for the rulers and employers to live this ideology and act within the system as though it were true. It normally functions to their profit, just as it normally functions to the detriment of the worker; but its contradictory role is shown by the way in which in times of social unrest, various spontaneous ideologies of freedom are produced which threaten the whole social order. The role of Marxist political organisation is to go beyond this ideology and show it to be a specific organisation of reality, i.e. a specific mode of production organised to the interests of one class, a mode that is in contradiction and necessitates these representations of freedom. But Marxism cannot abolish ideology because any social system needs to represent itself through subjects in certain positions, thinking along certain lines.

Ideology functions, then, by putting the individual at the centre of the structure, making the subject the place where ideological meanings are realised. In attempting to account for this, Althusser describes the process:

> All ideology represents in its necessarily imaginary distortion not the existing relations of production (and the other relations that derive from them), but above all the (imaginary) relationship of individuals to the relations of production and the relations that derive from them. What is represented in ideology is therefore not the system of real relations which govern the existence of individuals, but the imaginary relation of these individuals to the real relations in which they live (*Lenin and Philosophy*, p. 155).

The word 'imaginary' which is insisted upon as the real character of ideology is not quite that of the normal opposition imaginary/real, where 'imaginary' means merely 'that which is not real'. It also draws upon the term as used by Lacan, but its mobilisation by Althusser only acknowledges the inadequacy of the terms available in Marxism, rather than uses the full implications of the psychoanalytic term. Had he so used it, Althusser's theory of ideology might have been very much more effective. As it is, the term is limited to indicate the calling on the individual as a homogeneous, non-contradictory whole – or subject – which is then the coherent support for ideological representations. So when Althusser talks of a 'necessarily imaginary distortion', he indicates the process by which the individual is treated as a consistent subject in control of his own destiny, able to act. Althusser fails to present the subject as traversed and worked by social contradiction; as having an unconscious which is concomitant with his consciousness. This subject, traversed and worked by social contradiction, is nevertheless set in place as fully responsible, a controlling consciousness, consistent within one articulation. Brecht pinpointed this when he said (in 1926), 'The continuity of the ego is a myth. A man is an atom that perpetually breaks up and forms anew' (*Brecht on Theatre*, Methuen, London, 1964, p. 15). The product of the work of ideology at the level of the individual is precisely this 'continuity of the ego'. It puts in place the contradictory subject, puts him in positions of coherence and responsibility for his own actions so that he is able to act. This acting is the 'initiation' of acts: the subject appears to be the origin of his own activity, responsible for it and for its consequences.

This account does not show the construction of the subject in relation to social relations which are contradictory. As we shall see in the following chapter, Lacan's concept of 'the imaginary' is a more subtle instrument for understanding this process. Lacan demonstrates the construction of the subject in language, through a process in which the imaginary identification of self as a unified whole in a mirror is an essential part. This puts in place the subject (hitherto uncoordinated) in relation to a predicatable outside. But this is no simple process, because the imaginary wholeness which is identified in the mirror, is an identification which is retained as the prototype for all identifications as the child enters cultural and specific social formations as a language-using subject. Lacan's concept of the imaginary provides a route for understanding how the positioning of a subject in relation to language and, therefore, social relations is always accomplished in specific ideological formations. The identifications made by the infant in the process by which it produces itself in discourse are always already in ideology.

Thus the function of ideology is to fix the individual in place as subject for a certain meaning. This is simultaneously to provide individuals with a subject-ivity, and to subject them to the social structure with its existing contradictory relations and powers. The subject in ideology has a consistency which rests on an imaginary identification of self: this is simultaneously a recognition (since it provides subject-ivity, enables the subject to act), and a misrecognition (a recognition which involves a representation in relation to forms which include the work of ideology). The consistent subject is the place to which the representations of ideology are directed: Duty, Morality, and Law all depend on this category of subject for their functioning, and all contribute as institutions to its production. The individual thus lives his subject-ion to social structures as a consistent subject-ivity, an imaginary wholeness. Ideologies set in place the individual as though he were this subject: the individual produces himself in this imaginary wholeness, this imaginary reflection of himself as the author of his actions.

It was Althusser who first emphasised the term subject within a theory of ideology. He drew it from Law, which in his theory of the State, functions at once as an ideological and a repressive apparatus. Law is concerned with policing the limits of ideology, with the moments where this subjection fails to make people 'fully responsible' for their actions, and it condemns in the name of this free consistent subjectivity. In the written ideology of Law,

> the texts say: the subject of law is the general and abstract expression of the human person; they also say: what makes this expression effective is the *general capacity* of man to be his own master, and therefore to be acquisitive. They say finally: that if this capacity is the mode of being a subject, it is because the subject can be/wants to be/consents to be/is free to be his own master and to be acquisitive (Edelman, *Le Droit saisi par la photographie*, p. 20).

Here is the unity of the free subject with the subject whose motivation is acquiring property with the subject who is consistent in consciously willing his condition. The Law has a pivotal function in reinforcing this representation, and its elaboration of the fundamental category of the subject thus spreads into other ideologies. As Althusser writes: 'classic dominant bourgeois philosophy (including even its modern byproducts) is built on the ideology of Law, and its "philosophic objects" . . . are the categories or entities of Law: Subject, Object, Freedom, Will,

Property(s), Representation, Person, Thing, etc.' (*Eléments d'autocrit-ique*, p. 37). If ideology puts every individual in place as a consistent subject, then the Law ensures that those who go wrong are judged in the name of this consistent subjectivity. As Barthes puts it, 'How much penal evidence is based on a psychology of consistency!' (*Le Plaisir du texte*, p. 3). In *Mythologies* he shows that this judicial notion of the consistent subject is exactly a representation: 'this particular psycho-logy, in the name of which you can very well be guillotined, comes straight from our traditional literature, what is known in bourgeois style as the literature of the Human Document' (p. 45).

Ideological representations fix the category of subject as a closure, a structural limit. The subject is constituted of, and in, contradiction, but sociality necessitates that there should be a subject in order that any predication, and therefore communication, can take place. This (neces-sary) subject of sociality only ever appears in a specific ideological formation, that is it appears as the fixed relation of the subject to what it predicates, and this relation must necessarily be ideological. Thus the imaginary identity of ideology closes off the movement of contradic-tions, calling upon the subject as consistent. It puts the subject in the position of a homogeneous subject in relation to meaning, a subject who thinks himself/herself to be the point of origin of ideas and of actions. Ideology is thus a material practice in both senses of the term: first be-cause it is produced and reproduced in concrete institutions; second, because it produces fixed relations and positions in which the individual represents himself, relations and positions which are a material force in the process of the social formation. Ideology produces the individual in a relation to representation within the social process in which he or she is situated, as an identity (a point of self-reference) rather than a process. The practice of ideology then expresses a will, a purpose, a fixed position or tendency. These tendencies, these positions can work in a way that reproduces the existing relations of contradiction within political and economic practice. The contradictions in which the indivi-dual is constituted in capitalism would thus be 'settled to the profit of the ruling class' (Althusser, *For Marx*, p. 236). Ideology is a system of representations which entail certain subject positions. As these have their conditions of existence in certain social practices, it can operate to reinforce those practices. In bourgeois ideology, a subject can repre-sent itself as free, homogeneous and responsible for its actions because the social relations of capitalism are exchange-relations. For the social practice of wage labour to continue, these exchange-relations must presuppose such a free subject. Thus existing representations are delivered to this place, to this subject as he is constructed in sociality; he produces himself in their imaginary relation to the real relations of production and reproduction as part of the social relations. It is worth recalling here, Marx's claim that there is no ideology in general. In other words, it only appears in the dynamic of the specific mode of production, as existing representations, as the production of the subject in these existing representations, and as the constant transformation of social relations.

Thus ideology is a specific social practice: an articulation of the fixed relations of representation to a specific organisation of reality, relations which establish the positions that it is possible for the individual to inhabit within the social totality. It closes off the contradictions of the human subject with the imaginary identifications of unity. But this Marxist account does not show how the contradictory processes of the individual subject are themselves constituted: this in turn means that it cannot analyse moments of ideological crisis where these subjective processes enter into contradiction with the functioning of ideology itself; where these subjective processes are overdetermined by the contradictions of other practices. In other words, Marxism which does not ask itself these questions cannot account for the notion of practice, without falling into banal humanism, with its belief in 'the revolutionary will', etc.

Any attempt to analyse ideological processes leads inevitably to the problem of language since, as we have shown, ideology necessitates a theory of the relation of subjects to signification. For such an analysis, Marxism also requires an encounter with psychoanalysis, since it is only the latter which can provide a scientific elaboration of subjective processes and their construction in relation to language. This would involve a precise notion of the status of language, in articulation with, but not subsumed to, ideology. It would also involve an elaboration of the place of the unconscious, the site of interaction between psychic representations and a contradictory outside, produced in the process of the construction of a language-using subject. This would be a theory of the processes by which the structural limits of a society are established and transgressed.

It is precisely the dialectic between language and ideology that Marxist theories of language have not established. Marxist thought has only been capable of negative formulations about language: it is not reducible to ideology, nor is it reducible to a passive medium of communication with no effective determinacy of its own, etc. Worse, there is a persistent tendency to try and reduce language to being an element of ideology, motivated by the economistic use of the metaphor of society as superstructures where politics and ideology are built on the economic base.

One result of this tendency was the vacuousness of Soviet linguistics from the 1930s to the 1950s, dominated by N. Y. Marr's assertion that language is a superstructural form. Stalin produced a key text in opposition to this tendency, even though his political policies were themselves the result of an economic determination which saw development of the economy as the means of creating a communist state, and completely neglected ideological struggle. For this reason, Stalin could only produce negative formulations about the nature and role of language. He showed that language is not reducible to the superstructure by asserting that national languages are not the exclusive property of one class, but are the common means of speech of all the people; in addition he asserts that a language is not the product of one economic base, but of the whole course of history through many different economic formations. This is not to say that language is unaffected by history or independent of ideology. It is *worked by* ideological practice: language at any historical moment is riddled with styles, rhetorics, 'ways of speaking' which impose a specific social position, a definite view of the world. These ideological discourses are the product of the articulation of ideology in language. Language is more than these discourses, just as ideology is more than just ideas.

In addition, we can say (in opposition to Stalin) that language is not just a means of communication. It is not a carrier of meaning that exists outside it in some way. Language and thought are inextricable: thought conceptualises through language, and it is not a matter of one being the instrument of the other but of each engendering the other: language makes thought possible, thought makes language possible. This much Stalin acknowledges, but he does not draw the consequences from this idea. If language is not the servant of thought, then it is equally not just a container which transfers a thought from one brain to another, as the theory of language-as-communication implies. Oratory and rhetoric bear witness to the emotional level of language which goes beyond the communication of content: rhetorical speeches behave like a double speech, arousing emotional response across the 'communication' of the manifest content. Poetic language functions similarly by exploiting music, intonation and rhythm. We have seen how Lukács and Goldmann based their realist aesthetic on precisely this confusion of language with its chief social function of communication; the results are that they cannot deal with poetry (whose reality remains 'inexpressible' for them) and that they support a form of representation that is produced in bourgeois ideological practice. The fundamental problem with the conception of language as communication is that it tends to obscure the way in which language sets up the positions of 'I' and 'you' that are necessary for communication to take place at all. Communication involves more than just a message being transmitted from the speaker to the destinee: the speaker is at the same time the destinee of his own message, because he is capable of deciphering a message as he is speaking it and because he cannot say anything that he does not in some way understand. Thus the message which is intended for the other person is in one sense intended for the person who speaks: you talk to yourself from the place of another. Equally, the destinee can only decipher what he is capable of speaking himself. Thus communication involves not just the transfer of information to another, but the very constitution of the speaking subject in relation to its other, and the way in which this other is internalised in the formation of the individual. This area, the area of the constitution of the speaking subject, is the terrain of psychoanalysis whose very raw material is language, whose object of study is the subject in so far as he speaks.

Thus it can be seen that the process of language is not reducible to any Marxist model of society, either to that of base and superstructure, or to that of three practices. On the other hand, language is an active (and perhaps the vital) constitutive part of social relations: it is co-extensive with thought itself; it sets up the positions that enable social intercourse to take place. We have seen that it is not univocal, not just a carrier of something else but has a reality of its own. And it is also evident that this reality is material both in that it is constituted in several institutions (speech, writing, gesture) whose importance and forms differ from society to society; and in that its role is determining, playing a part (which remains to be deciphered) in the social process, in social contradictions. It is for these reasons that it is necessary to propose the process of language as a fourth practice: *signifying practice*. Christian Metz defines the space of this practice:

> Signification has more buried and permanent springs (ones by definition less visible, less striking to the mind) whose validity extends, in our present state of knowledge, to the whole of humanity, i.e. to man as a biological 'species'. Not that the symbolic is something 'natural', non-social; on the contrary, in its deepest foundations (which are always structures and not 'facts') signification is no longer just a consequence of social development, it becomes, along with the infrastructures, a party to the constitution of sociality itself, which in turn defines the human race. . . . There is always a moment after the obvious observation that it is man who makes the symbol when it is also clear that the symbol makes man ('The Imaginary Signifier', *Screen*, Summer 1975, p. 30).

It is Kristeva who draws the implications of this idea for conventional Marxism, recasting the notion of the subject in ideology:

> Marxist political economy asserts that a social formation is shaken by the contradictions between the productive forces and the relations of production: it thus introduces into every closed structure the possibility of its being surpassed both in thought and in historical development. We want to assert that along with this contradiction occurs that of the signifying process which makes an element of potential change out of every agent of the structure, and introduces the dimension of signification without which no links are possible between the 'base' and the 'superstructure' (*Tel Quel*, no. 60, p. 26).

Signifying practice thus provides, through psychoanalysis, what the Marxist notion of ideological practice elides: it shows the constitution of a necessary positionality, which is the language-using subject (Lacan calls this the symbolic). But it also shows how that positionality only appears in an ideological formation; it hence shows the nature of the movement of subjective contradictions, the moment of individual practice, of action. Marxism on its own is unable to account for major social crises which take the form of an overdetermined contradiction between subjective processes and the closure of ideology, crises such as that of fascism, a mass movement of reaction. Philippe Sollers states that

> at the same time as an economic analysis [it is necessary to employ] the irreducible discovery of psychoanalysis. If any historic explosion *proves* the fact of the sexual unconscious, it is Fascism. It does so at every level of human reality, in its very way of producing, of reproducing, of destroying, of identifying, or representing itself (*Le Monde*, February 1976).

It is outside the historical materialist analysis of society constituted from three practices that we must go to find the specific materiality in which these practices are articulated to constitute the human subject. It is to psychoanalysis that we have to turn.

This is not to say that Marxist thought has been able to ignore the problem of subjective contradiction. It has elaborated certain ideologies of its own to cover this area: perhaps the most pervasive and unacceptable of these is, as Althusser recognises, that of humanism. He sees humanism as an ideology (expressing a will) which has nothing to do with the later works of Marx, however much it may have contributed to his earlier writings. He defines humanism as a theory which seeks to 'explain society and history, by taking as its starting-point human essence, the free human subject, the subject of needs, of work, the subject of moral and political action' ('Est-il simple d'être marxiste en philosophie?', *La Pensée*, October 1975, p. 27). According to the humanist version of Marxism, this free subject is 'alienated' by social structures: the products of his activity return to him as objects which are set against him in the form of religion, commodities, etc. Communism, then, is the reinstating of the essence of this free subject as the centre of society. We are familiar with this free subject for he is none other than the subject of law, that homogeneous non-contradictory subject which many criminals are accused of not having been. In other words, in seeking to account for the constitution of the real human being, Marxist humanism resorts to an ideological notion of 'human essence' which functions to close the objective contradictions which constitute the individual.

Althusser goes further, by saying that Marxist humanism not only adopts an ideological representation as its basis, but also, in doing so, mistakes the very basis of Marxism itself.

> Marx shows that what determines a social formation in the last instance, and what provides knowledge of it, is not the spirit of an essence or a human nature, not man, not even 'men', but a *relation*, the relation of production. . . . This is not a relation between men,

a relation between persons, nor is it inter-subjective, psychological or anthropological, it is rather a double relation: a relation between groups of men concerning the relation between these groups of men and things, the means of production. It is one of the greatest possible mystifications of theory to think that social relations are reducible to relations between men, or even between groups of men: for it is to suppose that social relations are relations that only concern *men*, whereas they also concern *things*, the means of production, drawn from material nature (ibid., pp. 27–8).

Thus man is not the origin of society, it is rather that society is the origin of man. The result is that the Marxist analysis of society treats men, real concrete men, as the bearers, the supports, of these relations which determine them. Althusser situates this movement of thought exactly by saying that Marx, in his writing about economic and political practices, always treats men as bearers of a function within the process. He explains:

This is emphatically not because he reduces men in their concrete life to the simple bearers of functions: he considers them as such because the capitalist relations of production reduce them to this simple function in the infrastructure, in production, i.e. in exploitation (ibid., p. 28).

He concludes by showing that this analysis is not enough to account for the reality of human beings, and that Marxism on its own cannot do this:

In the 1857 Introduction, Marx said: the concrete is the synthesis of multiple determinations. We can take this up and say: concrete men are determined by the synthesis of multiple determinations of the relations in which they are seized, in which they participate (ibid., p. 30).

Clearly, there is something missing in the Marxist analysis of the subject. The concrete is the synthesis of multiple determinations: the furthest that the Marxist analysis of the concrete individual can go is to show it as *determined by* a synthesis of multiple determinations.

What is missing is an idea of the materiality of the human subject in which this synthesis articulates itself. In order to examine the psychoanalytic discovery of this materiality, it is necessary first to open out the Marxist notion of the contradictory subject which is contained in the philosophy of dialectical materialism. Dialectical materialism thinks the concepts of historical materialism: the concept of contradiction, which has remained in a practical form so far in this exposition; the concept of the subject which has been dealt with only in terms of exploitation and closure in ideology.

Unlike previous philosophies, Marxism has as its specific aim the transformation of the world; we have seen this in the discussion of practice as the transformation of specific givens. It is this notion that really separates Marxism from previous philosophy: it makes philosophy a revolutionary activity; there is reason for revolutionary change. Historical materialism, the science of history as the objective process of the class struggle, is not simply a mode of understanding and explaining the world, but a science whose philosophy posits a new subject. This is a subject who no longer simply 'understands' but also transforms reality by practice. Only this conception of the subject can describe the true subject of materialism, stressing process rather than identity, struggle rather than structure, seeing it as part of a heterogeneous (contradictory) totality rather than logical development.

If these aspects are not emphasised, historical materialism can only be left open to idealism with its vision of things as isolated, static and unchangeable. According to idealist thought, any change that takes place can only be an increase or decrease or a change of place, and most importantly, the cause of these changes is always considered to be external. In other words, it is attributed to a transcendent cause or consciousness, which operates reality and thought as if it were the origin of those things. Materialism, as Sollers claims in *Sur le Matérialisme*, is not the simple opposite of idealism: it is the repressed of Western philosophy, in that it has never been dominant and that materialism can be found in contradictory moments of idealist philosophy. Nevertheless, the place attributed to materialism as the enemy of the State, always in combat with idealism results from its revolutionary notion of man (defined by his practical activity) and of the continuous process of the transformation of the existing state of things. The function then of materialism can only be political; it defines itself as militant in that it sees the negation of all existing states of being. To understand this is to disengage the real basis of Marxism and this real basis is to be found in the exposition of dialectical materialism. Marx described the revolutionary content of the dialectic:

> In its rational form [the dialectic] is a scandal and abomination for
> the bourgeoisie. . . . As it includes in the understanding of the given
> the simultaneous understanding of its negation and necessary destruc-
> tion, as it conceives any mature form as in motion . . . and is in its
> essence critical and revolutionary (*Capital*, as translated in Althusser,
> *For Marx*, p. 90).

Lenin saw the philosophical content of historical materialism, that is, dialectical materialism, to be the logic of *Capital*. Marx always intended to write a 'method' like Hegel's *Science of Logic* after coming to terms with political economy; he never wrote this intended work, but Lenin noted, 'If Marx did not leave behind him a Logic, he did leave the logic of *Capital*' (*Philosophical Notebooks*, p. 319). Lenin described the essential features of this logic:

> In his *Capital*, Marx first analyses the simplest, most ordinary and
> fundamental, most common and everyday relation of bourgeois
> (commodity) society, a relation encountered billions of times viz,

the exchange of commodities. In this very simple phenomenon (in this 'cell' of bourgeois society) analysis reveals *all* the contradictions ... of modern society. The subsequent exposition shows us the development (*both* the growth *and* movement) of these contradictions and of this society in the sum of its individual parts, from its beginning to its end. ... Such must also be the method of exposition (or study) of dialectics in general (*Philosophical Notebooks*, pp. 360–1).

Lenin clearly indicates here how dialectical materialism, with its chief feature, the law of contradiction, is the basic exposition of the materialist process in *Capital*.

Dialectics makes it possible to think of a materialist process since it aims at the simultaneous recognition of 'things' both as objects and as processes. In other words, dialectics aims at grasping things in the double-articulation of totalities: grasping things immediately in their isolatedness, and mediatedly in their full relation to other things, and finally grasping the unity and disunity of both.

Hegel first elaborated the dialectical method, but within a philosophy that was finally idealist. The cause and organisational principle of the process is Negativity, which is not the same thing as negation. Negativity dissolves and transforms structures; it is an 'ineffable' movement of determination: 'negation is determination'. As such it must be understood as the productive dissolution of structures. Every time a term is determined by another term, it is simultaneously negated, and transformed into a new term. To posit one term is to posit its limits at the same time: to posit its outside determinants as well. The negative of this process becomes the positive of a new term. Negativity in this case could be called affirmative negativity.

Hegel's idealist problematic proposed that the necessity of movement was engendered from an initial unresolvable gesture: the Idea. The process is then one of simple development or logical progression. The figures of transition are not really destroyed, but because of the accumulative nature of the process they reappear in a superior form. The dialectic is convergent on a defined conjuncture, that of Absolute Knowledge, and the subject is an entity whose identity of self is already completed. The finished, perfect subject who already knows the end of the process is the fundamental hypothesis of the Hegelian dialectic. It is even named as the substratum of the process, being called 'self-consciousness'. The Hegelian dialectic is then purely logical, linear and hierarchical; as one element comes into co-existence with another, both dissolve into unity in the endeavour to transcend the limit imposed by otherness.

Kristeva points out that there is an ambiguity in this dialectic of consciousness. In the process in which the mind creates itself in the struggle to overcome its own contradictions, consciousness is both of the object, and of itself. Experience is the central unifying term in the struggle to resolve this split of consciousness, a split that results from the fact that consciousness only becomes certain of itself in its object, i.e. consciousness of an other. This is also necessarily self-consciousness, since, for Hegel, each is the mediating term of the other. As soon as consciousness 'knows' the object, it reveals itself to itself; and what it reveals is an unacceptable state in which self-consciousness is determined by an external object, a non-self-consciousness. Self-consciousness exists in and for itself only by the fact that it already exists for another; but at the same time 'consciousness of self' is the basis of consciousness of anything whatsoever. This ambiguity is resolved by Hegel in the notion of self-mediation. *The Phenomenology of the Spirit* describes the way in which consciousness tries to appropriate this otherness and make itself self-determinate. This is the solution of an idea of Absolute Spirit, knowing its end in its beginning, whose aim and intentionality makes man mediate its production by purposeful interaction with the world-object. In this way, the Hegelian dialectic suppresses the notion of the determination of consciousness by a heterogeneous outside, by using the idealist presuppositions of Beginning, God and Subject. Before this recuperation, the process shows up the annihilation of consciousness and subjective unity which should underlie the subject of revolutionary practice in the Marxist dialectic.

> On this level, as in the whole of its trajectory, the Hegelian dialectic starts by dissolving the immediate unity, the sensible certitude; but after having noted the moments of its division, of its doubling-over, and its mediation in relation to the other, it returns to the same, refills it and consolidates it. . . . The self is divided and doubled to reunite itself in the unity of consciousness of self. The ambiguity of the idealist dialectic is here; it locates division, movement and process, but brings them to light in the same gesture in the name of a superior, metaphysical and repressive truth, differentiated but uniquely, in the closure of a unity which will be consciousness of self, and its correlate on a juridical level, the State (Kristeva, *La Révolution du langage poétique*, pp. 123–4).

In contrast to Hegel's idealism, the Marxist dialectic is dealing with practical activity, products and objects, and not merely ideal concepts: the practical activity of men governs their mental relations in opposition to the unfolding of the idea. Determinacy therefore is *not* the immediate negation of that which is determined. Because the dialectic is historical, the moment of negation and the moment of determinacy can be temporally and spatially separate. As Lenin remarked, it was on the question of history where Marx and Engels made the greatest advance, and where the Hegelian notion of 'the spreading out of God in a particular determined element' became antiquity. The totality is no longer built up through an accumulated logical series of determinants, achieved through the supersession of elements, but is, rather, a heterogeneous totality, made up of the co-presence of many determinants and many negations. There is no place in Marxist thought for the idea of a simple beginning which is the characteristic of metaphysics. The emphasis is on practice; theory never starts anything on its own. There can never be a zero point since the movement of knowledge has always already begun and includes practice as one of its terms. Reality, then, is an ever pre-given, complexly structured totality, characterised by disjunctions, irregularities, uneven development and partial, fragmented movement. Thus the Marxist dialectic suggests a way of understanding structural relations which does not imply structural equilibrium but rather both structure and process simultaneously. It is the notion of contradiction, called by Lenin the kernel of the dialectic, which enables this understanding of the heterogeneous totality as being simultaneously process and structure. It is still Althusser who has given the most adequate exposition of the materialist process:

> If every contradiction is a contradiction in a complex whole, structured in dominance, this complex whole cannot be envisaged without its contradictions, without their basically uneven relations. In other words, each contradiction, each essential articulation of the structure, and the general relation of the articulations in the structure in dominance, constitute so many conditions of the existence of the complex whole itself. This proposition is of the first importance for it means that the structure of the whole and therefore the 'difference' of the essential contradictions and their structure in dominance, is the very existence of the whole; that the 'difference' of the essential contradictions (that there is a principal contradiction, etc., and that every contradiction has a principal aspect) is identical to the conditions of existence of the complex whole (*For Marx*, p. 205).

It is the emphasis on both process and practice which has characterised Marxism in its demarcation from idealist philosophy, and these are both to be found in the 'kernel' of the dialectic, the primacy of contradiction over identity with the concomitant emphasis on the irreducibility of struggle, movement and transformation of one thing into another, on antagonism and non-antagonism and finally on the notion of process. The theory of contradiction therefore has been central to any elaboration of the theoretical bases of Marxism.

First, Engels, engaged with Marx on the project to establish the objectivity of the real revolutionary movement, that is the material basis of the class struggle, in the face of contemporary Utopian socialism, tended to subordinate the dialectic to materialism. Although it appears from his historical analyses that Engels was working towards a dialecticisation of theory, nevertheless in his general philosophical writings, this subordination, which even extended into natural sciences, was very much in evidence. This may have been an historical exigency; the need to oppose Utopian socialism with scientific socialism. But the result was that Engels did not consider contradiction to be the principal motor of movement. He described the dialectic as 'the science of the general laws of movement' (*Ludwig Feuerbach*) and 'the science of connections' (*Anti-Dubring*). Thus he 'prioritised the theory of liaisons and inter-dependencies over the theory of contradictions' (Badiou, *Théorie de la contradiction*, p. 31). He wanted to establish that the dialectic itself grew out of the materialist thesis; that it reflected the objective laws of natural science. Crude economism is one of the descendants of this philosophical tendency, and it is crude economism which is still one of the principal hindrances to revolutionary socialism. Engels's suppression of the dialectic is insufficient to counteract such tendencies. In the *Dialectics of Nature*, Engels outlined what for him constituted the three laws of the dialectic. They were, the law of passage of quantity into quality; the law of interpenetration of contraries; and the law of the negation of negation. The dialectical principle itself is missing, that is the primacy of contradiction over identity, and, without this, none of the other laws can develop fully. The law of unity of contraries and the movement of one contrary into the other, is missing in Engels; the notion of a heterogeneous totality and the idea of qualitative breaks resulting from quantitative accumulation are suppressed, and what results is that the way is left open for a notion of evolutionism which gives priority to unity rather than to contradiction.

It was Lenin who really saw the centrality and revolutionary signifi-cance of the dialectic. He reactivated the principle of contradiction as the underlying principle in the separation of materialism and idealism, and emphasised the development of 'the subtle, revolutionary dialectic' as the instrument against evolutionism. Lenin achieved a qualitative advance in the realm of philosophy. This advance was 'no more, no less than the restitution and the extension of the basis of marxism, present in the texts of Marx and Engels themselves' (Sollers, *Sur le Matérialisme*, p. 94). The key to this basis was the elaboration of contradiction as the motor of the materialist process, the 'recognition of the contradictory, mutually exclusive, opposite tendencies in all phenomena and processes of nature (including mind and society)' (Lenin, op. cit., pp. 359–60). But this conception of reality as the movement of contradictions does not fall into the trap of being either metaphysical or ontological: Lenin 'distinguishes between the philosophic categories of matter and the scientific concepts of matter, between relative and absolute truth' (B. Brewster, *Theoretical Practice*, 3/4, p. 25). Dialectics is therefore the theory of knowledge of Marxism. The notion of contradiction 'in the very essence of things' is something which even Hegel recognises to be challenging a fundamental prejudice and misunderstanding inherent in bourgeois thought: 'Usually contradiction passes for something acciden-tal in reality as well as in thought, as if it were something abnormal, a morbid and passing paroxysm' (quoted in Sollers, op. cit., p. 117). Lenin recognised that contradiction is the principle of all internal movement at every moment and in each historical conjuncture.

The misunderstandings of 'contradiction' indicate, Sollers claims, the feebleness of thought which continually returns to the idealist project of unity and logical progression. He points to the difference between the Hegelian metaphysical unity and the dialectical use of the term as 'unity of opposites':

> When writing about the Hegelian unity, Lenin noted that it would be better to talk about inseparability: here he touches on the basis of dialectical materialism where it is necessary to recall ceaselessly that development as a unity of opposites is a process of doubling over (the doubling of one into contraries which are mutually exclusive and interrelated) (Sollers, op. cit., p. 117).

To avoid idealism, the emphasis should be on one dividing into two rather than the logic of two fused into one — the latter being a logic which characterises and gives an idealist form to mechanical materialism. The emphasis should not be so much on the unity of opposites, as on the division of that unity. 'The doubling of one and the knowledge of contradictory parts is the basis of the dialectic' (ibid.). What takes priority in this conception of the dialectic is the struggle of contraries, always in movement, in which identity is only one moment of this struggle. 'Unity (coincidence, identity, equal action) of opposites is conditional, temporary, transitory, relative. The struggle of mutually exclusive opposites is absolute' (Lenin, op. cit., p. 360). Mao has made it easier to understand the relativity of identity by developing the principle of contradiction with the thesis of principal contradiction and the assymmetricality of contradictions. There is a qualitative determination of the historic moment by the principal contradiction: secondary contradictions, which are specific and sometimes autonomous, develop internally from their own articulation with the principal contradiction. In the same way that the principal contradiction fixes the qualitative nature of a process, each contradiction is qualitatively specified by a principal dominant term. For example, Britain is a capitalist country not just because the principal contradiction is between the middle class and the working class, but also because in this principal contradiction there is a principal aspect which is the domination of the middle class. Struggle is then the only absolute principle of dialectical thought; its essence is to change the basis of reality.

Lenin brought the dialectical method definitively into existence. He insisted on the significance of the Hegelian dialectic in order to restore the crucial aspect to Marxist philosophy, that of the primacy of struggle over identity. 'Hegel brilliantly divined the dialectics of things (phenomena, the world, nature) in the dialectics of concepts' (Lenin, op. cit., p. 196). Hegel had shown movement

> by leaps, catastrophes, by 'solutions of continuity', the transformation of quantity into quality; the internal impulsions of development provoked by contradiction, the shock of forces and diverse tendencies bearing on a given body, in the framework of given phenomena

or in the lap of society; the interdependency and the straight liaison, indissoluble, of all aspects in all phenomena; a liaison which determines the universal process of movement, a unique process governed by laws — such are certainly the traits of the dialectic as doctrine of development (Lenin, op. cit., *passim*).

In elaborating this basis of Marxism it is significant that Lenin retained the Hegelian notion of negativity. He marked a passage where Hegel dismissed the simplicity of the three-termed dialectic, and stressed the need for the fourth term, that is, negativity as 'the necessary liaison and immanent genesis of differences' (ibid., p. 97). His dialectical materialism thus accepted the notion of 'internal negativity' as the objective principle in 'all natural and spiritual life' (ibid.), as being the motor of contradiction. Lenin once wrote that it was at the summit of a contradiction that diversities became active in relation to one another, and acquired the negativity which is the internal impulsion of all spontaneous life movement. In returning to Hegel, both Marx and Lenin acknowledged his very real grasp of reality as process, subsumed as it was under idealism. It provided a way of understanding that any fixity is negated. Practice, productive forces, and the economic base in general, occupy the dominant place in producing a certain fixity and identity of the historical moment, but this will always be negated and changed.

It is practice which determines this aspect of dialectical materialism, and practice presupposes a subject. Logically the subject of a process whose motor is negativity can only be a subject in process: a subject whose identity is in crisis. It can never be what Althusser suggests in claiming that Lenin revealed 'a process without a subject'. Althusser makes the Hegelian equation of Beginning, God, Subject, and then goes on to suggest that it follows logically that the subject also disappears in Lenin's removal of the Beginning and God from the dialectic. But in suppressing these notions, Lenin does not remove the category subject. What in fact he proposed was not the suppression of the subject, but the simultaneous reflection on the separation and reciprocal action of the two categories of subject and object in the general movement of the process. Nor did he exclude the possibility that the subjective factor may at some points be the key to the movement of the process. 'If one considers the relation of subject to object in logic, one must take into account the general premises of Being of the concrete subject (life of man) in the objective situation' (Lenin, op. cit., p. 202). The subject therefore remains in the process, but remains as the problem of the contradictory movement between the subjective and the objective. The unilaterality of the concepts subject and object is no longer tenable. To separate them is a metaphysical operation; to suppress either one or the other can only ever be either absolute idealism or its inverse, mechanical materialism.

Kristeva indicates how dialectical materialism with its emphasis on practice must inevitably point to the contradictory process of subject and object:

> The logical expression of objective processes, negativity can only yield a subject in process, the subject which constitutes itself according to the law of negativity, that is, according to the laws of objective reality: it can only be a subject crossed over by this negativity, opened onto by a non-subjected free objectivity in movement. A subject immersed in negativity ceases to be 'external' to objective negativity, a transcendent unity, a monad to specific rules, but rather places itself at the moment which is the 'most interior, the most objective in the life of the spirit' (Lenin) (*La Révolution du langage poétique*, p. 103).

Such an understanding of the materialist process does not dispense with the subject but leaves it divided. Objective contradiction must imply a struggle in identity; the identity which it is the task of idealism to preserve. If history is that of modes of production and not that of the unified subject in its self-presence, then dialectical materialism ought to suggest the subject as 'a contradiction which activates practice' (Kristeva), that is, a subject crossed by and constructed in this negativity.

But materialism has developed in such a way that only a fraction of this negativity has been retained in relation to the subject. This fraction is the subordination of the subject (as a complete unity) to the social and natural process. Forms of Marxist thought bracket out the problem of the subject, and concentrate, in a totally mechanistic fashion, on the mode of production, or hypostatise a fixed identity which usually appears under the ludicrous notion of 'false consciousness'. This can only ever return to the idealist problematic if the subject is presupposed as having some essential human nature, which is alienated and distorted by ruling ideology. It is a presupposition which is very far from the materialist process proposed by Marx.

It has been pointed out by Kristeva that it is the Feuerbachian reversal of Hegel which still underlies these very idealist readings of Marx. Feuerbach's 'reversal' was achieved by the fact that he totally ignored the possible dissolution in relation to the subject and the unity of consciousness proposed by Hegel. Feuerbach stressed nature and society as the bases of the production of man, rather than the progress of self-consciousness. But in positing this unified notion of man, he lost the movement of negativity and the dialectical principle itself. The subject in his case is reduced to a desiring ego: a human 'being' which is only motivated by society or its surroundings, and which can never be negated. Thus metaphysical notions of being and presence are affirmed by the suggestion of the suffering, lacking man who is the origin of desire. (We will see in the following chapter how this notion of desire differs from that of Lacan, which is precisely produced in this negativity.) Feuerbach's notion of desire proposes a theological view of man which underlies the human community, society, and finally the State. In other words, he simply transferred the thrust of religion into the social domain. In the *Grundrisse* and *Capital*, with his reconsideration of the Hegelian dialectic, Marx moved away decisively from the naturalist metaphysic of Feuerbach. He rehabilitated the dialectic, the notions of struggle, contradiction and practice in an attempt to describe a materialist process of transformation, both for society and man. Despite this dialecticisation, and despite all the developments of the dialectic which we have described, Marxist doctrine nevertheless still inherits something from two essential moments of Feuerbach's thought.

The first is this tendency to posit 'human unity' in the form of the man of lack. In Marxist thought this is usually the working class who are seen as the route for the realisation of the complete and total man, the man of mastery who is without conflict. Man in this case is first and foremost a solution to conflict:

On the one hand, therefore, it is only when objective reality universally becomes for man in society the reality of man's essential powers, becomes human reality, and thus the reality of his *own* essential powers, that all *objects* become for him *objectification of himself*, objects that confirm and realize his individuality, *his* objects, i.e. *he himself* becomes the object (K. Marx, 'Economic and Philosophical Manuscripts' in *Early Writings*, Penguin/New Left Review, 1975, pp. 352—3).

The second is the direct and exclusive anchoring of man in the State or more generally in the social machine and in social relations, which are then seen as relations of need and suffering. The machine may be contradictory and determined by social conflict, production and class relations, but man remains untouched as a unity, in conflict with others but never with himself. In this case, the subject will always remain neutral, oppressor or oppressed, leader or exploited, but never a subject in process, corresponding to the process of society and nature, revealed by dialectical materialism.

Socio-political movements of the twentieth century which have tended to develop according to the dominance of one or other of these two views, have either attempted to change the relations between 'men', or to transform the structure of the State, but none has touched on the dialectical principle of the negation of fixity in relation to the subject itself. As we have seen, it is only with this notion that the theory of contradiction can develop as the principle of dialectical materialism. Unless the subject is seen to be a process, 'an effect of the intersection of matter in movement' (Sollers), which activates practice, there will only ever be a mechanical view of the movement of the superstructures and therefore of the social totality as a whole. Bourgeois ideology remains in dominance because of the plurality allowed to it by its having as its fundamental hypothesis the unity of the subject. Until Marxism can produce a revolutionary subject, revolutionary change will be impossible.

Without a move in this direction, Marxism will remain unable to account for fascism and other conjunctures where ideology is a principal determinant. Ideology will not be understood until Marxism produces an understanding of language, since the materialist dialectic must now be seen as the dialectic between history, language and ideology. To analyse the structure without the subject can only be a form of metaphysical materialism; to analyse language without its object can only be idealism; and to analyse ideology without language will only ever be mechanical materialism, since all of these forms of analysis deny the determinacy of the symbolic system as it is imposed on the human subject in its construction in history and ideological formations. It is here that the importance of the work of Lacan resides, for in positing that the theory of signification is the theory of the subject, Lacan is proposing an understanding of the subject as the materialist process itself. And it is only with this theory of the subject that Marxism can move towards a destruction of the division between subject and object, which underlies its return to idealist thought.

6 On the subject of Lacan

It may seem strange to situate the relevance of Lacan's work in a close connection with the philosophy of dialectical materialism and the problems of ideology in Marxism, but it is precisely in drawing these connections that his re-reading of Freud has most significance. For it provides the foundation of a materialist theory of the subject in the social process, a subject constructed as always already included by those social processes, but never simply reducible to being a support. Lacan's subject is therefore this new subject of dialectical materialism: a subject in process. Lacan asserts that the discoveries of Freud open on to the mobility of which revolutions are made. They point to the 'missing area in human sciences, that of the process of meaning in language and ideology, the process of the "I" in history, an area which would operate in the same space as dialectical materialism itself' (Kristeva, *Tel Quel*, no. 48).

Access to the subject in process is based on Lacan's emphasis on the determinacy of the signifier (that is, language) in the construction of the individual as subject. He analyses the determinacy of the symbolic system as it is imposed on the human subject in its construction in history and ideological formations. The emphasis on language provides a route for an elaboration of the subject in the social process, the subject demanded by dialectical materialism. It suggests a notion of the subject produced in relation to social relations by the fixing of its signifying chain to produce certain signifieds. But in that he also specifies the 'symbolic system' – the positions necessitated in order to be able to use language at all – Lacan avoids the reduction of language to ideology. 'Symbolic relations', whose determinacy can be traced in the history of the unconscious, are the positions necessitated by predication, i.e. a subject different from and able to differentiate within a predicatable outside. As such, according to Lacan, they are different from and not reducible to specific ideological relations. At the same time, they are not to be separated from ideology, as somehow 'coming before' it. The symbolic relations, a subject in position of predication, are always manifested within ideological formations. It is therefore a subtle and careful notion of language and the subject which avoids previous confusions.

This is achieved by the very material of psychoanalysis, whose object is the unconscious: for Lacan this is produced by the same movement by which the subject enters the symbolic universe. Thus its disruptive relation with consciousness, bearing witness to what is heterogeneous and appears irrational and illogical, demonstrates the price for producing a subject in sociality, that is a subject in a position of predication. This distinct operation is opened to analysis as a result of Lacan's notion that the process of signification is the process of the subject itself. Through this, the process of the construction of a subject in relation to social relations becomes a process available to scientific analysis. In the same movement, the notion of a unified subject of self-consciousness becomes untenable. The erratic and devious presence of the unconscious, without which the position of the subject cannot be understood, insists on hetereogeneity and contradictions within the subject itself. Therefore it provides the most rigorous criticism of the presupposition of a consistent, fully finished subject, and of the social sciences that base themselves on such a presupposition.

These assertions, which are developed in this chapter, underlie the claim that the work of Lacan has provided a radically different way of situating the problems of language, ideology and the subject. The relations to social relations are fixed in the same process by which the subject is produced, able to predicate an outside. It is ideology which necessitates the limiting of this relation to a specific predicate; it produces a specific articulation which necessitates a certain subject for its meanings. Positioning takes place in the same process by which the subject enters into language, but is never finally limited to this early stage. Nevertheless, Lacan's psychoanalysis has demonstrated the importance of the sexual and familial in the fixing of ideological discourse, an importance which is intuitively felt, but consistently repressed in Marxist thought.

The way in which Freud's discoveries are taken up by Lacan to illuminate the problematic of the subject in language results from the importance that he attributes to the structure of language in the unconscious. Before Freud, he claims, the unconscious simply was not. All theories of the unconscious were merely the ensemble of all the divergent meanings given to the word 'darkness'. He cites eight definitions, collected by Dwelshauvers in 1916, in which are included: acquired formations in the memory, telepathy, automatism from which habit is developed, and co-consciousness, that is the existence of the double personality. For Lacan, despite their disparateness in terms of psychological objectivity, all these definitions display the central error of psychology: 'This error is to take as unified the phenomenon of consciousness itself' (Lacan, *Ecrits*, p. 831). The refutation of this 'given' of the unity of the subject in traditional psychology (a given which Lacan has clearly identified in its use in American exploitation by directing an adaptive cure) is based on a re-reading of Freud that radically subverts the notion of the unified subject of consciousness. In every way, this reading is opposed to idealism, and cannot therefore contribute to that idealism which serves existing society.

In Freud, consciousness is too 'frail a concept' for the unconscious to be seen simply as the negation of it. What is more, the Freudian unconscious participates in the functions of ideation and even thought, which is what leads Freud to use the paradoxical term 'unconscious thought'. In all theories of the unconscious before Freud, it is always in some way associated with a hidden will, existing prior to consciousness. The Freudian unconscious has, at all points, something homologous with what occurs in the network of the individual. This was evident to Freud in the work on dreams. Here he found that something may be said 'in person' without, however, issuing from the first person (in the grammatical sense), but in the alienated form of the second or third person. Thus he was led to posit that the data of consciousness is incomplete and that the gaps in the conscious discourse, its inconsistencies and contradictions, could be made coherent only if the unconscious formations were interpolated in these gaps. Freud's discoveries can therefore justly be compared with the revolution in the organisation of the conceptual field brought about by the discoveries of Copernicus. As with the Copernican revolution, the question once more is the place man assigns to himself at the centre of the universe. The pursuit of a topology of the unconscious through work on linguistics which is the specific model of Lacan's work, aims at accounting for the constitution of the subject considered as a signifying process. This constitution is accomplished in negativity: the negativity of the signifying process itself and of desire. Such, according to Lacan, are the implications of the discovery of the unconscious. How have these claims developed?

The principal development has taken place through the model of linguistics which offers 'a solid prop for the elaboration of the unconscious' and which assures us 'that there are, under the terms of the unconscious several things that can be qualified, are accessible and objectifiable' (*Ecrits*). What Freud anticipated in his work on dreams, which begins the royal road to the unconscious, are the formulas of Saussure:

> necessary to any articulation of analytic phenomena [is] the notion of the signifier, as opposed to that of the signified, in modern linguistic analysis. Freud could not take into account this notion which postdates him, but I would claim that Freud's discovery stands out precisely because, although it sets out from a domain in which one could not expect to recognise its reign, it could not fail to anticipate its formulas. Conversely, it is Freud's discovery that gives to the signifier/signified division the full extent of its implications: namely, that the signifier has an active function in determining certain effects

in which the signifiable appears as submitting to its mark, by becoming through that passion the signified (ibid., p. 688).

To understand this claim, it is necessary to retrace some of the developments of Saussurean linguistics and also the developments in the work of Lacan that have lead to this stress on the *signifier* as the crucial term in Freud and modern linguistics under its most influential exponents Saussure and Jakobson. Lacan points to the formula

$$\frac{\text{signifier}}{\text{signified}}$$

as the foundation for the emergence of linguistic science. The formula is what has made possible the exact study of the proper relations of the signifier in the production of meaning. This has already been discussed in earlier chapters as what founded structuralism and semiology, made possible through the concept of difference, showing that 'no meaning is sustained by anything other than reference to other meaning' (ibid., p. 498).

Saussure disposed of the problem of origin that had been the major preoccupation of nineteenth-century bourgeois linguistics, replacing it with a model that takes *a priori* the human semiological system; this stresses the systematic reality of language: 'in language there are only differences'. In attempting to explain the necessity for understanding language in this way, Laplanche and Leclaire in their article 'The Unconscious' (*Yale French Studies*, no. 48) call the reader to imagine a mythical construction of language little by little. They use the well-known example of the 'Fort/Da game' from Freudian psychoanalysis, where the child's game is seen to be an attempt to master, and repeat, its mother's absence (see below, p. 104).

> If (in this hypothesis) by allowing him to master them, the opposite pair of phonemes A—O come to symbolise for the child the presence and absence of the mother, is it not by the same movement that the presence and absence are themselves constituted as the two categories into which the child's whole universe is divided whereas previously it was wholly and without mediation satiety or void (ibid., p. 153).

This is to show, even though this myth of origin of language is deliberately banal, the co-extension of the two systems (signifier and signified): the four terms in this example are 'presence' and 'absence' as signified, and 'O' and 'A' as signifiers. A refers to presence only in so far as it refers to its phonematic opposite O. This leads to the conclusion that:

> If a signifier refers to a signified, it is only through the mediation of the entire system of signifiers: there is no signifier that doesn't refer to the absence of others and that is not defined by its position in the system (ibid., p. 154).

The determinant then is to be understood not by a link between the thing and the sign, but by the relation of signifiers: Saussurean linguistics does not look for identity but for difference; each element is distinct from its own origin, different at each new instance of its repetition, and similar or identical only in its opposition to all other elements in the signifying chain. It is taken for granted that each individual enters into a pre-existent linguistic world.

The logical development of this position is to see the signifier as the crucial determinant in linguistic science. It is possible to attempt to describe the limits of the signifier by taking as the starting point the fact that it is structured only in so far as it is part of an articulation. Lacan describes these limits in his paper 'The Insistence of the Letter in the Unconscious' (*Ecrits*). The units of the signifier are submitted to the double condition:

(1) of reducing to its distinctive features, that is, to phonemes. These do not have a fixed or static status, but are part of the synchronic system by which sounds are distinguished from one another in a given language. The letter is therefore seen as the essentially localised structure of the signifier;
(2) that the units combine according to a closed order; from this Lacan is led to posit the necessity for a topological substratum which he calls the signifying chain.

These two instances provide a description of what makes up the signifier; they point out that examination of grammatical laws can only illuminate meaning if based on the relations between signifiers. From this he is led to propose the notion of the constant sliding of the signified under the signifier. This disposes of the illusion that the signifier functions as the representation of the signified: 'it is in the chain of the signifier that meaning insists, but none of its elements "consists" in the meaning of which it is at that moment capable' (*Ecrits*, p. 502). Language is seen to have the dizzying effects of a dictionary: each word, definition by definition, refers to the others by a series of equivalents; every synonymous substitution is authorised. Language results in tautology, without at any moment having been able to 'hook onto' any signified at all. In the face of this endless tautology, in which resides the origin of the incessant sliding of the signified under the signifier, what does Lacan suggest to explain the fact that language lends itself so readily to the 'effects of meaning'? Why, as Laplanche and Leclaire ask, does the word 'x' only have a group of meanings 'b, c, d', rather than opening endlessly on to an alphabet of meanings? It is here that Lacan introduces his '*points de capiton*' (usually translated as 'spaced upholstery buttons', the buttons that are used to stud down a couch). These are privileged points at which the direction of the signifying chain is established. The *point de capiton* is located in the diachronic function of the phrase, in that meaning is only ensured with its last term, that is, retrospective meaning. Only in so far as language is used by a subject who intends meaning within a signifying practice does it possess deep structures, through which categories like the logical, the semantic or the intercommunicational are articulated. The question which therefore imposes itself is how the subject is constructed in relation to meaning. The incidence of the chain of signifiers on the signified, i.e. the production of meaning, represented in the fictional model of the *point de capiton*, is an incidence which can only occur if speech can evoke a third term as witness to its meaning, and thereby complete the signifying chain.

The signifier, then, is seen as the mark of separation by which identities and differences can be established. It is not, however, a simple matter of the subject learning to ascertain relations of contiguity and difference: it is also a matter of the subject's own identity being achieved by this same process of differentiation, marking out of separations between itself and its own surroundings in order that it may find itself a place in the signifying chain. Identifications of this structural nature are necessary for the subject to represent himself in the system of differences which is learned language. This claim for a necessary positionality in language to determine the direction of the discourse is elaborated in Lacan's discussion of the mechanisms of the unconscious.

Freud himself claimed that his work on dreams contained the essential concepts of his discoveries concerning the unconscious. In the description of the elements of timelessness, lack of contradiction, condensation and displacement in dreams, Freud uncovered the mechanisms of the unconscious system. The analysis of dreams produced an interpretation which suggested that the unconscious has the same structure as that through which 'the signifier in ordinary discourse is articulated and analysed'. Where traditional psychology had always maintained that dreams had no meaning, Freud demonstrated that they exhibit a constant sliding of meaning. This is the constant sliding which characterises the primary process, the sliding of condensation (the process which enables all the meanings in several threads of associations to converge on one idea at the point of their intersection), and displacement (where an apparently trivial idea comes to be invested with all the depth of meaning and intensity originally attributed to another one).

The structure of language makes it possible for us to read dreams. There is no fixed original meaning, just the dream-text with its distortion and production, that is, the dream-work.

> The dream-thoughts and dream-content are presented to us like two versions of the same subject matter in two different languages. Or, more properly, the dream-content seems like a transcript of the dream-thoughts into another mode of expression, whose characters and syntactical laws it is our business to discover by comparing the original and the translation (Freud, *Standard Edition*, vol. V).

Freud emphasised the primacy of linguistic analysis in describing the dream-content as a rebus. Although the dream-content is expressed as if it were a pictographic script, Freud dismisses the attempt at reading these characters according to their pictorial rather than symbolic value. This is the error that led his predecessors to 'non-sensical and worthless' interpretations. The dream-as-a-rebus has to be understood as a picture-puzzle; a proper judgment of it can only be formed 'if we put aside criticisms . . . of the whole composition and its parts [as being inconsistent or incongruous] and if, instead, we try to replace each separate element by a syllable or a word that can be represented by that element in some way or other' (ibid.). This attempt to locate the syntactical laws of operation of the unconscious is what underlies Freud's whole discussion of the dream-work.

Distortion was recognised by Freud to be the 'general pre-condition for the functioning of dreams' (*Ecrits*, p. 511). It is the overall effect of the dream-work by which latent thoughts are transformed into their manifest form, which is not immediately or easily recognisable. Lacan identified this as the same tendency as that described by Saussure as the constant sliding of the signified under the signifier. The two central modes of the functioning of the unconscious processes are condensation and displacement. Condensation is the process which explains why dreams are brief, meagre and laconic in comparison with the range and wealth of dream-thoughts. Freud points out that a written description of a dream in recollection might cover half a page of writing; the analysis might produce an inexhaustible amount of associations. The dream of the Wolf Man in *The History of Infantile Neurosis* (*Standard Edition*, vol. XVII) is one of many examples whereby a brief dream in analysis produces a wealth of associations. Displacement is the process by which the original emphasis of an idea is detached and passed on to other ideas, a 'veering off of meaning'. Lacan has pointed out the similarity between these modes of functioning and those of language in ordinary discourse. This type of signification is not, however, like logical categories, the object of modern linguistics, but rather a signifying process which contains many heterogeneous elements.

The signifying function as such is made up, according to Lacan, of metaphor and metonymy. These are the two processes of the signifier by which meaning is constituted, 'the two great poles of language'. The direction of the signifying chain is determined by the effects of combination and substitution in the signifier: the signified – meaning – is generated by these effects. Metonymy, with its word-to-word movement (thirty sails can be understood as thirty boats), is seen to be the same process as that of displacement. Metaphor retains a hidden signifier when one signifier takes the place of another. It does so through the fact that the hidden signifier has a metonymic relation to the rest of the signifying chain. This process is equivalent to that of condensation, with the same superimposition of signifiers. These modes of functioning are by no means exclusive; however, certain forms of articulation can be dominated by one or another. Jakobson was the first to insist on these processes as the essential modes of functioning of language, and he categorised certain artistic practices in which one or the other predominate. Barthes refers to these in *Elements of Semiology*:

> To the metaphoric order (in which associations by substitution predominate) belong the Russian lyrical songs, the works of Romanticism and of Symbolism, Surrealist painting, the films of Charlie Chaplin. . . . To the metonymic order . . . belong the heroic epics, the narratives of the Realist school, films by D. W. Griffith (p. 60).

The consequence of these developments was the recognition of the formative role of the signifier in the production of meaning; it was the same formative role that Freud, without realising it, had found in the unconscious through his analysis of dreams, which endlessly employ the elementary mechanisms of language.

> The unconscious from Freud onwards is a chain of signifiers which somewhere in another scene (Freud's 'eine andere Schauplatz') repeats itself and insists so as to interfere in the breaks offered by the discourse and the thought that the discourse informs. In this formulation . . . the crucial term is the signifier, revived from ancient rhetoric by modern linguistics (*Ecrits*, p. 799).

These modes of functioning are characteristic of the primary processes which belong to the unconscious system. Waking thought, judgment, reasoning, logic, all belong to the secondary processes. Unlike primary processes, where psychical energy flows freely by means of displacement and condensation, in the case of secondary processes, energy moves in a more controlled way. Satisfaction is delayed while the mind tries out different ways to satisfaction. This regulatory functioning is made possible by the construction of the ego. This regulatory function results from the process of the construction of the ego and its world of objects, and is the same process as that by which the subject is constructed in language. In Lacan, this construction is a complex matter, since it involves a notion of the 'splitting', or separation, of the subject: first from its sense of continuum with the mother's body; then with the illusory identity and totality of the ideal ego of the mirror stage; and finally a separation by which the subject finds itself a place in symbolisation. It is this construction which creates the subject and the unconscious, and involves imaginary and symbolic relations.

In this discussion of Lacan's notion of subjectivity, we are stressing the construction of a meaning-producing subject from a system of differences, and the notion that the unconscious is concomitant with this. This is in order that the states of the imaginary and the symbolic can be seen in their relation to signification. For a further elaboration of the process of the drives in their relation to signification, see the following chapter 'The Critique of the Sign'.

The process of the construction of the subject occurs from the moment of the child's birth. Lacan produces a mythical hypothesis of the child in its existence before it becomes a language-using member of society. This myth can only ever be mythical precisely because any knowledge that one has of the processes pre-existing language and the unconscious are known only through language with its symbolic relations. The myth suggests a state dominated purely by the drives, that is, by pressures or forces towards certain objects. At the moment of its birth the child is like a 'hommelette' — a little man and also like a broken egg spreading without hindrance in all directions. But as this child is always already submitted to the division of matter and to the constraints of, in our society, the family, the drives are limited and are contained in what is known as 'erotogenic zones'. These are cuts or gapings inscribed on a surface, for example the lips or the anus: it is this cut or aperture on the surface of the body which allows the sense of 'edges', borders or margins, which differentiate the body from the organic functions associated with these apertures, thus marking out that part of the body as area of excitation. Because these cuts or apertures are described on the very surface of the subject, they have no outside that they represent; it is this which enables them 'to be the "stuff" or rather the lining . . . of the very subject that one takes to be the subject of consciousness' (*Ecrits*, p. 818). In other words, the division of matter of the subject's own body in relation to the heterogeneous outside, is the 'stuff' out of which the conscious subject is produced.

Freud's hypothesis of charges or pressures travelling across the body was developed from the standpoint of an economic principle. These pressures, due to their interrelatedness and their relation to socio-familial constraints, can enter into unpleasurable tension. He did not suggest any absolute and original notion of pressure; he was led to hypothesise the 'drive' after noticing the transformations undergone by desire in relation to its objects. (Freud uses the word 'Trieb' which we translate, following Lacan, as 'drive'. The *Standard Edition* of Freud consistently uses the word 'instinct' which we retain only in direct quotation.) These were particularly obvious of the sexual drives which undergo several changes in regard to their objects, aims and excitations. The hypothesis of their existence resulted from the fact that a concomitant reduction at another point was noticed when pressure was spent in achieving certain aims. The emphasis, then, was not on the stability of the aim, but on the irresistible nature of the pressure. As such, it is far from being an energic or substantialist conception. These pressures are only known by their delimitation in certain zones, by their sites and the transformations of the object choice, so there is no notion of a 'pure' unlimited drive. The object is what is deemed capable of satisfying the aim of a drive: 'the object of an instinct is the thing in regard to which or through which the instinct is able to achieve its aim'. 'It is what is most variable about an instinct and is not originally connected with it, but becomes assigned to it only in consequence of being peculiarly fitted to make satisfaction possible' (*Instincts and Their Vicissitudes, Standard Edition*, vol. XIV, p. 122). According to Lacan, objects propose themselves from outside 'as substitutes for the lost anatomical complements' as images capable of filling in the lack and re-establishing a lost connection, for example, the mother's breast.

The economic hypothesis of the functioning of these drives in relation to the construction of the ego, was formulated precisely in relation to the aims of the drives. This principle is the pleasure principle originally suggested by Freud as one of two principles (the other being the reality principle, see *The Two Principles of Mental Functioning, Standard Edition*, vol. XII) by which the ego and its world of objects is constructed according to the economic principle of the avoidance of unpleasurable tension. This principle therefore involves the question of the arrangement and activity of the drives. Unpleasure is due to the increase of quantities of excitation, and pleasure is their reduction. The amount of unpleasurable tension or the resolution of tension (unpleasure and pleasure) relies on the relation of objects to the structural arrangement of the drives. It should be emphasised that these are not necessarily real objects: the term object refers to what the drive aims at, its goal. The source or resolution of tension can always be the interaction between the body and the outside. The aim of the drives therefore is to eliminate states of tension either by introjecting an object deemed capable of closing the sense of loss, or by projecting an aim which produces an excess of tension. It is this function of the object which defines its status of 'good' or 'bad'. In that the drives work as a pressure to realise the object of satisfaction, they are a 'demand made on the mind for work' (*Standard Edition*, vol. XIV, p. 122). As such, they inhabit the turning point between the body and the conscious subject. Gradually, Freud came to realise the dominance of the modality of the pleasure principle in establishing the outside world as separate and different from the subject. At first the subject attempts to coincide with everything which is pleasurable (its own body is divided into pleasurable and unpleasurable parts, just as the outside is). This endeavour is what leads to the introjection of good and the projection of bad objects. In Freud's early writing, this leads to the location of all unpleasure outside the subject. The article on 'Negation' (*Standard Edition*, vol. XIX, pp. 235—9), however, suggests that the process of introjection and projection sets up the outside as radically 'other' to the subject and therefore producing the possibility of predication, i.e. the subject/object relations.

This process of introjection and projection establishes, or at least traces, marks of similarities or difference in objects. These enable the drives to attach themselves to a certain signifier in order to know the object of their aims. They can therefore repeat their direction without repeating the painful process of learning. This tracing occurs even at the stage where the child's satisfaction is auto-erotic or bound up totally in the mother's body. It is the same process which establishes the child as separate from the mother's body, thus establishing an 'outside' for the subject. The dialectic of introjection/projection is the movement which can eliminate unbearable tension by setting up an outside which is radically 'other' to the ego, definitively separated and 'outside' the ego. It should be stressed at this stage that Lacan does not suggest a simple relation of subject/real; this process is more concerned with the production of the conscious subject, able to construct sentences in which it separates itself from objects. As such, it does not exclude the imaginary attributes of the ego. 'Reality' as such is only established with the so-called reality-principle, i.e. the ability to re-find the object. Discrimination between good and bad object, and the control of states of tension associated with these objects becomes possible with the establishment of an outside which is signifiable. This formation of an outside also forms the ego by 'cutting it out', separating it from its implication in its surrounding, and placing the subject in a position of possible predication. What is significant in this context is the process by which the child, in tracing connections and differences in matter and in attributing to them states of pleasure and unpleasure, begins to construct a differentiated universe of objects, and itself as different from these objects, thus establishing the possibility of signification.

However, at this stage, the connections and differences which are established are not under the dominance of the system of differences which is learned language. The identities of subject and its objects emerge in the operation which differentiates the subject from its surface and equates it with their difference. Connections and discontinuities are established, for example, acoustic, visual and tactile similarities and differences can be traced. These marks of separation (elementary signifiers) can have several directions of signification condensed in them. Such are the activities of the primary processes which involve the free flow of libidinal energy along the routes of condensation and displacement; small units, such as phonemes, correspond to large units of conscious discourse which express complex meanings.

Freudian interpretation, through the cajoling of meaning from the associations produced by the dreamer, has exposed the activity of these processes, and demonstrated that these form the basis of unconscious activity. In dreams some things are barred from signifying, and typical dreams have 'moments of silence' where the dreamer fails to produce the association which would decipher the dream. This highly subjective dissemination of meaning in the dream, in which the expression of desire is always to be sought, reiterates the same question of the production of meaning from the apparently limitless movement of metonymy and metaphor. The study of dreams confirms what Freud had begun to realise in the study of hysteria; that the unconscious is essentially made up, not by what consciousness can call up at some point but by what is refused entry into consciousness. It is made up of contents inaccessible to consciousness and is dominated by the modality of signification of the primary processes.

In this way we are led to the question of what is the repression which forms the unconscious; Lacan places a great deal of emphasis on the two stages of repression — primary and secondary — suggested by Freud. For Lacan, primary repression occurs with the acquisition of learned language, which necessitates that the signifiers (marks of separation and difference, whose tracing we have just examined) reappear reduplicated in conscious language, in different arrangements.

We have reason to assume that there is a primary repression, a first phase of repression, which consists in the ideational representative of the instinct being denied entry into consciousness. With this a fixation is established; the representative in question persists unaltered from then onwards and the instinct remains attached to it (Freud, *Standard Edition*, vol. XIV, p. 147).

Thus the identities traced by the movement of the drives persist but are refused entry into conscious language. It is the reduplication of these traces or marks in conscious language which therefore constitutes repression. An example of this reduplication is given in the analysis of the dream by Laplanche and Leclaire in their article 'The Unconscious'. In this, a certain signifier, for example 'li' which appears in several words in the dream, especially in the name Lilianne, is found to be attached as a representative to a drive in the unconscious, but also appears in normal discourse. The acquisition of language produces a first stage of repression which results in a specific organisation of the primary processes. But this is no simple matter; its organisation, as we will see, is contingent on the production of desire by the acquisition of the symbol to master satisfaction of needs. At this point we must concentrate on the production of the symbol, and therefore the function of judgment, as a continuation 'along the lines of expediency' of the original functioning of the pleasure ego by which objects were introjected or projected according to their relation to the arrangement of the drives. It is worth considering the Fort/Da game in this context since it is the game which led Freud to posit the relation between the operations of the pleasure principle and the acquisition of symbolicity.

The Fort/Da game was elaborated by Freud in *Beyond the Pleasure Principle* where he observed the infant's apparently obsessive repetition of presence and absence in the game of throwing the toy from the cot, and repeating 'Fort' ('there it goes'), and 'Da' ('here it is') when it was returned to him. In these repetitive utterances, Freud deduced the infant's attempt both to master its abandonment by its source of satisfaction, i.e. the mother, and also the beginnings of symbolisation. By raising its need to the level of symbolisation, the infant's action destroys the object, which it can cause to appear and disappear at will. In this action 'it raises the sign to the function of a signifier and reality to the sophistication of signification' (Lacan, 'Subversion of the Subject',

Ecrits). On the trace of nothingness, presence is constructed of absence in the production of the symbolic universe, 'through the word — already a presence constructed out of absence — absence itself comes to giving itself a name in that moment of origin whose perpetual recreation Freud's genius detected in the play of a child' (Lacan in *Language of the Self*, ed. Wilden, p. 39). 'From this pair of sounds modulated on presence and absence — there is born a particular language's universe of sense in which the universe of things comes into line' (ibid., p. 39). This can be seen to refer back to our original mention of the Fort/Da game whereby one was called on to imagine the construction of language through the oppositions of pairs of phonemes. There, we stressed how a signifier only refers to a signified through the entire system of language. By this we are led to see that the child's mastery of absence both in the game and in its progress to destroying the isolation of the imaginary image, submits to the entire 'signifying battery', that is the whole system of language. Inter-subjective communication is only possible with the completion of the signifying battery, installed in the first term of these primary attempts to master the symbolic function.

Thus the differentiation which allows the acquisition of the existing signifying system is a continuation of the modality of functioning of the pleasure ego. The establishment of the object (the mother) as definitively separated and able to be re-found in the mind by the symbol, allows the extension of the ego to the function of judgment. The totality of the reference can be controlled and manipulated through the representation of needs by a 'stand-in': the sign. This is the reason why Freud can make the claim in 'negation' that the two poles of linguistic judgment — affirmation and negation — are a continuation of the original mechanism by which the ego introjected or projected objects as the source of pleasure or unpleasure.

However, the process of the construction of the ego is not as simple as it may appear for, according to Lacan who follows Freud very closely at this point, the subject undergoes a separation or splitting in order to find a signifying place from which to represent itself, even if only by means of a 'stand-in'. For in order to use language, it is necessary that the subject finds himself at the axis of the division signifier/ signified, taking up a position in regards to meaning. This positionality is possible after the initial 'splitting' of the subject to form itself as distinct from an outside. It is achieved through two dominant states, the mirror-phase and the castration complex (which also correspond to dominance of imaginary and symbolic attributes). The accomplishment of positionality is what produces secondary repression which operates as a retrospective determinant of the primary processes and creates the conscious subject.

This repression involves the barring of certain signifiers from entry into consciousness: the subject must then recognise himself in the organising structures of the signifier. The mechanism of this repression is anti-cathexis: because ideas to be repressed are permanently invested with energy from the drives, they can only be kept unconscious if an equally constant force is operating in the opposite direction. Repression presupposes two interrelated economic principles. The first is the withdrawal of psychic energy (cathexis) from the unpleasurable drive; the second is anti-cathexis whereby the energy released in the withdrawal is used to construct an opposite aim. It is therefore the energy which prevents certain ideational representatives from appearing in consciousness. This process is analogous to the model of metaphor, where a signifier falls to the position of signified, while being retained as the latent signifier.

> Metaphor must be defined as the implantation into a chain of signifiers, of another signifier by dint of which the one it replaces falls to the rank of a signified, and as the latent signifier, perpetuates the interval onto which can be grafted another chain of signifiers (Lacan in *La Psychanalyse*, vol. IV, p. 12).

It is a metaphoric structure which shapes the process by which the signifier is refused entry into consciousness. The introduction of a new signifier creates a new meaning which alters the direction of the original chain of signification.

> Between the two chains . . . those of the signifier as opposed to all the ambulatory signified that circulate because they are constantly in the process of sliding . . . the pinning down or capping point (*point de capiton*) is mythical, for no-one has ever been able to pin a meaning to a signifier; but on the other hand, what can be done is to pin one signifier to another signifier and see what happens. But in that case something new results . . . namely the appearance of a new meaning (Lacan, unpublished seminar, quoted in Laplanche and Leclaire, op. cit., p. 155).

The hidden or repressed signifier becomes, through the passion, or the energy, of the anti-cathexis, the signified. There are certain key signifiers which determine the metaphoric structure of the repression. For example, one of these is the myth of the Name-of-the-Father, which as we shall discuss later involves the establishment of positions in the symbolic resulting from relations to the 'phallus'. This determination of the unconscious processes by the imposition of symbolic relations is retrospective, and involves the acceptance of the structural function of the phallus as signifier of difference. This function then imposes a certain development of desire on categories of difference (e.g. absence/presence) which have previously been established and which have made possible the acquisition of language.

This description of the primary processes and of primary and secondary repression is given schematically at this stage, in order to substantiate Lacan's claim that the unconscious is structured like a language; in order to demonstrate its specific signifying formations and its dependency on the acquisition of language. Thus 'the unconscious is a concept forged on the trace of what operates to constitute the subject' (*Ecrits*, p. 830). It is important to realise that language may be learned before the subject acquires a position in the symbolic (the relations governed particularly by the family, perhaps also by the state, religion, etc.). But it is only when this positionality has been achieved that the desire of the subject will develop according to the constraints imposed by these formations. 'The register of the signifier institutes itself, in that a signifier is what represents the subject for another signifier' (*Ecrits*, p. 840): the discovery of the primacy of the signifier in the determination of the signified indicates the necessity to elaborate the function of the subject and its realisation of 'fixed' positions, in order to understand the production of meaning.

The structuration effected by secondary repression is not absolute. In order to acquire a position as place of intention in learned language, the subject is forced into a separation from the movement of the primary processes. The signifiers marked out by the primary processes will therefore only ever be able to be articulated across (despite) the symbolic relations. But they do persist, reduplicated in the unconscious, and this unconscious chain is easily re-invoked in consciousness by a metonymic relationship with the signifiers in conscious language. They appear in the stumbling of the logical discourse of consciousness, in dreams, in jokes, in slips of the tongue, puns and so on. Here there appears to be an intentionality, but it is in a strange relation to time and logical thought. The subject feels surprised by what appears in these discontinuities in logical speech; they are both more and less than he was expecting. In *Jokes and their Relation to the Unconscious* (*Standard Edition*, vol. VIII), Freud describes these mechanisms in detail.

We have outlined above the construction of the subject and the unconscious in relation to the signifier, where the signifier is the mark of separation carried out on a surface, a marking of differences. This marking of differences is as much differentiating the subject from its outside, and it is this which demonstrates that the subject is constructed by the signifier. Hence Lacan affirms the materialist assertion that 'man speaks, but it is only that the symbol has made him man'. The network which is the subject is made up of the properties of language. The subject is 'effects in which are to be found the structure of language, of which he becomes the material . . . and through this there resounds in him the relations of speech' (*Ecrits*, p. 689). Lacan attempts to clarify that this advocacy of man's relation to the signifier has nothing to do with 'a "culturalist" position in the ordinary sense of the term. . . . It is not a question of the relation between man and language as a social phenomenon' (ibid.). By the 'ordinary sense of the term', Lacan is meaning here a crude conditioning model, which attempts to instate a mechanistic interpretation of the mental process. It is not in any way a rejection of the necessity to understand the cultural conjuncture in which the history of the subject is realised. Empiricism, with its 'question-begging appeal to the concrete', is built, Lacan claims, on a metaphysical notion 'conveyed so pitifully by the term "affect" '. The formative role of the signifier in the construction of the subject is to be rediscovered in the laws governing that other scene, that is the unconscious. As it is never a question of repressed emotion, but of repressed representation, that is, what is not realised, the effects 'are discovered at the level of the materially unstable elements that constitute language' (*Ecrits*, p. 689).

From this it is clear that the subject is not to be understood in any ontological sense as having any pre-existent essence which language somehow conditions, but as an 'absent' subject, able to signify because of his production, positioned in relation to the signifier. Without the signifier, there would be no subject: 'the effect of language . . . is cause introduced in the subject. . . . Its cause is the signifier without which there would be no subject in reality, and it wouldn't know how to represent anything except another signifier' (*Ecrits*, p. 835). It is not possible to speak of a subject, it speaks him, and it is necessary that he apprehends himself in language.

Thus it can be seen that the laws 'that govern that other scene' are to be found in language, and that these are intertwined with the representation of the drives.

What is the process by which mankind is constructed as a result of his linguistic nature, in eccentricity to himself, in subject-ion to the structure of language? What is the 'dialectic of desire' in which this subjection occurs? Although Lacan often refers to Hegel in a 'totally didactic fashion', the dialectic of desire as it appears in Lacan is in no way comparable to Hegelian idealism. It can in no way be seen as the same as the alienation of self-consciousness of the *Phenomenology of the Spirit*. On the subject of the accusations levelled at Lacan of idealism, produced by his constant reference to the Hegelian dialectic, J.-A. Miller asked:

> 'Surely the definition of a being born into, constituted in, and regulated by a field external to him, is very different from the alienation of self-consciousness?'. Lacan replied: 'Yes, indeed . . . it is much more a case of Lacan versus Hegel' (*Le Séminaire*, vol. XI, p. 195).

But Lacan is forced to stress frequently that the concerns of the Freudian unconscious are closer to those of ethics and philosophy than they are to the concerns of traditional psychology. For in his discoveries, the properties of speech and language are governed by the principles of the dialectic of consciousness of self. It is therefore without any allegiance to the system of thought, that Lacan often refers to the Hegelian dialectic. He sometimes emphasises the importance of the subject proposed by Descartes in the formulation, 'Cogito ergo sum' ('I think therefore I am'). At the same time he insists that this is the most blatant form of the stupidity of thought which posits a subject completed and finished in its identity, knowing always exactly where it is going. He considers it to be important that the Cartesian subject should not be ignored out of philosophical pretensions. For the place man assigns for himself in knowledge is what makes possible communication and meaning, even if that place is ascribed to him long before he 'knows' anything about it. In Lacan, the dialectic of consciousness of self is the necessary structuring of the signifying process, by which verification of the individual speech act (man's place in truth) is attained only through calling on a third term as witness. By this the subject is decentred in the structure.

The process of calling upon a third term as witness is what underlies the Lacanian concept of the Other. It is a term used with bewildering frequency but is of crucial importance since it occupies a central place in the dialectic. In that a signifier must refer to a condition outside itself in order to signify, the Other can be seen as the place of the signifier. It is the intervention of a third term which completes the chain of signifiers and verifies the individual speech act, by situating the subject in a position by which meaning becomes possible. It is a difficult concept, and will become clearer in the exposition of its function of situating the subject in the process of signification.

If linguistics and Freudian analysis both point to the necessity of understanding the knotting of the subject into signification as the way of understanding what determines meaning, it becomes necessary also to understand how a subject finds its signifying place: 'the discovery of what it articulates in that place that is in the unconscious enables us to grasp at the price of what splitting it has been constituted' (*Ecrits*, p. 689).

In the history of the subject in the way it is reconstituted in Lacan's theory of the unconscious, two moments are dominant in which the subject finds his place in the process of signification. These are the mirror-phase and the castration complex.

The thesis of the mirror-phase as formative of the function of the 'I' was originally developed as early as 1936 from the observation of the infant's behaviour in front of the mirror, observations which indicated to Lacan that the 'I' was constructed rather than pre-existent. 'It is an experience which leads us to oppose any philosophy directly issuing from the Cogito' ('The Mirror Phase', *New Left Review*, no. 51, p. 71). Lacan describes the infant's fascination with his mirror image as an 'identification, . . . a transformation which takes place in the subject when he assumes an image' (ibid.). It is to be seen as the 'spatialisation' necessary for a position in language by which the subject is able to communicate. For the mirror-phase is seen by Lacan to be the moment at which the infant's first movement towards a unified sense of itself is set in motion. Prior to this, the infant is dominated by the constant flux of instinctual energy across its body. Although these drives are always already in a state of alteration, by virtue of the social and familial situation into which the child is born, until the moment of the mirror-phase, the child is dominated by these drives and their constant need for satisfaction. The identification of the image in the mirror is the first moment in which the infant comes to form an image of itself, separate from the fragmented mobility of the drives, dominated by its relation with the mother. In order to grasp hold of the image of the unified whole with which it is confronted, as well as with the representatives of the drives which coagulate in this image, the infant is forced to situate its identity in separation: the body. The specular image makes up the prototype for the 'world of objects'. 'The position of the imaged "I" introduces the position of the object, itself separated and signifiable' (Kristeva, *La Révolution du langage poétique*, p. 44). This threshold of position is what opens the way to the apprenticeship of language. This can be seen as a violent and dramatic conflict between the position/separation identification, and the mobility of the energy of instinctual needs. It is in the mirror-phase also that the notion of the Imaginary is introduced. The distinction of the Imaginary, the Symbolic and the Real is an important distinction in Lacan, and is central for any understanding of the role of ideology in language.

The Imaginary is the state which characterises the mirror-phase, in that the ego of the human infant is constituted on the basis of the image of the specular counterpart. From this it can be seen that, as regards inter-subjective relations, the imaginary is the basically narcissistic relation of the subject to his ego. The dual relationship based on – and captured by – the image of the counterpart, belongs to the imaginary order. A counterpart can only exist by virtue of the fact that the ego is originally another. In other words the ego is an *Ideal-ich* (ideal ego), another self which characterises all later identifications.

The way in which it does this resides in the imaginary identification of a unified position, a unity which is characteristic of the ideal ego. This is at the root of the necessary misrecognition (*'méconnaissance'* also connoting mis-knowing and mis-apprehending) by which identifications of the ego are inaugurated. This 'imaginary capture of the ego by its specular reflection, and . . . the function of misrecognition that remains attached to it' (*Ecrits*) is the only homologous function of consciousness, and the apparent transcendence of the subject of the enunciation supports itself in the appearance of unity that the ideal ego constructs. There are two simultaneous moments implicit in the narcissistic identification of the mirror-phase, and these correspond to the distinction between the ideal ego and the ego-ideal. The first, the ideal ego, is the imaginary identification of the real, corporeal image as a unified image. The second, the ego-ideal, involves the fact that in order to see its fragmentary being in the place of the image that confronts it, the child sees its being in relation to otherness. The ego is a projection in whose apparent unity the subject misrecognises himself. This fictional ideal totality is broken into with the entry into language: the symbolic. But the ego-ideal is a function by which that image of ideal unity is taken back by the subject after the entry, but invested with new properties, that is 'admonitions of others' or the 'awakening of his own critical judgment' (Freud, 'On Narcissism', *Standard Edition*, vol. XIV, p. 94). These would be identifications resulting from the acquisition of the capacity of judgment. In other words, the ego-ideal is seen as the identifications made after the breaking up of the fictional direction of the ego, which allow the retention of its original narcissistic ideal. The super ego functions as the basis of these identifications. In this way, the mirror-phase demonstrates the two functions of the ego, resulting from the response to the speculary reflection. This double aspect of the mirror-phase shows the mechanisms by which the ego preserves its narcissistic self-regard. This is an important area since it points to the mechanisms of the imaginary which are at the basis of the ideological fixing of the subject in identifications, and positions of exchange in the symbolic. It is able to do this because the subject able to signify is produced as a result of a process of acquiring a position in which the image of the mirror-phase is a part.

The mirror-phase shows the production of the possibility of a unified subject, a possibility which is necessary for establishing social communication: there has to be a subject in order for there to be a subject of a proposition. The coagulation of identity in a structure of otherness is a stage in the process of the ego 'on the path of subjectivation to the signifier' (*Le Séminaire*, vol. XI). It represents a premature acquisition of the structure of communication:

> The jubilant assumption of the specular image by the little man at the infant stage . . . would seem to exhibit in an exemplary situation the symbolic matrix in which the 'I' is precipitated in a primordial form, before it is objectified in the dialectic of identification with the other, and before language restores to it, in the universal, its function as a subject (Lacan, 'The Mirror Phase', *New Left Review*, no. 51, p. 72).

It is a premature acquisition because the infant is as yet unable to make identifications which ensure social communication. The positionality which characterises language — in which meanings exist for a subject who functions as the place of the intention of those meanings — commences with the separation of subject and object. The situating of the image as separate through the intervention of the third term, the other, is paralleled by the dialectic of introjection and projection. It demonstrates here how language constructs itself from a state of otherness. The self-presentification of the subject arises from primary alteriority; the subject represents itself by a 'stand-in'. The subject is constructed through its acquisition of language from the place of the Other. 'The signifier producing itself in the place of the Other, which is not yet marked out, makes the subject surge up there — the subject of being which does not yet have speech, but at the price of coagulating it. . . . It was there, and it is no longer there' (Lacan, 'Alienation', *Le Séminaire*, vol. XI). This is precisely the operation anticipated by the mirror-phase, where the self-presentification of the subject arises from its speculary reflection. The Other is defined as:

> the place where the signifying chain is, which controls everything that will be able to be presented from the subject, it is the field of this living being where the subject is destined to appear. . . . It is from the place of this living being, called to subjectivity, that the drive is essentially displayed (Lacan, *Le Séminaire*, vol. XI, p. 185).

It is the site prior to the pure subject of the signifier; it is where the subject finds its signifying place 'by means of a logical anteriority to any awakening of the signified' (Lacan, 'Subversion of the Subject', *Ecrits*). But the imaginary unity of the mirror-phase and the fictional direction of the ego has to be broken by the fact of difference before signification is possible.

We have already seen in the Fort/Da game and the tracing of difference in the primary processes that difference, even learned language, pre-exists the full acquisition of sociality: the Oedipus complex. For, in order to complete meaning from these differences, the signifier must appear to have a referent, and it is this which means that the use of language occurs from the place of the other, as the third term by which the subject is submitted to the signifier as produced by it. The detachment from the dependency on the mother as source of satisfaction of needs is completed in the second moment as the subject finds his signifying place. This is the castration complex, which has often been pointed out as the central thesis of the Freudian reconstruction of the unconscious. Any discussion of this as it has been elaborated by Lacan is impossible to separate from the question of desire and the construction of the unconscious.

The castration complex was first developed as an abstract theory in the case of Little Hans, where Freud elaborated the crucial notion that 'castration bears the transmission of culture' (Mitchell, *Psychoanalysis and Feminism*). From the formulations concerning the case of Little Hans, Freud found in clinical observations that the castration complex in the unconscious

> has the function of a knot:
>
> (1) in the dynamic structuration of symptoms in the analytic sense of the term . . .
>
> (2) in a regulation of the development that gives its ratio to this first role: namely, the installation in the subject of an unconscious position without which he would be unable to identify himself with the ideal type of his sex, nor even respond without grave risk to the needs of his partner in sexual relations, or even to accept in a satisfactory way the needs of the child who may be produced by this relationship' (Lacan, 'Signification of the Phallus', *Ecrits*).

In other words, the reproduction of the species is ensured by the ratio installed by this complex. Implicit in the claim that the castration complex orders the development of sexuality in a way that produces the sexed individuals – boy and girl – is the notion that drives are, prior to this complex, bisexual. The notion of bisexuality of drives was developed in the analysis of the case of the Wolf Man, which is a fascinating account of the structuring of these drives and the problems that Freud encountered over terminology. Lacan points out this strange position that Freud found himself in, forced to posit that mankind assumes the attributes of a sexed individual only through the threat of privation. 'In *Civilisation and its Discontents* Freud, as we know, went so far as to suggest a disturbance of human sexuality, not of a contingent but of an essential kind' (*Ecrits*, p. 685). This disturbance cannot be solved by any reference to biological givens, which Lacan takes to be the explanation for a 'man of science' such as Freud, resorting to a myth underlying the structuration of the Oedipus complex. The Oedipus complex, which Freud found widely in his clinical cases, is seen to be the body of contradictory wishes which the child experiences towards its parents within the nuclear structure of the family. These wishes are both active and passive, loving and hostile. Laplanche and Pontalis in *The Language of Psychoanalysis* point to the two sides of the complex:

> In its so-called positive form, the complex appears in the story of Oedipus Rex: a desire for the death of the rival – the parent of the same sex – and a sexual desire for the parent of the opposite sex (p. 283).

Like all the complexes of Freudian theory, the Oedipus complex does not represent an absolute origin, the founding moment of a universal condition (as Jungian thought would suggest with its return to the archetypical symbols). It has rather a structural function operating as the start of the establishment of a series of differences. Freud found numerous instances resulting from this complex, like, for example, guilt at an imagined occasion of incest.

The child cannot transcend the Oedipus complex and achieve identification with the father or the mother, by which 'sexed' reproduction is ensured, without having overcome the castration crisis, the anxiety about castration. In the instance of the male child, there has to be the confrontation of the realisation that the penis cannot be used as an expression of his desire for his mother. The castration complex, therefore, as Freud saw has to be understood as part of the cultural order. The 'threat of castration' is what guarantees the prohibition of incest, and is the Law that founds the human order. Lacan emphasises this 'structural nature' of the Oedipus complex, and shows how the myth expounded by Freud in 'Totem and Taboo' (*Standard Edition*, vol. XIII), is precisely such an attempt to situate the structural function of the Oedipus complex.

The myth introduced by Freud was an attempt to locate the prevalent phenomena of totemism and exogamy (the prohibition of intercourse with any one from the same clan). He suggests a mythical situation of the murder of the primal father by a band of sons, with equal fraternal rights. This was because of the father previously keeping all the women to himself. After the murder, the father was eaten in a totemic meal,

> The totem meal, which is perhaps mankind's earliest festival, would thus be a repetition and a commemoration of this memorable and criminal deed, which was at the beginning of so many things — of social organisation, of moral restrictions and of religion (Freud, 'Totem and Taboo', *Standard Edition*, vol. XIII).

In the totemic repetition of this feast, there are two taboos in operation; that against the destruction of the totem figure which represents the dead father, and that against incest, which are the same as the taboos of the Oedipus complex.

Lacan indicates how the work of Lévi-Strauss has 'shown us the truth of the totemic function' (*Le Séminaire*, vol. XI, p. 137) in his description of the structures of exogamy as the primary classificatory structure of human society. In *Elementary Structures of Kinship* Lévi-Strauss describes how it is the prohibition against incest which is the minimal condition for the differentiation of culture and nature. In other words, it is the structures of marriage relations, not the development of the natural family, which is the all-important condition for the inauguration of human culture. This work on the laws of exogamy has offered confirmation to the substance of the mythical hypothesis of the primal murder; that the symbolic system has arisen through the sexual reality of the laws governing marriage exchange.

What is confirmed is that the continuation of the species is ensured only with the maintenance of the 'sexed' individual, differentiated in the two poles of male and female, located in relation to reproduction. The knowledge that human society is founded on this terrain has been clarified, as we have already seen, by contemporary structuralism, 'showing that it is in the network of marriage, in opposition to the natural generation in the biological line, that the fundamental exchanges have operated — in the network of the signifier, that is, — and it is there that we find again the most elementary structures of the social function which are inscribed in terms of a combination' (Lacan, *Le Séminaire*, vol. XI, p. 138). It is in this area that we find the most consistent use of the term, the Symbolic, by Lacan. The three orders, the Imaginary, the Symbolic and the Real, all intersect in the subject.

The idea of the Symbolic order which structures all inter-human relations was introduced by Lévi-Strauss. Human law, sociality, is identified as identical to the order of language, 'for without kinship nominations, no power is capable of instituting the order of preferences and taboos which bind and weave the yarn of lineage down through the succeeding generations' (*Language of the Self*).

The reference to the Symbolic order, in this instance, is then quite clearly referring to the law of a pre-established human order, in which the subject has to find itself. This Lacan has designated by the notion of the Name-of-the-Father, a notion used for the explanation of the cultural origin of law, as embodied by the myth of the father as figure of the law. Thus, the Oedipus myth and the castration complex are not the source of being. They do not function as a sort of theology in Freud's work, but as parts of a myth representative of the construction of the symbolic law, through which human exchanges become possible and meaningful, in the accumulation of codes. 'The existence of law shows that language is other (than the speaking subject), has been constituted over the ages' (Lacan, *Le Séminaire*, vol. XX, p. 10). In this sense it becomes possible to say that the unconscious is structured like a language; the processes which constitute the language-using subject, i.e. produce the subject in symbolic relations, constitute the unconscious in the same movement. Linguistics has shown language to operate in a combinatory game which is played in a pre-subjective fashion. The symbolic order is often designated by Lacan to be a structure, whose discrete elements operate as signifiers, or more often, the order to which such structures belong. It is this structure which gives its regulation to the unconscious, in that the signifiers in this overall structure or order organise the elementary relations of the human being before any formation of the subject. It is then necessary that the subject recognises himself within these organisations.

The castration complex is seen to complete, in its establishment of differences, the process inaugurated by the mirror-phase and the Fort/Da game in which subjectivity is organised by the same structures as language. In other words, the castration complex situates the subject at the axis of the division signifier/signified — in a position by which a chain of signifiers is produced in incidence with the signified. It is because of this notion of language as a structure, that the symbolic is increasingly used to designate the order which locates the subject in relation to meaning. The castration complex manifests itself in the child in the following ways,

(1) . . . the little girl considers herself if only momentarily, as castrated, in the sense of deprived of a phallus, by someone; in the first instance by her mother, an important point, and then by her father, but in such a way that one must recognise in it a transference in the analytic sense of the term;

(2) in a more primitive sense, the mother is considered by both sexes to possess the phallus, as the phallic mother;

(3) the signification of castration takes on its effective weight as far as symptom-formation is concerned only on the basis of the discovery of the castration of the mother' (*Ecrits*, p. 686).

These three points lead to the question of the reason for the phallic stage. The localisation of all pleasure, even pleasure which exceeds the available limits for its articulation (that is, *jouissance*) in the phallus, is characterised by the Imaginary dominance of the phallic attribute.

Before we discuss this, it is necessary to elaborate on the preceding points in more detail. Castration anxiety is seen to proceed from the problem of the anatomical difference of the sexes, becoming a nodal point in the discovery that the mother, or woman lacks a phallus. In referring to the process of 'transference in the analytical sense of the term', Lacan is pointing to a significant feature through which human law is transmitted with the accession to sexual difference. For transference is the dramatising in the place of an other (in the case of analysis, the other is the analyst) the symptoms or complexes of anxiety. In using the term here, Lacan is drawing attention to the mechanism by which unformulated anxiety acquires a cultural form in the transference of castration anxiety to the figure of a castrator, the mother or the father. In this structure is to be situated the myth of the Name-of-the-Father as the dramatisation of the castration anxiety, whereby it receives a cultural form through which identifications can be made.

To return to the question of the dominance of the phallic attribute is to return one to perhaps the most contentious area of Lacan's rereading of Freud. For in the claim for this dominance, the phallus is seen to be 'the signifier of desire' and, as such, the means by which all desire is organised. To see this issue in its proper perspective, it is necessary to stress that the phallus is not the penis. The term 'phallus' is used throughout Lacan's writing, in the way it was used in classical antiquity, as the figurative representation of the male organ: a simulacrum. Yet despite this representation of the reality of the organ, it still is necessary to account for the paradoxical privilege of the phallus in a theory of the construction of subjectivity which has as its main substance culture and not biology. This privilege is based on the theory of the phallus as signifier. He refers to it as such, not because it appears in articulation, but because it is a mark of difference which refers to a condition outside itself that makes articulation possible. This is precisely the meaning we have attributed to Lacan's use of the term elsewhere. The condition outside itself, to which the phallus refers in order to make articulation possible, is the situating of subjectivity in the symbolic order. Before the emergence of the castration complex, the mother occupies the place of alteriority in that she is the receiver of all demands, and is the place of all narcissistic aspects and satisfactions. The discovery of castration — the mother lacks a penis — detaches the subject from its dependence on the mother, and makes the phallic function into the symbolic function. It is the recognition of the structural function of the phallus, by which reproduction of the species is ensured through the establishment of difference, which enables the subject to detach itself from the mother and to acquire a position of signification, by situating itself in the cultural or symbolic order. Difference, making possible symbolic relations, the production of subjects and meanings, is established to break up the imaginary direction of the ego. And this difference, arranging itself around the 'to have' or the 'not having' of the phallus, imposes its regulation retrospectively on all the markings out of difference which preceded it: 'the living part of the being in the primarily repressed finds its signifier only by receiving the mark of the repression of the phallus (by virtue of which the unconscious is language)' (*Ecrits*, p. 693). Thus the individual being is situated in a position whereby meaningful communication can be ensured, that is, between the signifier and the signified. This is a difficult philosophy to grasp, and it is necessary to repeat some aspects slightly differently to make it clearer.

It is not a question of the assumption by the subject of the traits of the Other, but rather that the subject has to find the constituting structure of his desire in the same gap opened up by the signifiers in those who come (through transference) to represent the Other for him, in so far as his demand is subjected to them. This is central for the understanding of the dialectic of desire proposed by Lacan in which the phallus occupies the pivotal role, in that the relations between the sexes revolve around the question of the 'to be' or 'not to be' and the 'to have' or 'have not' of the phallus. What is proposed here is the way in which desire is constructed through the relation of the subject to language. In that language and the symbolic order pre-exist the individual's entry into them, the signifier gives its ratio to the development of demand and, as demand is always formulated to the Other, and this is represented for the infant by the mother or father who are already constituted as sexed human individuals, then the child must submit to the effects of the signifier. Thus the submission of the subject to the signifier (language) in order to master his dependency in needs through the acquisition of a separated signifying place in language, means submission to the cultural order by which human sexuality is regulated.

Signification is only possible with the construction of the Other as the place of the signifier; that is, the construction of an outside referent by which the individual speech act or word is verified. The symbolic relations of the cultural order, within which the phallus has a structural function as the inauguration of a series of differences, is the structure in which the subject is forced, by the existence of discourse, to find its place. The strange antinomy that mankind only assumes his sexed identity under a threat thus becomes clearer. Symbolic relations necessitate that the subject finds his signifying place in the laws of culture; if he does not he will fall ill.

The entry into language and the law of culture results from the whole structure of the division need/demand/desire.

The phenomenology that emerges from analytic experience is certainly of a kind to demonstrate in desire the paradoxical, deviant, erratic, eccentric, even scandalous character by which [desire] is distinguished from need. This fact has been too often affirmed not to have been obvious to moralists worthy of the name (*Ecrits*, p. 690).

In 1946, Lacan drew attention to the Hegelian notion of desire, organised through a hierarchy of mediations,

> The very desire of man (Hegel tells us), is constituted under the sign
> of mediation; it is desire to make its desire recognised. It has for its
> object a desire, that of the other, in the sense that there is no object
> for man's desire which is constituted without some sort of mediation
> — which appears in his most primitive needs: for example, even his
> food has to be prepared — and which is found again throughout the
> development of satisfaction from the moment of the master—slave
> conflict through the dialectic of labour (*Ecrits*, p. 111).

For Lacan, the presence of signification, even in its most primitive
structures of simple sign systems, necessitates a deviation in man's
needs: 'in the sense that in so far as his needs are subjected to demand,
they return to him alienated' (*Ecrits*, p. 690). This is not as a result of
the kind of dependence on a structure that a mechanistic tendency in
structuralism proposes to examine in the interrelations of a network
which is established in a relationship of exteriority to the subject. It is
rather 'the turning into signifying form as such, from the fact that it is
from the locus of the Other that the message is emitted' (*Ecrits*, p. 690).
The crucial term of mediation in Lacan's philosophy is demand.
'Demand in itself bears on something other than the satisfactions it calls
for' (*Ecrits*, p. 690). The point about demand is that it is articulated. It
is the formulation of the need, that is, setting it in the chain of signifiers. This occurs through the fact that demand constitutes itself in the
knowledge that satisfaction is primarily situated in an other, first the
mother:

> It is demand of a presence or of an absence — which is what is mani-
> fested in the primordial relation with the mother, pregnant with that
> other to be situated within the needs that it can satisfy. Demand
> constitutes the Other as already possessing the 'privilege' of satisfy-
> ing needs, that is to say, the power of depriving them of that alone
> by which they are satisfied (*Ecrits*, p. 691).

Lacan sees the nature of the articulation of the demand of the infant
for the mother, who represents the Other of the satisfaction of the
child's needs, as abolishing the particularity of the child's needs. Oral
satisfaction ensuing from the feeding of the child does not satisfy the
multitude of needs of which the infant's body is a complex. Therefore,
to ensure the presence of the mother as the locus of satisfaction, the
particularity of the needs is articulated in the 'unconditionality of the
demand for love'.

> In this way, demand annuls the particularity of everything that can
> be granted by transmuting it into the proof of love, and the very
> satisfaction that it obtains for need are reduced to the level of being
> no more than the crushing demand for love (all of which is perfectly
> apparent in the psychology of child-rearing, to which our analyst-
> nurses are so attached) (*Ecrits*, p. 691).

This mediation of demand which abolishes the particularity of need produces desire:

> It is necessary then that the particularity thus abolished should re-appear beyond demand. It does in fact re-appear there, but preserving the structure that the unconditionality of the demand for love concealed. By a reversal which is not simply the negation of a negation, the power of pure loss emerges from the residue of an obliteration. For the unconditional element of demand, desire substitutes the 'absolute' condition: this condition unties the knot of that element in the proof of love that is resistant to the satisfaction of a need (*Ecrits*, p. 691).

In other words, when demand is articulated for the satisfaction of a single need, for example the cry for food, the reason of the demand for love is then removed. Even though the need for the food may have been satisfied, the co-existent totality of needs, such as the need for oral satisfaction, remains unsatisfied. Satisfaction, then, can only be a frustration producing a sense of loss, almost an anguish, at the lack of universal satisfaction obtainable from the other. 'Thus desire is neither the appetite for satisfaction, nor the demand for love, but the difference that results from the subtraction of the first from the second, the phenomenon of their splitting (Spaltung)' (*Ecrits*, p. 691). This splitting is produced by the sense of lack in the other, and the border produced by that splitting is desire:

> Desire outlines itself in the border where demand tears itself away from need, this border being that which demand, for which the name is only unconditional in the place of the Other, opens under the form of possible failing that demand can bring to bear on it as not providing universal satisfaction (*Ecrits*, p. 814).

This is to show how desire situates itself in a dependency on demand (the articulation of needs):

> in articulating itself in signifiers (demand) leaves a metonymic residue which runs under the chain of signifiers, an indeterminate element, which is at once absolute, but untenable, a necessary and misunderstood element called desire (Lacan, *Le Séminaire*, vol. XI, p. 141).

The experience of the loss is what sets in motion this metonymic process of desire. As Lacan has more recently pointed out, 'there is no such thing as cause, unless there is something amiss'. Without this gaping of a Lack, there can be no cause either of language, or, therefore, the subject. The primary processes, tracing a route of condensation and displacement appear as the impulsion in the unconscious; they can now be seen to be the effective presence of desire and it is for this reason that Lacan claims that desire, 'more than any other point on the human spectrum makes the presence of the unconscious felt'.

Now we can see the full implication of the claim that the unconscious is constructed in the same process by which the subject acquires language. It results from this structuring of need/demand and desire. The 'cause' of the subject and the unconscious is the same process that introduces the subject to the symbolic universe and for this reason Lacan often refers to the unconscious as the discourse of the Other. The subject and language arrange themselves on a negativity, a logical zero point, 'the metonymy of the lack of being'. The claim that the phallus is a signifier the symbolic function of which produces the desiring subject in the place of the structure which already included him or her becomes clearer. The assumption of castration creates the lack through which desire is produced in a way organised to cultural ends: i.e. it forces the transition from the imaginary to the symbolic.

> Freud revealed to us that it is thanks to the Name-of-the-Father that man does not remain in the sexual service of the mother, and that aggression towards the father is at the principle of the Law and that the Law is at the service of desire, which it institutes through the prohibition of incest. It is therefore the assumption of castration which creates the lack through which desire is instituted. Desire is the desire for desire, the desire of the Other and it is subject to the Law. It is the default of the phallus that mounts up the symbolic debt. Desire reproduces the subject's relation to the lost object (*Ecrits*, p. 852).

It is desire then that resides within the unconscious, as a 'metonymic residue', likely to be called up into consciousness by a metonymic relation of signifiers.

This conception of desire simultaneously situates the process of the beginning of the subject across and beyond needs or drives. It is the movement which skips the limits of the pleasure principle and invests in a reality which is already structured as signifying. It invests in this reality through the presence of the third term, the Other, where it is included, although included as a divided and mobile subject. The movement of desire results from the profit to be gained in the detachment from the dependence on another for the satisfaction of needs. This detachment is achieved in the articulation of needs. Thus desire is,

> an effect in the subject of the condition which is imposed on him by the existence of a discourse, to make his need pass through the defiles of the signifier . . . if we must ground the notion of the Other as the locus of the deployment of the Word. . . . It must be posited, as a facet of an animal at the mercy of Language, man's desire is desire of the Other (*Language of the Self*).

In this interpretation, desire results from the process by which the subject is produced in a system of finished positions, that is, signification, in order to master dependence on an unpredictable source of satisfaction. *Desidero* (I desire) is according to Lacan the Freudian *Cogito*, since what is essential in the primary process (the play of combination and substitution in the signifier which determine the institution of the subject) traces the route of desire.

Thus we come to the phenomenon that was central in the discovery of the Freudian unconscious, which is: its subjective status. Freud said about dreams that everything blooms from a central point. Lacan therefore requires the recognition that everything that flowers in the unconscious diffuses itself from the nodal point, like the mycelium, and that this nodal point is the subject. Thus Lacan's work proposes a way of understanding language and discourse which denies every vestige of the notion of the 'wholeness' of identity and consciousness, 'man can never be the "total personality" while ever the play of displacement and condensation in which he is doomed in the exercise of his functions, marks his relation as subject to the signifier' (*Ecrits*). Lacan was quite correct in anticipating the indignation that this re-reading of Freud would provoke: it is the indignation of humanism, which refuses any theory of subjectivity, 'it is humanistic man and the credit, affirmed beyond reparation, which he has drawn on his intentions' (*Ecrits*, p. 528).

7 The critique of the sign

The understanding of the subject in signification produced by both Marxism and psychoanalysis suggests the necessity of seeing the sign as only one moment in the process of signification. It is the moment which produces and fixes meaning but it is not an absolute, pre-given relation. It is the sign, the relation between signifier and signified, which is fixed in the construction of positions for the predicating subject. Such an understanding emphasises the activity of the signifier, whose limitation to produce certain signifieds therefore becomes a question of positionality in sociality and social relations.

There is a need to consolidate these theoretical developments: first to provide a rigorous examination of the idealism implicit in sciences which construct themselves uncritically on the notion of the sign, from the perspective opened by Marxism and psychoanalysis; second, to develop a theory of language which sets out from the recognition of the primacy of the signifier and its activity. It is the analysis of poetic language that attempts to provide an analysis of modes of signification in which the activity of the signifier is evident.

This double movement of theory is necessitated by an attempt to sustain the radical potentiality of the encounter of psychoanalysis and Marxism. As with Marxist theories, the discoveries of psychoanalysis are often taken up in a way that ignores their contribution to a revolutionary understanding of the subject in sociality. Such interpretations tend to emphasise the *structural* aspects of Lacan's work: symbolic relations are stressed as somehow pre-existing the work of ideology and specific social relations. Kristeva aims at an analysis which establishes the inseparability and mutual dependency of these two aspects in the positioning of the subject, but without either being submerged in the other. In this way, she can sustain an analysis of practice at the same time as observing the limitations of sociality and the work of ideology.

Work of this kind has only become possible with a re-examination of the place of the sign, since as we have seen, this notion has become problematic with the developments of Marxism and psychoanalysis. In recent years the notion has been submitted to such a critical examination. At the head of this work has been Jacques Derrida, whose work shows his consistent attempt to restore the materiality of the sign which is systematically repressed in 'Western discourse'. Despite the radical potentiality of Saussure's work on the sign, the very notion of sign is deeply implicated in the flight from materiality: 'it is in its roots and implications metaphysical through and through' (Derrida, *Positions*, p. 27). The radical potentiality is seen by Derrida to reside in the decisive critical role played by showing 'against tradition that the signified was inseparable from the signifier, that the signified and the signifier are two aspects of one single production' (ibid., p. 28). From this position, it became possible to emphasise the ongoing production of meaning in actual speech acts. Saussure's stress on the differential and formal characteristics of semiological functioning pointed to a way of challenging notions of a fixed unit of consciousness which corresponds to a meaning that is external and anterior to the process of production of that meaning. For these reasons, Saussure opened up the possibility of the criticism of 'the metaphysical appurtenance of the sign' (ibid., p. 27).

However, Derrida shows that Saussure did not and could not avoid confirming the idealist tradition by his use of the notion 'sign'. Although the distinction signifier/signified was emphasised – the distinction with the greatest potentiality for prising open the idealist tradition – he nevertheless went on to retain the concept 'sign', justifying its use 'because we do not know what to replace it with; common language does not suggest any alternative'. But common language is not innocent and neutral: it is the language of Western metaphysics, and is therefore riddled with presuppositions which bind it to idealism.

This is why the radical potentiality of the sign is foreclosed. There are two principal tendencies in this foreclosure. By maintaining the rigorous distinction between the signifier and the signified, and by equating the signified with the concept, the possibility is left open of thinking of a signified concept *in itself*, independent of language, that is, of the system of signifiers. This grants a right to the classical idealist demand for what Derrida calls the 'transcendental signified', 'which supposedly does not in itself, in its essence, refer back to any signifier but goes beyond the chain of signs, and itself no longer functions as a signifier' (Derrida, *Positions*, p. 23). In this way, the distinction or equilibrium of the notions 'signified' and 'signifier' in the sign allows the metaphysical belief of a reserve or an origin of meaning which will always be anterior and exterior to the continuous productivity of signification.

The second tendency towards the foreclosure of the radical potentiality is the 'logocentricism' inherent in Saussure's philosophy. Saussure, like innumerable linguists before and after him, suggests that there is a privileged bond between the voice and meaning, between speech and meaningfulness. The spoken word, and everything which links the sign with the 'phone' (the acoustic image, basic acts of speech, i.e.

sounds), is privileged in that it transparently presents fullness of meaning. He even presents the possibility of a natural link between thought and voice, between meaning and sound. This idea of speech is part of an idealist nostalgic recourse to the possibility of a meaning existing in meaning-fullness which is prior to any exteriorisation in language or material form. This sense of a reservoir of 'purified' meaning existing prior to language is paralleled by certain texts of Lévi-Strauss, especially in *Tristes Tropiques* where he persistently implies that the acquisition of writing brings about the end of innocence. Lévi-Strauss's nostalgia for a paradisal illiterate innocence displays the same tendency as Saussure's suggestion that the voice represents the immediacy of intercourse and experience: 'the phone is the signifying substance that gives itself to consciousness as the most intimately linked to the thought of the signified concept' (Derrida, op. cit., p. 32). The voice from this perspective is seen to be the presence of consciousness itself: the intention of meaning. In other words:

When I speak, I am conscious not only of being present at what I am thinking but also of keeping close to my thought or to the 'concept', a signifier . . . which I know as soon as I emit it, which seems to depend on my pure and free spontaneity, not to require the use of any instrument, any accessory, or any force taken from the world. Not only do signifier and signified seem to unite, but in this confusion the signifier seems to be erased or to become transparent so as to let the concept present itself, just as it is, referring to nothing but its own self-presence (ibid., pp. 32–3).

It is these two tendencies which have lead to Derrida's assertion that a philosophy of language based on such a notion of the sign is 'profoundly theological'. 'Sign and deity have the same place and same time of birth.' The pyramid (referent–signified–signifier) ends by resolving itself into the hypostasis of a signified which always culminates in god: 'the epoch of the sign is essentially theological' (ibid., p. 25). Because this metaphysical tendency has dominated Western culture since Plato (furnishing the distinctions body/soul, matter/idea, etc.) even semiology, which set itself the task of the scientific and formal elaboration of meaning, was constituted with fundamental concepts and presuppositions which 'can be located very precisely from Plato to Husserl, passing through Aristotle, Rousseau, Hegel etc.' (ibid., p. 33). In this way semiology is deeply committed to the idealist problematic which presupposes the existence of meaning, 'prior to the appearance of the ego and knowable by it . . . but never calling into doubt the unity of the ego – precisely the guarantee of such knowledge' (Kristeva, *Semiotext(e)*, vol. 1, no. 3, 1975).

Semiology, influenced by the work of Hjelmslev, tended to split off the theory of a pre-existent meaning, like a 'substance', from its 'formation' in an expression, which is either a proposition or a sign assumed 'by a thinking subject. Hjelmslev wrote: 'we can thus see that in different languages, the sequences have, in spite of all their differences, a common factor: meaning itself which, considered in this way, presents itself provisionally as an amorphous mass, a non-analysable grandeur, defined by its external functions alone' (Hjelmslev, *Prolegomena to a Theory of Language*, p. 75). This statement represents quite clearly how early semiology asserts that it is the function of language that determines the form of this amorphous meaning. It is only by the intervention of this form and function that meaning obtains a possible existence. The presupposition of an expressible meaning is therefore fundamental to this conception of language despite the fact that this meaning is located as being beyond the form of content and the form of expression, as something beyond the substance of content and the substance of expression. These semiological functions of expression and content locate the semiological project in phenomenology's area of concern. For, in phenomenology also, content and expression function as stages between a pre-given meaning, always already positioned in some way, and its linguistic or semiological utterance. In the same way, the semiological factors grow out of the sign in that the sign is the sign of an object which is suggested as existing 'out there': 'it seems correct that the sign is the sign of something and that this "something" remains in some way outside the sign itself' (ibid., p. 82). For these reasons, semiology includes the ambiguity which Derrida attributed to the notion of the sign and which enables the idealist interpretation of a pre-existent meaning, grasped by a thinking, unified subject. As Benveniste has remarked, 'the semiology of language, paradoxically, has been blocked by the very instrument that created it: the Sign' (Benveniste, *Problèmes de linguistique générale*, vol. II, Gallimard, 1974, pp. 65–6). The development of a theory of the productivity of meaning is inhibited by thinking of the signified concept as independent from the system of signifiers. This reaffirms the premises of all idealist thought: identity, presence and the unity of the thinking subject. 'Semiology then poses a communication implying a transmission charged with making the identity of the signified object, of a meaning or of a concept, pass from one [completed] subject to another' (Derrida, op. cit., p. 34).

Derrida indicates the impossibility of simply escaping metaphysics: it is not possible to simply reject such notions as 'concept', 'signified', etc.; 'they are necessary and today at least nothing is thinkable without them' (*De la Grammatologie*, p. 25). It is not a matter of refusing these ideas but rather of 'shaking up' the tradition of which they are a part. The sign is the 'kernel element of our culture' and it is the primacy which it is given in theories of meaning and language which has enabled the repression of materialism. Yet, because of its ambiguity, the sign also opened up the possibility of the assertion of materialism. For as soon as the notion of 'signified' is questioned, the sign itself becomes problematic, suggesting that language is the movement of signifiers. But the movement from this problematicity to a materialist theory of signification is a difficult one. Derrida himself has attempted a critique of the idealist self-presence of the subject, implicit in logocentric theories of language, by extending the Saussurean idea of language as a series of differences. He has done this by stressing the primacy of writing (*écriture*) in the establishment of differences by which all language, including speech, functions. The central terms in his theory are '*trace*' or '*gramme*' which are both structure and movement; language is 'the systematic game of differences, of traces of differences, of spacing by which the elements enter into relation with one another' (ibid.). He calls this notion of difference '*différance*'. He changes the last syllable to 'ance', from 'ence' to include also the action of differing (*différant*). This inclusion is used to show how all signs (in this case the written word) include traces of other signs. Thus, he points to the spacing, the temporal constitution by which generation and transformation of language are achieved. But while the development of 'grammatology' enables the challenging of the dominant notion 'sign—meaning—concept', it nevertheless is unable to account for language as a social practice, that is, meaningful communication between two subjects. This failing in a theory which has been able to envisage making 'the transcendental signified' redundant, is symptomatic of the difficulties involved in formulating a truly materialist critique of the sign. As Derrida himself realised, a critique of the sign would involve the project of the deconstruction of the whole of Western metaphysics. The opposition materialism/idealism is not an absolute opposition as seems to be implied in Derrida's work. Materialism can be found as an 'abundance' and 'excess' which is repressed in the positing of the transcendental signified. The positionality seen by Lacan as a necessary constraining factor involves a materialist analysis of its construction. It is not a retreat from the problem of meaning which underlies Derrida's own position of *différance* as movement without matter, in which everything is finally unknowable. This is ultimately idealist. Idealist thought appropriates the constraining factor that Lacan analyses, and fixes it as a point of origin, thus affirming 'presence and identity', and repressing the process of construction. That is why this process can be found in certain idealist philosophers or writers as an 'excess'.

It is from this perspective that Kristeva has developed the work of the examination of the sign in *La Révolution du langage poétique* (the revolution of poetic language). It is called this because the texts she examines of Lautréamont and Mallarmé are representative of a certain *avant-garde* experience in the second half of the nineteenth century in which the crisis of the bourgeois state, paternal law and religion dissolves the fixed relation between the subject and its discourse. The socio-symbolic limits (sign, religion, family, state), in which the syntactical structures are normally constrained, are broken down in these texts with the result that the subject is put in process by an excess of language.

In an extensive theoretical introduction, she examines the possibilities of a materialist re-reading of theories of meaning and language to see how the position of the sign influences the conception of the subject. It is not, as many people think, an emulation or adoption of Hegelian or phenomenological perspectives, but rather a re-examination of these perspectives in the light of the knowledge of the subject produced by Marxism and psychoanalysis. This knowledge has suggested the possibility of a materialist theory of signification which can distinguish language from other signifying practices and therefore see the linguistic sign simply as a stage in the process of signification. This stage would be qualitatively different from other stages and dependent on, or produced by, a positioned subject. We have already seen how Barthes and Kristeva assert that this understanding of the subject imposes itself in a close reading of an *avant-garde* text. The signifying practices of these texts (Kristeva calls them 'poetic language' after the term introduced by the Russian Formalists) are complex processes which contain the possibilities of transformations and changes; the subject of these texts is no longer beyond the realm of understanding, but can be analysed in the alterations of its discourse without being reducible to the formal structures of language. Poetic language not only dissolves narrative but also puts the identity of meaning, the sign, and the speaking subject, into crisis, producing a musicality, rhythmic and acoustic functioning. This 'subject in crisis' of the *avant-garde* texts, and the possible understanding of the subject produced by Marxism and psychoanalysis, both demand attention to the question of the 'extra-linguistic', that is the processes of production of the relation between subject and meaning (meanings produced for a subject included as the place of their intention). It is this question that Kristeva claims has been repressed by contemporary linguistics with their understanding and use of the 'sign'. We have discussed in Chapter 2 the implications of this notion of the sign in structural linguistics: it represses the question of the subject in its concentration on the formal laws of functioning and structural transformation. We have seen how modern linguistics forecloses consideration of 'meaning'.

The work of Chomsky is seen by Kristeva to be particularly significant in having raised the question of the extra-linguistic, which is so rigorously excluded from the formalist conceptions of language. This results from his original idea of the generation of syntactical structures. In some respects, he remained close to his original influence: post-Bloomfieldian linguistics. This is a structural, analytic description which breaks down the sentence into self-contained strata. It is the principle called 'the separation of strands' (phonematic, morphemic, etc.); each strand functions in itself, so in undertaking a phonematic study, for example, it is not possible to refer to morphology. This linguistic theory proposes an empirical description of the spoken chain, without considering the speaker or its role in the construction of the sentence.

The theory deludes itself with this empiricism that it is 'neutral' or 'objective'. Chomsky stayed faithful to the demand for a rigorous, neutral and formal description, and also to the distrust of the signified. But he was also anxious to solve certain difficulties such as categorial activity, which a syntagmatic analysis — analysis of the linear relations between signs — showed itself incapable of solving. He attempted to create a new theory of grammar which could account for the functional role of phenomena which usually fall to the realm of pragmatics, without having to resort to semantics.

In the place of the analytic approach to structures, Chomsky introduced the idea of a synthetic description. This no longer functions by breaking down sentences into their immediate components, but rather by a process of synthesis which brings the components into a syntagmatic structure, or transforms the structure into a different structure. In the last instance, this operation relies on the implicit intuition of the speaker who is the only criterion for whether a sentence is grammatical or not:

> The fundamental aim in the linguistic analysis of a language 'L' is to separate the *grammatical* sequences which are the sentences of L from the *ungrammatical* sequences which are not sentences of L, and to study the structure of the grammatical sequences. . . . In this respect, a grammar mirrors the behaviour of the speaker who, on the basis of a finite and accidental experience with language, can produce an indefinite number of new sentences. Indeed, any explication of the notion 'grammatical in L' . . . can be thought of as offering an explanation for this fundamental aspect of linguistic behaviour (*Syntactic Structures*, pp. 13, 15).

In this way, Chomsky is led to reject the idea that grammaticality, and therefore syntax, reflect a pre-existent meaning since a sentence can be grammatical but meaningless, e.g. 'colourless green ideas sleep furiously', and indeed the same words can be arranged into a non-grammatical sequence, 'furiously sleep ideas green colourless'. It is this development which shows quite emphatically that as soon as a notion as apparently formal as grammar is extended, then a theory of the sign itself can no longer be avoided.

In attempting to formulate the ideological foundations of his theory, Chomsky is led to question the speaking subject that Bloomfieldians wished to exclude from their analysis. Bloomfield, in a reaction against what he saw to be the imprecise 'mentalist' tendencies in such linguists as Sapir, had presented a totally behaviourist idea of language in his book *Language* (Allen & Unwin, London, 1933). His extremely mechanistic view was made famous by his schema of language as stimulus and response, where a resonance is said to be produced in the listener which is then translated into a practical response. It is a theory which is totally unable to account for the complexities of speech or the act of discourse.

Chomsky on the other hand faced the problem of recognising the activity of thought in the formal structures of the signifier. In *Cartesian Linguistics* he located the antecedents of his theory of the speaking subject in the *'cogito'* of Descartes and the subsequent Cartesian theories of the subject. These ideas imply the universality of innate ideas of the subject which is the guarantee of normality (Chomsky calls it 'grammaticality') of thoughts and statements. As a result of this theory, Chomsky extended the Saussurean model of *Langue/Parole* to include 'the recursive processes underlying sentence formation' in terms of Competence/Performance. Competence is the capacity of the speaking subject to make and recognise grammatical sentences in an infinity of possible constructions in language; and performance is the concrete realisation of this capacity. Rejecting the suggestion of language as 'a system of habituals' given by Bloomfield, he chose instead the Cartesian idealist solution of 'innate ideas': the universal character of these ideas necessitates a highly abstract theory, developed from specific concrete instances, to find the universal formulation which is valid for every language and of which every language is a specific realisation.

Grammar, for Chomsky, is less an empirical description than a theory of 'language' and as such it ends in 'a condition of generality'. His approach, nevertheless, offers a dynamic view of the syntagmatic structure, which is absent from structural grammar, by admitting the activity of thought in the formal structure. He suggests a notion of language as the process of production in which each sequence and rule corresponds to a coherent group centred on the consciousness of the speaking subject. This examination of syntactic structures shows language as a group of co-ordinated terms, in opposition to the fragmentation or atomism implicit in previous studies.

The subject in Chomsky is free in the possession of innate ideas and it controls their transformation. This transformational analysis presents the syntactic schema of a psychic process which is contained by a certain rationalist conception of the subject. It is an analysis which does not concern itself with the diversity of language and signifying practices; it demonstrates the coherency of the logical system of subject–predicate. Chomsky thus developed a notion which follows very closely the idea of the subject in Husserlian phenomenology. His explicit reference to this subject is symptomatic of the fact that Husserlian philosophy has been at the basis of signification theories in this century, and, consciously or not, explicitly or not, at the basis of modern linguistics. This is exposed by the fact that generative grammar, developing after the work of Chomsky, like 'distributionalism' and syntactic theories of enunciation, is completing the structuralist reduction to a pure signifier without a signified, a grammar without a syntax, the index in the place of the sign which therefore is no longer the central term. And this reduction is accompanied by a rediscovery of the same epistemological space as Husserl. In order to dispense with the empirical subjectivity in linguistics, generative grammar had to reduce the constitutive elements in a spoken sentence, convert signs into indexes or marks, in order to demonstrate that the elements have no other meaning than their pure grammaticality. By returning to the constitutive subjectivity and re-finding there the Cartesian subject as generator of meaning, 'transformational grammar chose an eclecticism which, for a while, reconciles a psychological theory of the subject with an indexation of increasingly inexpressible linguistic components' (Joyaux, *Le Langage, cet inconnu*, p. 252). Kristeva offers two alternatives facing this temporary reconciliation. The formal indexes will have to be invested with the ability to signify and this will need to be integrated into a theory of 'truth' and the 'subject'. The alternative is to separate these concepts of 'truth' and the 'subject' as incapable of explaining the indexed order. In this development, a Cartesian grammar would become redundant and linguistics would have to orientate itself to a different view of the subject, one in which the subject is destroyed and re-made in the signifier — a theory which, as we have seen already, both Marxism and psychoanalysis would favour.

Kristeva gives a great deal of significance to Husserl. This is partly because she feels it important to make a strategic intervention in elaborating the epistemological space in which contemporary linguistics is now locating itself. It is also because she thinks Husserl demonstrated, although in a way which committed him to an idealist perspective, the fundamental logic of signification. While she divorces herself from any theory of an immanent meaning, anterior to language, or from theories of language as thought, pre-conditioned by 'natural' given factors, she nevertheless considers that certain Husserlian terms do, or can be made to, accommodate a materialist theory of language using the Lacanian development of the idea of a necessary positionality in language. She makes this intervention of a materialist re-reading of Husserl at a time when he is being rediscovered and used for metaphysical assurance in linguistics. It should be stressed that she is never anything but critical of the fact that his theory is elaborated from within a totally idealist perspective; the perspective in which the grammatical order and the configuration of signs is always accounted for in terms of 'generalities' and the purely logical.

What interested Husserl was to account for the way in which objects are constructed as objects through mental relations and acts. He set out to explain the cognitive bases of logical categories and to explain the discrepancies between the epistemological foundations of knowledge and the logical aspects of knowledge. He wanted to explain the presuppositions of logic, to produce a self-criticism in logic, to show that logical concepts are not just items to be analysed and defined in terms of a similar nature, but are the product of categorial activity. This categorial activity leads to a theory of an object-constituting subjectivity.

Without producing a general theory of the sign, Husserl nevertheless brought such a theory into his consideration of mental relations and acts by distinguishing between two types of signs: one expresses or means something (expression), the other type does not have any meaning, and Husserl called it 'mark' or 'index' which is established through relations of convention and association. These distinctions are easily confused and ambiguous: what is significant in them is that in *Logical Investigations* (1900–1), Husserl locates the sign in a judgment about something which is an expression of meaning: 'the articulated phonic complex . . . becomes the spoken word, communicative discourse in general, only because he who speaks produces it with the intention of thus expressing himself about something' (quoted in Joyaux, op. cit., p. 216). This 'intentionality' is a mental relation and therefore involves a mental act, and 'while it does not imply the extra-mental existence of the object of such an act, it does presuppose the existence of a *subject*, that is, someone who knows, hates, wants, etc.' (Pivcevic, *Husserl and Phenomenology*, p. 47). Intentionality describes the experience in which we stand in relation to an object. Husserl posits the inseparability of intentionality from the phenomenon of consciousness.

In this perspective, the sign (signifier/signified) opens onto a complex architecture where the intentional act forms the object for consciousness. This process occurs by the intentional act grasping material (Husserl's 'hyle') multiplicities. This 'hyle' in Husserl is the component of the purely sensorial and non-intentional in signifying matter. It is 'amorphous' sensory stuff and is only shaped by the form of intention. This is a new version of the matter/form dichotomy. The amorphous hyle, the material multiplicity, is activated only by the intentional form-giving acts. The intentional and strictly non-material component of an experience is described by Husserl as 'noesis' (*nous* means 'reason'). Noesis refers to the cognitive, intentional act, and it has a counterpart in the 'noema' which completes the act of understanding. The noema is the objective 'meaning-content', the ideal content correlate of noesis, that is the intentional act. Even a simple perception has a noema: it is the 'perceived as such', the recourse to the resemblance. It is through this schema that the 'phenomenological reduction' is accomplished. This is the reduction to essences and generalities from the analysis of the intentional structures and their grasping of material multiplicities. Husserl's idea of transcendental consciousness results from this phenomenological reduction. This method of deducing generalities posits what is essential and constitutive in our cognitive relation with the world. To discover these ultimate presuppositions of knowledge, he calls for the necessity to suspend all *a priori* assumptions about entities external to consciousness; to concentrate on what is given to the 'stream of experiences' not as empirical events but as intentional structures. To grasp these ultimate presuppositions, it is necessary to reduce consciousness into a 'stream of experiences', to reduce the individual consciousness to the transcendental consciousness, i.e. to a stream of transcendentally purified experiences. Transcendental subjectivity or consciousness is, in this analysis, what remains as a philosophical residuum after this phenomenological reduction.

What is signified here is transcendental since it is produced by means of a certain development of consciousness which finally is always that of judgment. For this reason, phenomenology disputes the so-called 'natural attitude', the existence of the external 'real' world. It is not concerned with the spatio-temporal existence of things, such concerns are simply bracketed out: if it is real to consciousness, then it is real. This reduction to 'pure' facts of the transcendental consciousness is guaranteed by the transcendental ego which unifies experience in which the noesis and noema shape the hyletic data. Consciousness cannot therefore be seen as the logical expression of, or as identical with, the world. It is the operation or act of predication, then, which produces the judging consciousness of the transcendental ego, because it positions both the signified 'being' (and therefore the object of meaning and signification) and the operating consciousness itself. The transcendental ego is that of a constitutive operating consciousness, produced in the act of predication. While intentionality, and with it the judging consciousness, are already given in material data and in perceptions, since it 'resembles' them (which allows us to say that the transcendental ego is always already given in a certain way), in fact the transcendental ego is constituted only in the act of predication. The subject is the subject only of predication, of judgment, of the sentence. In this way, a relation is posited between the signified object and the transcendental ego, the operating consciousness, which is constituted in position and positioning in the act of predication. Husserl calls this movement the thetic since it belongs to the realm of the thesis of position and pro-positions: 'it posits at the same time both the thesis (position) of "being" and the thesis of the ego. Thus the transcendental signified object and the transcendental ego are each given by predication or judgment which forms the thetic process' (Kristeva, *Semiotext(e)*, vol. 1, no. 3, 1975).

What interests Kristeva is not the metaphysical affirmation of 'being' or 'presence' as the origin of meaning, or indeed any of the metaphysical project, but the fact that he has drawn attention to this object-constituting subjectivity which produces positioned consciousness in the act of predication. Logical acts, concepts, propositions, etc., are not just a special class of items but involve mental acts of the judging subject. In elaborating this notion of subjectivity which in fact underlies structuralism, she draws attention to the fact that structuralism refuses to consider the implication of this thetic constraining factor of language. For this reason, structuralism will remain entrenched in a 'negative theology' since it refuses to consider what is constraining, legislative and socialising in the function of language. By ignoring this, structuralism thinks it has done away with the transcendental ego, but by ignoring the social and linguistic constraining factor, it reaffirms idealist notions and is unable to produce a valid theory of practice.

Certain linguistic theories have tackled this consideration head-on. The most significant has been that of Emile Benveniste who insists on attention to a constitutive subjectivity in language, which he calls attention to the subject of the enunciation. In Benveniste, however, the operating consciousness includes not only the logical modalities (categorial activities) but the relations between speakers. In this way, his consideration of the thetic consciousness (to continue to use phenomenological terms) admits a hetereogeneous outside; indeed, his subjectivity is developed in relation to 'otherness' and in this respect his ideas are very different from Husserl's idealist theologisation of this subjectivity as the source and origin of all meaning.

Nevertheless, Benveniste sees the function of predication in which coherent social identity, 'I', 'he', 'she', etc., makes possible meaningful communication between two subjects to be a central concern of linguistics. It is through language that man constitutes himself as a subject because language alone establishes the concept of the ego in reality: 'the subjectivity we are discussing here is the capacity of the speaker to posit himself as "subject". It is not defined by the feeling which everybody experiences of being himself: but as the psychic unity that transcends the totality of the actual experiences it assembles and that makes the permanence of consciousness' (Benveniste, *Problems in General Linguistics*, p. 223). He continues by asserting that this subjectivity is the fundamental property of language and the foundation of this subjectivity is in the linguistic category of 'person'. Thus all linguistic acts, inasmuch as they constitute a signified or a meaning that can be communicated in a sentence, are supported by a transcendental ego. Without this, it would be impossible to explain one, although not the only, function of language: the expression of meaning in communicable sentences between speakers. Social identity resides in this function:

Language is possible only because each speaker sets himself up as a subject by referring to himself as 'I' in his discourse. Because of this, 'I' posits another person, the one who, being as he is completely exterior to 'me', becomes my echo to whom I say 'you' and who says 'you' to me. This polarity of persons is the fundamental condition of language, of which the process of communication in which we share, is only a mere pragmatic consequence. It is a polarity moreover very peculiar in itself, as it offers a type of opposition whose equivalent is encountered nowhere else outside language. This polarity does not mean either equality or symmetry: 'ego' always has a position of transcendence with regard to you. Nevertheless neither of these terms can be conceived of without the other; they are complementary, although according to an interior/exterior opposition, and at the same time they are reversible (ibid., p. 225).

Benveniste thus introduces into a formal theory of language, the idea of a stratum previously seen only as the concern of semantics or pragmatics. This stratum is as we have seen, the subject of the enunciation which functions as a very deep 'deep structure'. It is at this level that are situated the modal relations between speakers. But as we have seen, Benveniste still gives priority to an idea of the transcendental ego to explain this subject.

Psychoanalysis enables us to see this thetic phase (the operating consciousness constituting, by predication, the real signified object, being and the ego as transcendental) as merely one stage in a truly heterogeneous process. The theory of the unconscious as elaborated by Lacan gives clear support to the idea of positionality that is necessary in meaningful communication between two speaking subjects. This positionality is seen to be acquired through the mirror phase and the castration complex. These stages produce an alteration in the mobility of the drives and make possible the movement away from maternal dependency and auto-eroticism by the introduction of the division signifier/signified, thus producing the possibility of signification. Signification therefore appears as a stage which is not fundamental but rather a frontier of the signifying process. The alteration signifier/signified is thus introduced as a result of social censure and, in that it enables the positions of language, it is the condition of signification. But at the same time this condition is no longer seen as the point of origin, as it is in Husserlian theories of language. The positionality which Husserlian phenomenology describes with the terms 'doxa', 'thesis', 'position' is structured according to psychoanalytic development by a break in the process of signification, which establishes the identification of the subject and its objects as the conditions of propositionality (meanings for a subject included as the place of their intention). This thetic positionality installs, according to Kristeva, the realm of the symbolic in language since the act of predication which constitutes and fixes the subject and its objects, is also the movement which establishes the universals of language, linguistic symbolism. It installs the ability to establish a relation of signification between one thing and another.

From this perspective the subject, in its acquisition of the sign and learned language through the thetic phase, is seen merely to be 'the tenant of a structural closure'. While the thetic represents the threshold of signification, the subject is certainly not reducible to this process. Signification is seen to be a complex heterogeneous process which demands consideration of the extra-linguistic, that is the arrangement of the drives, the body submitted to socio-familial constraints, the fixity of ideological positions, etc.

The work of such linguists as Benveniste in demanding attention to the subject of the enunciation has challenged the notion of the relation of arbitrariness and the equilibrium of the sign: which is the very notion on which formal linguistics justifies its neglect of the extra-linguistic. Psychoanalytic developments of theories of language have added further evidence to challenge this notion. But the challenge from psychoanalysis has revealed a very different modality of signification from that of the thetic (even though it still relies on the modality of the thetic as the condition of social communication). Kristeva calls this other modality the 'semiotic'. It concerns the possibility of a 'motivation of the signifier' by suggesting – as a result of the Freudian theory of the drives and the movement of the primary process, i.e. condensation and displacement – that 'empty signifiers' function in relation to the psychosomatic function; or at least that the drives enchain signifiers in a certain sequence of metaphor and metonymy. In this way, the notion of the arbitrary is replaced by the notion of an articulation.

Psychoanalysis has investigated the proceedings of the subject from the position of language, and through this it has changed the general conception of language itself. We have already seen the inseparability of the concerns of linguistics from those of psychoanalysis; the most obvious and most important reason is that psychoanalysis sees its object as being the speech of the patient: it has no other point of entry for the exploration of the patient's unconscious or consciousness. It is only in this speech that the analyst can discover the position of the subject. The other considerations which have drawn linguistics and psychoanalysis together are the ways in which the objects of psychoanalytic study are considered as languages, for example, dreams or symptoms. It is only in the discursive reality of the patient that the unconscious motivation can be ascertained – a motivation of which the symptom is a symbol. This unconscious motivation, which is the product of a vertical and historical process, presents itself in a horizontal discursive situation: the relation between patient and analyst. This relation recalls what Lacan holds to be true of the signifying process in general: all discourse is destined to another, and constructed in this relationship with another. Such a notion of discourse demands attention to the full complexities of the speech act, complexities which direct attention to the unconscious processes and the position of the subject. Psychoanalysis is concerned with a signifying practice in which language is only the edge, and not the total experience. In this sense language in its formal structures is secondary because, although the signifying system of the unconscious is in a close relation to formal linguistic categories, it nevertheless imposes its own organisations and its own specific logic.

Typical of these processes of signification is the example of dream language. As we have seen, Freud thought the dream signified like a rebus or hieroglyph. It signifies by using the processes of displacement and condensation which transform the latent thought of the dreams into the manifest content. In other words, dreams in general do not use the logical relations of formal linguistics. Either several thoughts appear condensed in one symbol, or the representation of unconscious desire is displaced into another symbol to accommodate dream censorship. But the form of dreams is not symbolism, it is a language in that it is a structure with its own logic and syntax. Nor is it limited to spoken language: the body also communicates in the symptoms of hysteria. This form of language is not that of formal linguistics, even though it achieves its expression in that language. It does not follow logical proce-dures but is composed of heterogeneous representations. As Benveniste points out, Freud's conception of language is 'supra-linguistic in that it uses extremely condensed signs which in organised language correspond to large units of discourse rather than small ones' (Benveniste, *Problems in General Linguistics*, p. 75). It is a notion of language which is trans-linguistic, studying how language functions, and includes therefore psychosomatic functions. In attending to this function, Freud avoids the metaphysical tendency of linguistic science. This is because it gives concrete support to what we have seen to be the radical potentiality of Saussure's theory: it allows the separation of the signifier and the signi-fied, by insisting that we think of the signified in the function of the signifier that produced it and vice versa. The object of psychoanalysis is productivity and differentiation since it aims at an understanding of the production of the subject and meaning in language. We have seen how this development in Lacan produced a theory of the primacy of the signifier over the signified; this is not the same as the structuralist mistrust of the signified, but rather an attempt to account for the signi-fied in relation to the signifier: 'the signifier in fact enters into the sig-nified' (Lacan, *Ecrits*, p. 500). The subject and the signified no longer exist: they are produced simply by the discursive work, and their presence can only be defined in terms of a topology. This mathematical analogy refers to the study of spaces and forms and their interrelation, and Kristeva uses it to indicate the necessity for studying the configura-tions of the discursive space of the subject in relation to the other and to discourse. 'For the uniform structure which is language for structural linguistics and its transformational variants, psychoanalysis substitutes the problematic of the production of meaning' (Joyaux, op. cit., p. 264). Productivity here does not mean what generative grammar under-stands by the term as it 'produces nothing at all and contents itself with synthesising a structure in the course of a process which never questions the foundations of that structure' (ibid.). This productivity revealed by psychoanalysis is an effective production which crosses discourse and statements to produce a certain meaning with a certain subject.

For Kristeva it is only by looking at signification in this way that one can begin to move towards a materialist theory of signification, which would locate the sign as a stage in a dialectical process which would be the process of the subject itself:

> A dialectic which generates across the unconscious that which is presented as having a meaning in judgment (in a sentence). But also dialectic as the truth and/or generation of the subject who holds this

meaning; as also dialectic of the bond between the subject and its heterogeneous outside (Kristeva, *Critique*, No. 285, p. 101).

She asserts that Freudian theory has enabled the specification of the signifying systems as articulations of the dialectic of signification which gathers together language, the body, and the material 'outside'. Dialectical materialism can only be genuinely realised through a consideration of this 'exteriority' of psychosomatic functioning, produced by Freudian theories of the drives as the turning-point between the body and the psychic representations. There can be no understanding of history, ideology or language which does not take account of the production of the subject, and therefore of signifying practices, in relation to the heterogeneous outside: in relation to the movement of contradiction. For Kristeva, the Freudian conception of drives is not only dualistic (life/death, etc.) but also hetereogeneous; this is important since it implies continuous movement and contradiction before and after signifying positions become established. This hetereogeneity reveals a permanent state of division: it is both assimilative and destructive, but is finally governed by the negative movement which Freud called the death drive.

Kristeva proposes that an elaboration of this area of Freudian thought could be the basis for a materialist re-reading of dialectical processes which, with their adherence to notions of subjective unity and the unity of the concept, have remained trapped in idealism. This re-reading would be able to include the movement of heterogeneous matter which is repressed in idealist uses of the dialectic. She claims that Freud's paper 'Negation' (*Standard Edition*, vol. XIX) demonstrates an implicit formulation which connects the movement of material contradictions (reflected in the structural arrangement of the drives) and the engendering of signification.

Like Lacan and Benveniste, she insists that 'Negation' can be read as a discussion of the production of signification itself. Freud reduced the polarity of linguistic affirmation and negation (that is, the function of judgment) to the biophysical mechanism of introjection into the ego, and projection/expulsion from the ego of certain objects according to the appreciation of the good or bad object. This is the operation in which the reiterated drives ascertain at which object they may aim in order to achieve satisfaction (or, in Lacanian terms, which object may satisfy the sense of gaping or lack in which the drive originates), and which objects must be rejected as producing unpleasurable tension. Judgment according to Freud is a continuation of the original mechanism by which the subject builds itself and its world of objects: 'a continuation along the lines of expediency of the original process by which the ego took things into itself or expelled them from itself according to the pleasure principle' (Freud, *Standard Edition*, vol. XIX, p. 239). He makes these claims after observing the functioning of the negative symbol in analysis; the repressed idea or fixation often made its way into consciousness but always as a negative, that is it appeared as 'I didn't think that' when that was precisely the content of the repressed thought: 'with the help of negation only one consequence of the process of repression is undone — namely, the fact of the ideational content of what is repressed not reaching consciousness' (ibid.). Benveniste demonstrates that the characteristic of this linguistic negation (as opposed to animals' appreciation of what is harmful or beneficial) is that it can only annul what has been expressed; a judgment of non-existence then necessarily has the formal status of a judgment of existence. Negation is first and foremost an acceptance: 'negation is a way of taking cognisance of what is repressed; indeed it is already a lifting of repression, though not, of course, an acceptance of what is repressed' (ibid., p. 236).

These implicit statements about the nature of the negation symbol in language are very close to the conclusions reached by the logician Frege, in his analysis of the problems of logic. He showed quite clearly that negative thought does not exist: he was starting out from the premise that the judging subject sustains all thought, and that this subject cannot therefore be negated. Thought, he suggests, is characterised by the inseparability of the positive and the negative. Frege thus concurs with Benveniste's extrapolations from Freud (Benveniste, *Problems in General Linguistics*, pp. 65–79) when he says that a denial in the interior of judgment is complementary to affirmation; indeed, it necessitates an affirmation as its prior condition. Negation internal to judgment is a negation of the predicate, which, of course, involves an affirmation of the predicated object. In other words, negation is simply a variation of the positive predicate, and is therefore impossible outside the syntactical relations of subject and predicate. From this, Kristeva is led to suggest that if we must understand the symbolic function as a syntactical function which consists essentially in situating a subject in relation to a predicate, then the symbol of negation must be seen as prior to or coinciding with the beginnings of symbolicity. It is a hypothesis which has been verified by the observations of linguists interested in 'language acquisition'. This has shown that the negative symbol occurs at about 15 months; this coincides with the mirror-phase and with certain concrete utterances and operations which show the acquisition of certain syntactical relations. These observations confirm Frege's idea that negation belongs to the act of understanding, in that it is simply a variation of the act of predication. It is this logic which leads to the assertion that Freud's 'Negation' is dealing with the economy of the production of the symbolic function itself, the movement producing the judging subject able to predicate.

Freud is therefore positing the production of this symbolic function from the formation of the ego which develops according to the socio-familial constraints into which it is born. Kristeva extends this by elaborating the concept *'rejet'*, meaning 'expulsion', and also indicating 'rejection' and 'projection': it is the opposite movement of the introjection/projection dialectic. This concept would enable one to 'propose a logical mechanism in which can be inscribed "negation" not internal to judgment but economic, productive of the signifying position itself' (Kristeva, *La Révolution du langage poétique*, p. 112). Kristeva gives this movement the same status as negativity in dialectical processes: the movement of the destruction and dissolution of 'sensible certitude' to produce the new concept, here located in the psychosomatic processes. The emphasis on expulsion/projection as the movement necessary to the production of the symbolic function 'in a time logically and genetically prior to its constitution' enables one to 'disengage the trans-subjective, trans-ideal, trans-symbolic movement of the separation of matter, which is constitutive of the conditions of symbolicity' (ibid., p. 108). It allows one to understand this movement prior and necessary to symbolicity as a process of marking and separation carried out on a surface, thereby tracing and establishing similarities and differences.

Freud described the process in this way:

The original pleasure ego wants to introject into itself everything that is good and expel everything that is bad. . . . Judging is a continuation along the lines of expediency of the original process by which the ego took things into itself or expelled them according to the pleasure principle. The polarity of judgment appears to correspond to the opposition of the two groups we have supposed to exist. Affirmation – as a substitute for uniting – belonging to Eros; negation – the successor [aftermath] of expulsion – belongs to the destructive drive (*Standard Edition*, vol. XIX, p. 237).

Kristeva gives the notion of expulsion/projection the fundamental status of the movement constituting the possibilities of signification. This movement traces the processes and arrangement of the drives, faced with resistance and facilitations, according to the pleasure principle. We have seen how this principle functions according to the establishment of good and bad objects which produce the structural arrangement of the drives. The aims of the drives are to eliminate states of tension either by introjecting an object deemed capable of closing a sense of lack, or by expelling an object producing an excess of tension: it is these actions, productive of the ego, which Freud equates with the functions of judgment, affirmation and negation.

Kristeva claims that the dialectic of introjection/expulsion is the movement which can eliminate unbearable tension by the setting up of an outside which is radically other than the ego, definitively separated and 'outside' the ego. This enables the discrimination between good and bad objects, and the control of states of tension associated with these objects. And it is this which in creating an outside, builds the ego and places the subject in a position of possible predication. Her use of the operation of expulsion is complex. It implies the fundamental movement of resolution of the tension of the body submitted to the division of matter and to its social relations. This fundamental movement is first seen in the so-called pleasure principle. Lacan points out that this name is somewhat ironic, since excess of pleasure (excitation) is discharged in order to avoid unpleasurable tension. It is this process which Freud equates with the genesis of the opposition between the ego and the outside world, between the subject and the object. 'In so far as the objects which are presented to it as sources of pleasure [are taken into the ego], it "introjects" them . . . on the other hand, it expels whatever within itself becomes a source of unpleasure (the mechanism of projection)' (Freud, *Standard Edition*, vol. XIV, p. 136). Drives and their resistances (produced by the reiteration of drives at a certain aim) have no fixed identity, they are continuously moving, dissolving, renewing and transforming, but it is nevertheless their movement and structural arrangement which produces the position of the subject (while also remaining the possibility of that subject).

The position of the possibility of the predicating subject of the thetic is produced by the activity of expulsion, which according to Kristeva is nothing other than 'the semiotic mode of a permanent aggressivity and the possibility of its position and therefore its renewal' (Kristeva, *La Révolution du langage poétique*, p. 137). Freud thought that permanent aggressivity was an essential part of libidinal economy; he developed the theory as a result of having noticed 'the possibility of a primary sadism directed towards the ego, before any isolation of the object, therefore a primary masochism' (Freud, *Standard Edition*, vol. XVIII). It is this activity which, in *Instincts and their Vicissitudes*, he saw as the mechanism of lifting tension, its reduction to inertia. He equated it with the death drive, his name for the basic category of destructive drives, drives which aim at destruction. In this case, it is the destruction of tension by the activity of the attempt to master, control and regulate the operations of the 'outside'. Because of the heterogeneity of the drives, however, the tension is perpetuated, but in a renewed form. This is the principle of the other pole of Freud's dualism Life/Death; the aim to resolve tension produces new tensions as it comes into contradiction with other forces, thus necessitating a further aim of destruction. It is for this reason that Freud claimed that the death drive ultimately underlies all the drives, but is unthinkable without the movement of heterogeneous contradiction of these other drives.

Thus the movement which establishes the 'object' in a position of alteriority, separated from the body and therefore signifiable, is seen to be part of the pleasure principle. Pleasure is created at the very moment in which the drives detach themselves from auto-eroticism and dependency on the mother, and are projected onto the outside. This difficult pleasure coincides with a loss, that is the loss of the dual relation with the mother, but it is a separation that does not mean a lack of pleasure but a production of pleasure. This pleasure is the excess which is attacked by the destructive drives, aiming at equilibrium, and projected onto the outside. It is this which provides the model for the notion of '*jouissance*', which is pleasure released in the destruction or resistance to drives: resolution of desire or tension is the moment where the death drive emerges at the surface. It is experienced as void, catastrophe and '*jouissance*'.

By this movement of projection/expulsion, the object which has been projected is definitively separated from the body of the subject; it is situated as 'out there', and as such only one relationship is possible in order to master this exteriority and gain satisfaction of needs. This is by the acceptance of the sign, that is symbolic relations and learned language. Acceptance makes it possible to represent the object in its absence, and therefore enables mastery of that absence:

> The antithesis between subjective and objective does not exist from the first. It only comes about from the fact that thinking possesses the capacity to bring before the mind once more something that has once been perceived by reproducing it as a presentation, without the external object having to be there. The first and immediate aim of reality-testing is, not to find an object in real perception which corresponds to one presented, but to refind such an object, to convince oneself that it is still there (Freud, 'Negation', *Standard Edition*, vol. XIX, p. 237).

The lifting of tension, by the projection of certain aims or objects with the concomitant attack on these objects, is shown in pre-verbal gestures and concrete operations. It is worth recalling the Fort/Da game in this context since it was the game which lead Freud to posit the relationship between the operations of the pleasure principle, the death drive and the acquisition of symbolicity. The activity of the child concerns its practical relations as a subject to its objects; it destroys them, serialises them and organises them. In this game, the child projects its dependency on the mother (that is, its total dependency in needs on the maternal body) by the acquisition of the symbol. It can then re-find the mother as object of its demands but in her absence, in this case in the symbol of the toy that is perpetually thrown away. The mother's body can be a source of unpleasure, in that the body is periodically absent. In mastering the ability to signify an outside, which definitively separates the child from its implication in the mother's body, the child's need can now be expressed in demand:

> The game in which the child plays at making an object disappear from his sight in order to bring it back again and then to obliterate it once more – an object basically undifferentiated from his nature – yet at the same time he modulates an alternation of distinctive syllables – all this game shows in its radical features the determinacy which the human animal receives from the symbolic system. Man literally devotes his time to deploying the structural alternative in which presence and absence take the one from the other their call. It is at the moment of their eventual conjuncture, the zero point of

desire, that the human object comes under seizure which, annulling its natural properties, subjects it henceforth to the conditions of the symbol. [The game provides] an illuminating insight into the individual's entry into an order the mass of which supports and welcomes him in the form of language, and which superimposes the determination of the signifier over that of the signified (Lacan, *Ecrits*, pp. 46–7).

Thus it is the movement of projection which gives the outside (the Other) the possibility of holding signification and therefore raises the subject from maternal dependency: 'this expenditure poses an object as separated from the body itself, and, at the very moment of separation, fixes it as *absent*: as *sign*. This expulsion installs the object as real object and in the same movement as signifiable, in the sense of already held as an internal object to the signifying system, as subordinated to the subject who poses it through or by the sign' (Kristeva, *La Révolution du langage poétique*, p. 114). The child invests in the symbol, the 'stand-in' for the object in order to be able to demand the return of the mother. We have seen how this produces desire which is the sense of something amiss producing the continuous metonymic movement of the subject towards an object, impossibly designated with the task of satisfying that lack. But we also see here the close link that Lacan asserts between the death drive and the acquisition of the symbol:

The subject is not simply mastering his privation by assuming it, but . . . is raising his desire to a second power, for his action destroys the subject that it causes to appear and disappear in the anticipating provocation of its absence and presence. His action thus negativises the field force of desire in order to become his own object to itself . . . the desire of the child has become the desire of another, of an alter ego . . . whose object of desire is henceforth his own affliction. So when we want to ascertain in the subject what was before the serial articulations of speech and what is primordial to the birth of symbols, we find it in death (Lacan, *Ecrits*).

The expulsion/projection which creates the possibility for the acquisition of language, and especially syntactic structures, is parallel to the alienation and aggression of the mirror-phase, in that symbolicity necessitates this definitive separation of the subject from the object. This separation is like the movement by which the child sees its image as separate and unified, a unit from which identifications are made. It is the constitution of the other as that which holds the possibility of signification which separates the subject from maternal dependency, and places the subject where he believes himself to be: at the axis of the division signifier/signified, and therefore at the origin of the production of signification.

The relationship of the sign thus established in a vertical dimension: speaking subject/outside, refinds itself projected into the interior of the signifying system in the horizontal linguistic dimension: syntactical subject/predicate. The outside, which has become a signifiable object, together with the function of predication then appear in indissociable solidarity as a halting of negativity — of projection (Kristeva, *La Révolution du langage poétique*, p. 114).

Thus Kristeva sums up how this movement, originating in the relation of the drives to heterogeneous contradiction, produces a predicating subject; and she shows how signification therefore appears as a stage which is not fundamental but is a frontier of the process of signification.

The notion of expulsion is very close to the notion of negativity in dialectics — the productive dissolution which is both the cause and the organisational principle of the process. But expulsion is able to retain the materialist requirements of objective contradiction, since the processes of the drives trace the turning point between the psychic and the body, submitted to social and familial relations: expulsion is used as a term which shows the movement of material contradiction that produces the arrangement of the drives. It is used as a term here because it shows the aspect of the drives, 'repetitive and trans-signifying' (ibid., p. 134), as a dynamic of signification. 'Expulsion is of the heterogeneous order since from the Freudian perspective, it belongs to the drives, the hinge between the psychic and the somatic' (ibid., p. 147). The functioning of expulsion/projection is the primary process, the condensation and displacement of free energies or drives, the shocks of energetic discharges and returns. This process traces the separation of matter which is a movement crossing the subject, symbolisation and ideation. It traces marks of separation on a surface, establishing differences and similarities at every new instance of repetition. It is this separation of matter which constitutes the conditions of symbolicity, engendering in a leap the symbol itself. This notion enables the demonstration of the underlying forces of the individual, the world and history, through the alteration and inhibited of the drives. It is here that Freud joined dialectical logic, for, in making expulsion constitutive of symbolicity, he made it possible to trace the objective processes of history and society in the very constitution of signification and the subject.

Psychoanalysis has traditionally concentrated on a demonstration of the 'normatisation' of this process of expulsion/projection, whose general movement is captured in specific forms. We have seen how Lacan has shown the arrangement of these drives according to the constraints imposed by social and familial structures. The normal route in our society by which the drives find themselves in fixed identifications is through the identifications and the path of desire necessitated by the Oedipus complex. The projection of the subject's own body as a separate image tends to be directed through the arrangement of the drives towards the identification with the body of the parent of the same sex, thus substituting relations of symbolic exchange for the narcissistic, imaginary relations which preceded it. This arrangement of the drives is produced by resistances and facilitations in the course of the movement of the drives. Where their passage produces a permanent reduction in resistance then facilitation is said to have occurred, and the drives tend to opt for those passages where the greatest reduction has already occurred. This is the route usually taken by sexual normatisation, that is, according to the constraints imposed by the social and familial structure. What occurs here is the 'positivation' of the movement of expulsion, achieved in a dialectic of expulsion/projection and identification. The constraints are imposed, as we have seen, in the fact that the subject finds his desire in the desire of the Other. The difference, absence/presence, which enables the first grasping of symbolicity and enables the expression of demand which institutes desire and the primary processes, finds a symbolic modality in the Oedipus complex. The undifferentiated, imaginary identity of the pre-Oedipal subject is installed in symbolic relations through the interruption of the fact of difference. It is the identification necessitated by the question of having or not having the 'phallus' (the signifier *par excellence* of difference) which forces the transition from imaginary to symbolic. It is not a question of the Oedipus complex making language possible; it is closer to a retrospective sanctioning of differences and separations, already traced, by the relations established in the Oedipus complex. The pre-Oedipal therefore only ever appears across the post-genital manipulation of language, the definitive imposition of the phallic. But without this stage, it would be impossible for the ideal-ego, the imaginary unity, to find a symbolic counterpart, the parent of the same sex. This privileged unifying instance is necessary to produce the coherence of the sign and sociality, without which linguistic communication is unthinkable, and without which ideology could not be articulated.

In this discussion of the arrangement of the drives in the production of symbolicity, we have returned to the question of the other modality of signification, the semiotic, which Kristeva claims has been discovered by the principle of motivated articulations in psychoanalysis, for example, psychotic disorders. We will return shortly to the actual form of expression of this modality, but first we need to establish its relation to symbolic relations (subject—meaning—position), and to understand its importance for the notion of signifying practices.

The semiotic is not something which only occurs before the acquisition of language and which is therefore somehow outside language; it is an essential part of the signifying practice even though it is heterogeneous. It always has a view to meaning, or is in a relation of negation or excess in regard to meaning. At the level of sexual identification this tendency can be quite clearly seen: the movement of the drives becomes 'positivised' around the relations of desire in the Oedipus complex, but they are never totally subsumed in this identification; the precariousness of the Oedipus complex is the most obvious witness to this. Thus Kristeva insists that 'the subject never *is*, the *subject* is only the *process of signification* and only presents itself as signifying practice, that is when it absents itself *in the position* from which social-historical-signifying activity unfolds itself' (ibid., p. 188). We have already seen how the knotting of the subject in predication, the acquisition of symbolic relations, leaves the subject as 'discontinuity in the real' (Lacan). Kristeva's emphasis of the process of expulsion allows a notion of language and the subject as signifying process in which the acquisition of the sign is only one stage. The activity of expulsion/projection is continuous, and as such it operates to put the subject into crisis by its operations in material contradictions. This crisis, if not destruction, questions and displaces the unity of the subject as source and origin of all meaning. The operation of transcendence which ensures meaningful communication between two speakers is decentred and broken up, and by this movement, is opened onto a dialectic in which syntactical and categorial understanding 'is only the preliminary moment of the process, itself always driven by its relation to the other which is dominated by the death drive and its productive reiteration' (Kristeva, *La Révolution du langage poétique*). It is easy to see here why Kristeva equates this movement to that of negativity, since its dissolving activity arising from a contradiction activates a new contradiction, which is then the motor of a new development. Expulsion then is activated by the movement of objective matter, and it can put into process the unity of the sign and subject. The acquisition of the sign is the 'positivisation' of the movement of projection; it occurs through the production of position by the reiteration of the projected drive from the place of the Other. This produces an immobilisation which is the halting or marking of the movement of projection, and which enables the lifting up of the drive from its dependency, the investing in, and identification with the laws of the historical formation. But without this halting and lifting up of the drive, there would be no production of a state of newness; projection would simply be the mechanical repetition of undifferentiated identity. If this were the case, there would be no evidence of a heterogeneous conflictual process, in either ideological or social practice, or indeed at the level of psychosis, language disturbance or *avant-garde* literary practice.

The possibility of a mechanical repetition of identity is untenable for Marxism, which separates itself from previous philosophy precisely on the grounds that it makes philosophy a revolutionary activity.
Ancient philosophies had as their aim the explanation of the world. Dialectical materialism, on the contrary, wants to transform the world, and it addresses itself to a new subject, and can only make itself understood by this subject: a subject who no longer simply explains, understands and knows, but a subject which is ungraspable since it is *transforming* reality. This subject which includes the former subject, accentuates *process* rather than identification, *projection* rather than desire, the *heterogeneous* rather than the

signifier, *struggle* rather than structure (Kristeva, *La Révolution du langage poétique*, pp. 160—1).

This activity can only produce a subject in process, an atomised subject oriented towards external relations, objectivity, the real. Marx attacked Feuerbach for not seeing human activity as objective activity, i.e. not seeing the primacy of practice in understanding. Lenin continued this emphasis by opposing Hegel's syllogism of the act with the logical exteriority of reality: 'man's practice, repeating itself a thousand million times, becomes consolidated in man's consciousness by figures of logic' (Lenin, *Collected Works*, vol. 38, p. 217). Mao has developed these commentaries in 'On Practice', where he stresses the personal and direct experience as the essentially materialist characteristic of practice: 'anyone who denies such [sensuous] perception, denies direct experience or denies personal participation in the practice that changes reality, is not a materialist' (Mao, 'On Practice', p. 9). Because of this, he agrees that the activity of production is the final determinant in all human life, but adds class struggle, political life and aesthetic activity to the list of practices. Mao's practical moment is a reversal of the Hegelian moment since it operates from 'apprehension' of 'exteriority' in its 'external liaisons': only the repetition of phenomena in the objective continuity of social practice produces the qualitative leap which is the emergence of the concept which installs the internal liaisons.

From this perspective, where history is that of modes of production and not that of the unified subject in its self-presence, dialectical materialism suggests the subject as 'a contradiction which activates practice, for practice is always a signifying practice, semiotic and symbolic, a place where meaning emerges or is lost'. In this way, subjectivity is seen to be the place of the highest contradiction: an atomised subjectivity which is the motor of practice and therefore of social transformation and revolution. The subject revealed by the Freudian unconscious, in the movement of projection, is precisely such a subject in process. This is crucial for any elaboration of the concept of practice, for it allows a genuinely materialist understanding of history and practice which no longer falls back into the traps of idealism. The description made possible by Freud can show the process by which the social contradiction articulates itself within the composition of the individual, bringing about the conditions which activate practice. The description traces the process of the speaking subject: stabilisation and expenditure which collide with social institutions in which it previously recognised itself; it thus coincides with the movements of rupture, of renovation, of revolution. Kristeva describes the process in this way: dialectical logic has shown how the unity and self-presence of the subject is dissolved in practical activity.

> The moment of practice puts the subject in relation to, and so in
> a position of negation of, objects and other subjects in the social
> milieu, with which it enters into antagonistic or non-antagonistic

contradiction. Although it is situated outside the subject, the contradiction within social relations ex-centres the subject, suspends it, and articulates it as a place of transit where opposing tendencies struggle, drives whose moments of *resistance* and theses (the *representamen*) are caught up as much in the affective (familial and loving) relations as in class struggle (Kristeva, *La Révolution du langage poétique*, pp. 179–80).

This ex-centring of the subject produces a return of the movement of projection across positions previously established by the reiteration of these rejected drives:

> ex-centring the subject, projection brings about a confrontation between the atomisation of the subject and the structures of social relations and the natural world; it runs up against them, repulses them and is dis-posed from them. At the moment of this projection, which thus implies the period of the annihilation of an old objectivity, a linking component which is symbolic, ideological and therefore positivising intervenes in order to constitute in language the new object which the 'subject' in process through projecting, produces across the process of projection. Thus practice contains as its fundamental moment, the heterogeneous contradiction which places a subject put into process by a social or natural exteriority that is not yet symbolised, into struggle with the old theses (that is, with systems of representation which defer projection and blunt its violence) (ibid., p. 180).

Because of this movement, the speaking subject is put into process and collides with social institutions in which it previously recognised itself; this practice atomises the subject which has to produce a new thesis in order to ensure social communication. This understanding of practice makes the idea of a 'free subject' in objective contradictions – the greatest flaw in some developments of Marxism – totally untenable:

> Practice includes the heterogeneous contradiction as the motor of an infinite dialectical movement – material and signifying. It is in practice that the *process* of signification is realised, since practice is determined by this moment in which the unity of consciousness is pulverised by a non-symbolised exteriority, setting out from the objective contradictions out of which the projected drives will create the new object with its determinations objectively existing in the material world outside (ibid., p. 180).

This is the destruction of the unity of consciousness; a unity which fixes the subject in a certain relationship with signification and therefore society. It is this destruction which activates practice, and therefore the production of 'newness'. Thus a theoretical elaboration is provided of signifying processes which is both a revolutionary theory and a theory of revolution.

Kristeva insists that the *avant-garde* texts show the clearest exposition of the destruction of subjective and metaphysical unity. Poetic language is an articulation of the semiotic mode of signification; it puts the identity of meaning, the speaking subject, and therefore transcendency into crisis because it refers to unconscious processes, to the drives and to the socio-historical constraints in which these processes are structured. Positionality in poetic language is shaken, if not destroyed, by the flooding in of the activity of the drives. In that poetic language functions with, and communicates, meaning, it shares the same signifying functions that phenomenology has traced. But it is not limited to meaning and communication. The predicating operation (the domain of positions and symbolic relations) is only one of the limitations. Admittedly, it is the limitation which constitutes relations of signification, but nevertheless it is not absolute; the activity of projection/expulsion is continuously transposing the fixed relations of the sign, predication and negation. This occurs through the accumulation of expulsions which then displace the stability of the positions from which the subject articulates itself. It is possible to study only meaning and signification in literature but to do this would mean the reduction of language to a phenomenological horizon,

> thus overlooking what it is in the poetical process which falls outside the realm of the signified and the transcendental ego and makes what we call 'literature' something other than a 'knowledge'; in other words making it, 'the very place where the social code is destroyed and renewed', thus as Artaud writes, 'giving vent to the anxieties of the time by magnetising, drawing to itself, taking on its shoulders the wandering anger of the times in order to relieve the era of its psychological ill-being'. (L'Anarchie sociale de l'art, O.C., vol. VIII, p. 287) (Kristeva, *Tel Quel*, no. 61).

Her analysis demonstrates that in poetical language and therefore, in varying degrees, in all languages, there is something which is heterogeneous to sense and signification. This would be the multiple, diverse and non-homogeneous elements, elements which can be seen in the obviously heterogeneous processes, such as psychosis, rhythms, intonations, etc. In poetic language, it functions through, despite of, and in addition to signification to produce the so-called musical effects of poetry (for example, the carnivalesque discourse examined by Baktin, certain texts of Mallarmé, Lautréamont and Artaud). The term heterogeneous is used because, although what is articulated is subject to certain rules and constraints, it is not, however, a modality which conveys meaning by a fixed relation between subject and sign: 'there is no sign, no predication, no signified object, and therefore no operating consciousness of a transcendental ego' (Kristeva, *La Révolution du langage poétique*, p. 13). This heterogeneous 'semiotic' mode of signification is produced by the activity of the drives: their structural organisation as well as the so-called primary processes which displace and condense energies. The arrangement of the drives, being the turning point between the psychic and the somatic, articulates a non-expressive totality made up of moments of facilitation and resistance. This uncertain and undetermined arrangement nevertheless has a mechanism of articulation. Kristeva calls it the *'chora'*, the Platonic word meaning 'receptacle'. She uses this to indicate a sort of tracing or marking of a shape around whose form signification constructs itself. 'It is not a position which represents something for someone, that is, a sign; nor is it a position which represents someone for another position, that is a signifier' (Kristeva, *Semiotext(e)*, vol. 1, no. 3, p. 22). This tracing or mark is produced by discontinuities marked provisionally in semiotisable material by the resistances and facilitations of the drives. For example, discontinuities and connections are established in things like voice, colours and gestures, as well as acoustic, visual and tactile differences and similarities. The connections and functions established in this way are articulated according to their resemblances and oppositions, that is by condensation and displacement, which is the movement of the primary processes, and indicates a close affinity between Jakobson's two axes of language (metaphor and metonymy), and the movement of the drives. It is for such reasons that the primary processes working by condensation and displacement are the fundamental expression in the semiotic: 'an expression which describes the relations between the zones of the fragmented body amongst themselves, and the relations between these zones and "external subjects and objects" ' (ibid.).

These texts are dominated by the 'semiotic modality': conventional theses of signification have been transversed, 'ruptured', allowing an influx of unconscious processes connected with the movement of the drives. Thus they trace the process of projection. This, like the movement of negativity in the Hegelian dialectic, is the movement of destruction (hence its equation with the death drive). This is experienced as *jouissance,* and underlies the critique formulated by Barthes in *Le Plaisir du texte* in a somewhat confusing way: 'the fading which seizes the subject in the midst of *jouissance'*; 'a text of *jouissance* imposes a state of loss. It is a text that discomforts, unsettles the reader's historical, cultural, psychological assumptions, the consistency of his tastes, values, memories, brings to a crisis his relation with language.' Kristeva suggests that these texts are often characterised by the proliferation of the negative symbol: the expression of the destructive drives allows the expression of material previously repressed. In the *avant-garde* text the semiotic produces the dissolution of fixed, uniform subjectivity. Characteristic are those twentieth-century texts which minutely examine their own matter: language, systems of signification, and the subject implicated in this signification. Joyce's mature work is an example of this tendency in which literature becomes auto-analysis, an implicit research into the rules of its own construction, exposing its components and its laws. In opening onto this process of construction, and in fragmenting the unity of the subject, these texts are no longer instruments of communication, but signifying practices which show the subject understanding and organising the real.

It is for this reason that Kristeva always insists on the correspondence of the signifying practices of these texts and revolutionary practice, since both rely on the destruction of fixed, unified, constant subjectivity knotted into the sign, governed by the thetic (social) requirements. This destruction in which heterogeneous elements return is the prerequisite for any transformation. The text explores the mechanism of projection in its heterogeneity since it is a practice which pulverises unity and constitutes a process which states and displaces thetic relations in language. However, Kristeva draws a distinction between texts which have heterogeneous contradictions as the indispensable condition of their signifying formation, and those which return them to a purely subjective and esoteric level. The former she calls 'practice' texts; the latter 'experience' texts: this distinction is based on Hegel's differentiation between 'experience' and 'practical activity'. Experience is the term for the mediation between mind and matter in which mind/consciousness creates itself in the struggle to overcome its own contradictions. It is this process which gives, despite its totally idealist resolution of the Absolute Spirit achieving its aims, the clearest exposition of the fragmentation of the unity of consciousness. The Hegelian dialectic closes off the movement of heterogeneous matter which produces the annihilation of conscious and subjective unity, by the assertion of the Absolute Spirit which knows its end in its beginning, whose aim and intentionality makes man act as the mediation of its production by his purposeful interaction with the world-object. Kristeva uses this analogy for those texts in which the heterogeneous contradiction is explored and articulated as an essential economy of the text, but which is limited to 'a strictly individual, naturalistic or esoteric representation' (Kristeva, *La Révolution du langage poétique*, p. 174). Such are the texts of Mallarmé. Although they show up the movement of projection by the provisional articulation of the semiotic *chora*, thereby exposing the movement of heterogeneous matter (drives and their arrangement), this articulation of projection is nevertheless returned to a notion of self-presence. As such they are acceptable to bourgeois ideology, which can accept experimental subjectivity.

But Kristeva claims that 'practice' texts (Sollers, Lautréamont, Joyce) express the same process as that of revolutionary practice: 'the one operates for the subject what the other introduces into society' (ibid., p. 14). These texts produce heterogeneous contradictions which explode the confines of experience and open onto the mobility of projection/expulsion in relation to the social outside, which underlies revolutionary practice. Whereas 'experience' texts can show the annihilation of the unity of consciousness, they fail to show the objective material relations which engender the conflict. In 'practice' texts, contradictions issue which demonstrate the struggle in the unifying closure of the subject of the symbolic: a struggle which passes into the processes of social transformation which cross the subject.

The practical moment [of these texts] objectifies the process of significance since it confronts the projection of the drives with material
contradictions, the class struggle for example, but at the same time it
renders these material contradictions internal to the process of the
subject (ibid., p. 181).

This process occurs because the functioning of the drives according to
the process of projection is forced to reformulate according to the encounter with the new object of the objective social conditions. Thus the
dispersion operated by a particular text in breaking down symbolic
relations or positions is also a process of renewal, since it re-poses these
positions in order to signify a new object. This process of positioning–
displacement–positioning is precisely Kristeva's ideal of textual practice. Fixed positions of signification are disrupted to produce a subject
in process, a subject crossed by the contradictory processes of society;
and these contradictory processes are articulated by the processes of
projection in relation to the symbolic function. 'The function of the
text consists of lifting, in whatever society, and whatever situation, the
repression which weighs on this moment of struggle in the subject,
menacing or dissolving the subjective and social liaisons but also conditioning its renewal' (ibid., p. 183).

This notion of textual practice links with the notion of the subject
and practice resulting from dialectical materialist reasoning. Textual
practice demonstrates the process which exposes the subject as a necessary area of struggle, since it is precisely the area or place of the play of
objective and subjective contradictions.

The notion of projection in relation to *avant-garde* texts provides a
re-reading of Freud which contests the function of the sign in idealist
thought, as well as providing a materialist theory of signification. The
theory suggests that the process of signification is the process of the
subject itself. It is only with an elaboration of Freud's notion of the
heterogeneity of the drives, their process of arrangement, and of desire,
that it is possible to understand the subject in the movement of objective contradiction. In developing the Freudian process of the subject,
it has become possible to see the sign, the cornerstone of idealist
thought, as simply a stage in the process of signification. It has been
accepted that this stage is vital as the frontier of social communication.
This frontier is theologised by idealist thought, and given a 'negative
theological' status by crude materialists who refuse to consider it. Thus
the historicity of ideological formations is only to be understood in
relation to the process of the production of fixed relations between
the subject and meaning, i.e. meanings for a subject included as the
place of their intention. The question of the production of symbolic
relations, their fixity, renewal and transformation, is vital for any real
elaboration of relations between ideology and the subject. It suggests
the materialist elaboration of language as ideology articulating with
the symbolic in the subject to produce its imaginary identification. In

this perspective the relationship between the subject and meaning in the sign is a stage, but a stage which is continually crossed, destroyed and reformulated. This movement is important for the theory of practice. It is in fact the theory which can produce the 'new subject' to whom Marx's dialectical materialism addresses itself. Thus the work of Kristeva on the process of signification as the process of the subject itself can be said to offer a real challenge to the 'metaphysical appurtenance of the sign', and to be the real beginning of a materialist theory of language, signification and ideology.

8 Conclusion

The principal aim of this book is to introduce the conceptual and theoretical work which supports and informs the revolution undergone by structuralist thought. It has only been possible to sketch the forms of concrete analysis that this has produced. There are several reasons why we have taken this course.

Much of the recent analysis of texts has concentrated, as the previous chapter indicated, on *avant-garde* texts which by definition can only be comprehended in their original language. It is virtually impossible to 'translate' because this notion involves a transference of a 'content', a positionality and discourse, from one (neutral) system of signifiers to another. To transfer the sliding of signifiers and the disturbance of positionality involves a difficult task, of writing the whole text anew. For our purposes, then, it is impossible to assume any prior knowledge of such texts.

That work on writing which has taken place in Britain has been severely handicapped by the lack of any theoretical reference-points. In order to develop at all, it has been forced to assume that readers share some common conceptual and political horizons, a presumption that has caused many misunderstandings and even hostilities.

This is not to say that the work, both in literature and the cinema, has not had a wide reception. The flood of translations and of introductions in layman's terms (i.e. within another conceptual framework, according to another view of the world) is witness to more than just a desire to neutralise this work. It shows that the traditional disciplines of linguistics, cultural criticism and literary criticism (with its cinematic subsidiaries) are dissatisfied with their own methodology and want to import a controlled dose of new concepts that can cope with 'problems' that have arisen. These traditional disciplines appropriate concepts in a piecemeal fashion to paper over their cracks, when in reality the cracks bear witness to the weakness of their theoretical foundations. They adopt a 'critical stance' which 'takes what is good in the work', and explains the 'obscurities' by the fact of its being foreign. The result is either traditional British eclecticism, or a peculiarly arid brand of structuralism, which claims to explain everything and has no reason for explaining.

Understood in its full complexities, the self-criticism undergone by structuralism and semiology has had far-reaching results. It is an example of how the encounter of two disciplines (psychoanalysis and Marxism) on the ground of their common problem (language) has produced a new understanding of society and its subjects. This theoretical horizon is not something which can lightly be appropriated, or just ignored. The problem itself — the encounter of Freud and Marx — is not exactly a new one. Fromm, Reich, Marcuse and Habermas, to name just a few, bear witness to the importance of such a question for this century. But the terms in which it can now be raised, as a result of the linguistic developments we have discussed, are very different. To discuss the presuppositions, advances and failures of previous attempts would take another book; but it would be fair to say that there has not yet been an adequate account of the relation of the epistemological foundations of these two disciplines.

Certain tendencies have dominated the way in which the interrelation has previously been discussed. Either the theoretical premises of one discipline are simply transposed onto the other, as in the work of Marcuse, or they are seen as providing accounts of different *stages*: there is first the sexual construction (object of psychoanalysis), then the operations of the social process (object of historical materialism).

We have tried to show in this book how the problematic of language has influenced the developments of both Marxism and psychoanalysis in a way that their encounter must necessarily produce a new object of knowledge. This new object is the scientific knowledge of the subject. The idealism implicit in such notions as 'identity of the subject', etc. can be avoided only in an encounter of these disciplines based on an extension of the study of language and discourse.

For Marxism, the question of language posed the problem of the subject in two ways. First, Marxism asked whether the role of language in the social totality is determined or determining, whether language is superstructural or not. In admitting — as linguistics seemed to insist — that it is neither of these oppositions, Marxism had also to admit the possibility that the theoretical oppositions base/superstructure were inadequate, and that analysis of language was not possible within a rigid and false distinction between the objective (mode of production) and the subjective (individual identity).

This parallels the second aspect, which involves the movement towards understanding ideology as an articulation. This would be the production of a certain meaning achieved in establishing an identity between signifier and signified. This itself is only produced in the fixing of the subject in relation to the sign.

Psychoanalysis, as elaborated by Lacan with his emphasis on man's linguistic nature, also leads to this problematic. Positing that there is no 'cause' of the subject prior to its constitution in discursive reality, Lacan clearly demonstrates how meaning was only established through the positionality of the subject. It is this concentration on language — language producing the subject and therefore the unconscious — which points a way to avoiding incorrect appropriations of psychoanalysis to Marxist thought. These are characterised by seeing the concerns of psychoanalysis as pre-existing the social operations analysed by historical materialism.

In brief then, both disciplines have demanded a critical re-examination of the concepts of sign and identity in response to the problems posed for materialist thought by linguistic analysis. The sign and identity can no longer remain as homogeneous and non-contradictory, but are rather to be understood as produced in contradictory processes. Fixed, transgressed and renewed, there is only the discursive space of the subject in relation to a contradictory outside and ideological articulations. And this is always in process.

In drawing the similarities of the two areas, there is a danger of subsuming their specificity. For example, the place of the unconscious, and particularly its relation to ideology, is in no way self-evident. And it is often easier to reduce its importance than to acknowledge fully its disruptive heterogeneous relation to discourse, and its role in ideological representations. A reduction of this kind is almost inevitable unless the articulation of the two disciplines is located in the perspective of what we have called a 'materialist theory of signification'. One such example of this reduction is the otherwise important book by Juliet Mitchell, *Psychoanalysis and Feminism*. This illustrates the pitfalls of an attempt to relate the notion of the Freudian unconscious to a Marxist analysis of society *without* a radical understanding of signification, of identity and the sign.

As a result of not considering signification, Mitchell ultimately discusses the unconscious in terms of a repository of the structural relations of patriarchy. The heterogeneity of the subject which underlies the Lacanian notion of the unconscious is ignored. Implicitly, therefore, Mitchell's unconscious must always serve a retrogressive function. It would return in the face of economic, political and ideological contradictions as the form of patriarchal sexual construction. In proposing a totally different notion of the unconscious, Lacan's analysis would be able to propose a less pessimistic understanding of the unconscious. In this, the unconscious does not *contain* the forms of the social, structural relations. It is rather made up of heterogeneous elements which are refused entry into consciousness in the production of the positioned subject to produce (ideological) meaning. Changes within the economic, political and ideological break down the fixed positionality in which ideological discourse sustained itself. The unconscious can then emerge as a disruptive, destructive force. In order that the subject may represent itself again at all, it has to produce itself in relation to a new object. Thus the old contradictions which formed the subject and the unconscious can emerge in relation to a new object or new contradictions.

This is not, by nature, either retrogressive or progressive politically. It is the renewing of positions after the dissolution of their fixity, but it is a renewal which retains and reforms all the elements of the former subject.

Thus the social phenomenon of fascism cannot be described *simply* as the return of the sexual unconscious, meaning by this the return of the patriarchal form of social relations. It has to be understood in a much more complex way as the accommodation of the disruptive effects of the sexual unconscious which emerge in socio-political transformations. And it is an accommodation achieved in accordance with the dominant (class) contradictions of the society.

The encounter of psychoanalysis and Marxism on the terrain of language leads to an analysis of the place of the unconscious as a vital element in ideological struggle. The expediency of attention to this area of the subjective contradiction is clear. By leaving the concerns of the subject to conservative forces (ranging from bourgeois psychology through to encounter group therapy, etc.), Marxism leaves these forces better equipped to reformulate positions of the subject in the breakdown of previous positionality.

In no other area is this more evident than in the crisis of familial institutions. The patriarchal reproductive functions of the family have entered into contradiction with the needs of capitalism. There is a need for a reduction in the reproduction of the work force; and contraception is now widely called for from as apparently disparate elements as feminists and 'economic specialists'. The last century has witnessed a significant change in the reproductive function of the family unit, and we now witness the appearance of female sexuality which is no longer organised to reproductive ends. However, the same capitalist relations that are responsible for this manifestation are also able to deal with it since the complex psychology that accompanies bourgeois individualism easily deals with contradictions experienced by women in this conjuncture. Until Marxism can produce a more adequate account of the role of ideology, subjective contradiction, and the role of the family, it will never provide a real alternative to such operations of bourgeois ideology.

Bibliography

This is necessarily limited to the central theoretical texts. The editions quoted are those for which numbered page references are given. Where the translation of a French text is given, the original publication data follows the title. However, we have chosen in most cases to translate quotations afresh in this book, in order to provide a standardisation of terms.

Althusser, L., *For Marx* (1966), Penguin edn, Harmondsworth, 1969.

Althusser, L., *Lenin and Philosophy*, New Left Books, London, 1971.

Althusser, L., *Eléments d'autocritique*, Hachette, Paris, 1974.

Althusser, L., 'Est-il simple d'être marxiste en philosophie?', in *La Pensée*, October 1975.

Backès-Clément, C., *Lévi-Strauss*, Editions Séghers, Paris, 1970.

Badiou, A., *Théorie de la contradiction*, Maspero, Paris, 1975.

Barthes, R., *Writing Degree Zero* (1953), Jonathan Cape edn, London, 1970.

Barthes, R., *Mythologies* (1957), Paladin, London, 1973.

Barthes, R., *Sur Racine*, Editions du Seuil, Paris, 1963.

Barthes, R., *Essais critiques*, Editions du Seuil, Paris, 1964.

Barthes, R., *Elements of Semiology* (1964), Jonathan Cape edn, London, 1967.

Barthes, R., *Système de la mode*, Editions du Seuil, Paris, 1967.

Barthes, R., *S/Z* (1970), Jonathan Cape edn, London, 1974.

Barthes, R., *Le Plaisir du texte*, Editions du Seuil, Paris, 1973 (translated as *Pleasure of the Text*, Jonathan Cape, London, 1975).

Benveniste, E., *Problems in General Linguistics* (1966), University of Miami Press, 1971.

Benveniste, E., *Problèmes de linguistique générale,* vol. II, Gallimard, Paris, 1974.

Chomsky, N., *Syntactic Structures*, Mouton, The Hague, 1957.

Chomsky, N., *Cartesian Linguistics*, Harper, New York, 1966.

Communications, Journal of the Centre d'Etudes de Communication de Masse, Editions du Seuil, Paris.

Derrida, J., *L'Ecriture et la différance*, Editions du Seuil, Paris, 1967.

Derrida, J., *De la Grammatologie*, Editions de Minuit, Paris, 1967.

Derrida, J., *Positions*, Editions de Minuit, Paris, 1972.

Derrida, J., *Speech and Phenomena* (1967), Northwestern University Press, Evanston, USA, 1973.

Edelman, B., *Le Droit saisi par la photographie*, Maspero, Paris, 1973.

Engels, F., *Dialectics of Nature*, Progress Publishers, Moscow, 1974.

Freud, S., *Standard Edition of the Complete Psychological Works*, Hogarth Press/Allen & Unwin, London, 1963.

Heath, S., *The Nouveau Roman*, Elek, London, 1972.

Heath, S., *Vertige du déplacement*, Fayard, Paris, 1974.

Heath, S., 'Touch of Evil', in *Screen*, Spring and Summer 1975.

Hindess, B. and Hirts, P., *Pre-Capitalist Modes of Production*, Routledge & Kegan Paul, London, 1975.

Hjelmslev, L., *Prolegomena to a Theory of Language*, University of Wisconsin Press, USA, 1953.

Husserl, E., *Logical Investigations*, Routledge & Kegan Paul, London, 1970 edn.

Jakobson, R., *Selected Writings*, Mouton, The Hague, 1962.

Joyaux, J., *Le Langage, cet inconnu*, collection 'Points de la question', SGPP, Paris, 1969.

Kristeva, J., *Semiotiké*, Editions du Seuil, Paris, 1969.

Kristeva, J., *Le Texte du roman*, Mouton, The Hague, 1970.

Kristeva, J., *La Révolution du langage poétique*, Editions du Seuil, Paris, 1974.

Kristeva, J., *Des Chinoises,* Editions des Femmes, Paris, 1975 (translated as *On Chinese Women,* Marion Boyars, London, 1977).

Kristeva, J., 'The Subject in Signifying Practice', in *Semiotext(e)*, Columbia University, New York, vol. 1, no. 3, 1975.

Lacan, J., *Ecrits*, Editions du Seuil, Paris, 1966.

Lacan, J., *Le Séminaire*, Editions du Seuil, Paris. Vol. I: 'Les Ecrits techniques de Freud', 1975; vol. XI: 'Les Quatre Concepts fondamentaux de la psychanalyse', 1973; vol. XX: 'Encore', 1975.

Laplanche, J. and Leclaire, S., 'The Unconscious' (1966), *Yale French Studies*, no. 48.

Laplanche, J. and Pontalis, J. B., *The Language of Psychoanalysis* (1967), Hogarth Press, London, 1973.

Lenin, V. I., 'Philosophical Notebooks', *Collected Works*, vol. 38, Lawrence & Wishart, London, 1972.

Lévi-Strauss, C., *Elementary Structures of Kinship* (1949), Eyre & Spottiswoode, 1969.

Lévi-Strauss, C., introduction to *Sociologie et anthropologie* by M. Mauss, PUF, Paris, 1950.

Lévi-Strauss, C., *Structural Anthropology* (1958), Penguin edn, Harmondsworth, 1972.

Lévi-Strauss, C., *Totemism* (1963), Penguin edn, Harmondsworth, 1969.

Lévi-Strauss, C., *Mythologiques*, Plon, Paris. Vol. I: 'Le Cru et le cuit', 1964; vol. II: 'Du Miel aux cendres', 1966; vol. III: 'L'origine des manières de table', 1968; vol. IV: 'L'Homme nu', 1968.

Lévi-Strauss, C., *Tristes Tropiques* (1955), Russell, New York, 1967.

Lukács, G., *The Historical Novel*, Penguin edn, Harmondsworth, 1967.

Macciocchi, M. A., *De la Chine* (2nd edn), collection 'Points de la question', Editions du Seuil, Paris, 1974. 1st edn translated as *Daily Life in Revolutionary China*, Monthly Review Press, 1972.

Macciocchi, M. A. (ed.), *Eléments pour une analyse du fascisme* (2 vols), Editions 10–18, Paris, 1976.

Macksey, R. and Donato, E. (eds), *The Structuralist Controversy*, Johns Hopkins Press, Baltimore, 1972.

Mao Tse-Tung, 'On Contradiction' and 'On Practice', in *Four Essays on Philosophy*, Foreign Languages Press, Peking, 1968.

Marx, Karl, *Capital* (3 vols), Lawrence & Wishart, London, 1974.

Marx, Karl, *Grundrisse*, Penguin edn, Harmondsworth, 1973.

Marx, Karl, *Early Writings*, Penguin edn, Harmondsworth, 1975.

Marx, Karl, with Engels, F., *The German Ideology*, Lawrence & Wishart, London, 1969.

Metz, C., 'The Imaginary Signifier', in *Screen*, Summer 1975.

Mitchell, J., *Psychoanalysis and Feminism*, Allen Lane, London, 1974.

Pivcevic, E., *Husserl and Phenomenology*, Hutchinson, London, 1970.

Reich, W., *Mass Psychology of Fascism*, Penguin edn, Harmondsworth, 1975.

Saussure, F. de, *Course in General Linguistics*, Fontana edn, London, 1974.

Screen, Journal of the Society for Education in Film and Television.

Sollers, Ph., *L'Ecriture et l'expérience des limites*, collection 'Points de la question', Editions du Seuil, Paris, 1971.

Sollers, Ph., *Sur le Matérialisme*, Editions du Seuil, Paris, 1974.

Stalin, J. V., *Marxism and the Problems of Linguistics*, Foreign Languages Press, Peking, 1972.

Tel Quel, Review published by Editions du Seuil, Paris.

White, A., 'Mediations in Hegel and Marx', unpublished thesis, University of Birmingham.

Index